ACCLAIM FOR TERRI BLACKSTOCK

" . . . [*Last Light*] is in leagu[illegible] fiction and bodes well for the series to co[illegible]

"A popular suspense author, [illegible] g with relationship threads in the fourth series entry [illegible]). This title should find its way onto public library shelves."

—*Library Journal* (on *Dawn's Light*)

"The Restoration series comes to a dramatic end. Blackstock is absolutely masterful at bringing spiritual dilemmas to the surface and allowing readers to wrestle with them alongside her characters. This is a fitting conclusion to this unique series."

—*RT Book Reviews*, 4.5 stars (on *Dawn's Light*)

"*Truth Stained Lies* is the first in what's likely to be a very popular new series for Blackstock. Her characters are flawed, faltering in their faith, and ultimately human. They're the kind of people you wish you had as friends. This latest novel should appeal to millions of existing fans and millions of new fans who just don't know it yet."

—*CBA Retailers + Resources*

"Short chapters and terse dialogue propel the fast-paced action . . . [and] the mother-daughter relationship strikes true emotional notes; the redemptive arc of evangelical Christian fiction is natural and resonant in a story of addiction. Blackstock's many fans will be pleased, and this story will also speak to families dealing with addicted children."

—*Publishers Weekly* (on *Intervention*)

"The second in Blackstock's Intervention series is a fast-paced thriller . . . the portrayal of the dangers of drug abuse and the effects after rehab are fascinating."

—*Romantic Times* (on *Vicious Cycle*)

"Crisp prose, an engaging story, and brisk pacing make this thriller another home run for Blackstock. Recommend it to readers who enjoy material by Lynette Eason and Erin Healy."

—*Library Journal* (on *Downfall*)

"*Shadow in Serenity* from *New York Times* best-selling author Terri Blackstock won't disappoint. It features page-turning suspense, believable characters, a straightforward but non-preachy Christian message of redemption, and just enough romance to satisfy without being sappy. Blackstock is a masterful writer; highly recommend this excellent title to fiction fans."

—*CBA Retailers + Resources*

"Blackstock's superior writing will keep readers turning pages late into the night to discover the identity of the culprit in this amazing mystery. The unique setting and peek into the Nashville music scene are fascinating. Suspense lovers are in for a delightful treat."

—*RT Book Reviews*, 4.5 stars TOP PICK! (on *Double Minds*, 2009 Nomination for Best Inspirational Novel)

TRUE LIGHT

ALSO BY TERRI BLACKSTOCK

THE MOONLIGHTERS SERIES

1 *Truth Stained Lies*
2 *Distortion (Available Spring 2014)*

THE RESTORATION SERIES

1 *Last Light*
2 *Night Light*
3 *True Light*
4 *Dawn's Light*

THE INTERVENTION SERIES

1 *Intervention*
2 *Vicious Cycle*
3 *Downfall*

THE CAPE REFUGE SERIES

1 *Cape Refuge*
2 *Southern Storm*
3 *River's Edge*
4 *Breaker's Reef*

NEWPOINTE 911

1 *Private Justice*
2 *Shadow of Doubt*
3 *Word of Honor*
4 *Trial by Fire*
5 *Line of Duty*

THE SUN COAST CHRONICLES

1 *Evidence of Mercy*
2 *Justifiable Means*
3 *Ulterior Motives*
4 *Presumption of Guilt*

SECOND CHANCES

1 *Never Again Good-bye*
2 *When Dreams Cross*
3 *Blind Trust*
4 *Broken Wings*

WITH BEVERLY LAHAYE

1 *Seasons Under Heaven*
2 *Showers in Season*
3 *Times and Seasons*
4 *Seasons of Blessing*

NOVELLAS

Seaside

OTHER BOOKS

Shadow in Serenity
Predator
Double Minds
Soul Restoration
Emerald Windows
Miracles (*The Listener*/*The Gifted*)
The Heart Reader of Franklin High
The Gifted Sophomores
Covenant Child
Sweet Delights

TRUE LIGHT

A RESTORATION NOVEL | *BOOK THREE*

TERRI BLACKSTOCK

ZONDERVAN

True Light

This title is also available as a Zondervan ebook. Visit www.zondervan.com/ebooks.

This title is also available in a Zondervan audio edition. Visit www.zondervan.fm.

Requests for information should be addressed to:

Zondervan, *Grand Rapids, Michigan 49530*

Library of Congress Cataloging-in-Publication Data

Blackstock, Terri.
True Light / Terri Blackstock.
p. cm.—(A restoration novel ; bk.3)
ISBN 978-0-310-25769-1
1. Regression (Civilization)—Fiction. I. Title. II. Series: Blackstock, Terri, 1957- Restoration novel ; bk. 3.
PS3552.L34285T78 2007
813'.54—dc22 2007006670

Published in association with the literary agency of Alive Communications, Inc., 7680 Goddard Street, Suite 200, Colorado Springs, CO 80920. www.alivecommunications.com

ISBN 978-0-3103-3780-5 (2013 repackage)

Printed in the United States of America

HB 03.12.2018

This book is lovingly dedicated to the Nazarene.

DEAR READER

THANK YOU FOR READING MY RESTORATION SERIES. I got the idea for these books as the world was preparing for "Y2K." The world was expecting a huge catastrophe as the clocks turned from 1999 to 2000. Computers were expected to crash, power grids to shut down, and the world as we knew it might come to an end. We all sat around our televisions the night of New Year's Eve, bracing ourselves for darkness. That darkness never came, and the catastrophe didn't happen. But the thought of what might have happened continued to germinate in my brain.

I asked a physicist friend of mine what kind of event could knock out our power grid and fry all our technology, and he told me to research electromagnetic pulses. These pulses could be caused by different things—solar flares, celestial events, E-bombs, and nuclear weapons exploding in our upper atmosphere. As I read and studied these situations and their repercussions, I became more and more aware that these things were real threats to our way of life.

At the same time, I was troubled spiritually by the cultural decline in America. Families (including my own) seemed to be eating most meals in their cars between ballet and soccer practice, the children were glued to video games and television, and parents were distracted by their smart phones. Our comfort had numbed us to the things God wanted to do in our lives. I became convicted that He was going to have to do something drastic to America to get our attention. What would that be? Would it be war? Famine? A nuclear attack?

That's when I decided to flesh out the idea for the Restoration Series and challenge a spoiled American family with a massive global power outage. The Brannings, who'd been used to fast food and take-out, now have to grow their own food and find water. Their cars don't run, their jobs are gone, the banks are closed, there's no communication . . . and this family has to decide if they will hoard what they have or share with their neighbors, when sharing might lead to their own starvation. All around them are desperate people, some willing to kill for food or the opportunity to get ahead.

Since I wrote these books years ago, there have been variations of this theme in television series and books by other authors. Mine are different because I chose not to focus on the military aspect, but on the changing character of the people suffering through this disaster. I fell in love with these characters as I wrote the four-book series, and so did many of my readers. Several years since the series was first released, people are still buying the books and sharing them with their friends. For that reason, we've decided to give the series a second life with new covers and a re-launch that will give new readers an opportunity to discover them. It's my hope that "rehearsing" this catastrophe with my characters will help prepare readers for catastrophes in their own lives. And if it gets the attention of God's people *before* He has to give us a wake-up call . . . well, that would be my idea of true success.

If you like the books, please tell others about them. And if you enjoy the way I tell a story, there are many other books where these came from. Learn more about all of them at http://www.terriblackstock.com/books.

Thanks again for reading my books!
Terri Blackstock

CAST OF CHARACTERS

Branning, Doug—forty-eight, father of four and husband to Kay Branning. He's a successful stockbroker who's never known failure until technology comes to an end and he's forced to provide for and protect his family from the dangers surrounding them. Although the circumstances of life threaten to defeat him when the power goes out, he manages to find the character and strength to do what needs to be done. He commits to studying the word of God, and becomes the pastor of a home church for Christians in his neighborhood.

Branning, Kay—forty-five, Doug's wife; mother to Deni, Jeff, Beth, and Logan. She was a spoiled soccer mom before the outage, living in a four-thousand-square-foot home with all the bells and whistles, and driving a brand-new Expedition. Now she faces a daily struggle to feed her family and help those around her who have less than she does.

Branning, Deni—twenty-two, Doug and Kay's spitfire daughter. Just before the outage, she graduated from Georgetown University in broadcast journalism and landed an internship at the NBC affiliate in Washington, D.C. When the power went out, she was on her way home to plan her wedding to Craig, an attorney who works for a prominent U.S. senator. But after a number of tragedies and trials, as well as an encounter with God, she becomes disillusioned with Craig and breaks off the engagement. Mark Green, a neighbor and high-school friend, begins to win her affections as her priorities change.

Branning, Jeff—sixteen, Doug and Kay's son. He's the star pitcher on his high-school baseball team, a true jock and a popular kid at school, but not very accustomed to work. But when the Pulses knock out technology, he's forced to grow up quickly. Saddled with adult responsibilities and the desire to help protect his family, he becomes a young man of integrity and grit, someone his family and friends can count on.

Branning, Beth—twelve, Doug and Kay's daughter, who looks up to her older sister. She's sensitive to the needs of the neighbors and tries to help when she can. She has turned from a pampered princess to a person who puts others' needs before her own. To distract the neighborhood children from the drudgery of life during the Pulses, she writes, directs, and produces plays that bring the community together.

Branning, Logan—nine, Doug and Kay's youngest child, who was raised on PlayStation, computers, DVDs, and television, and finds their new way of life boring and unfair. But he's enjoying spending more time with his dad now that Doug is home most of the time.

Green, Mark—twenty-two, Deni's friend from high school. He's good looking, strong, inventive, and skillful. He skipped college and went to work in construction. He's disliked in the neighborhood because of his dead father's reputation. But Deni and her family know that Mark is just what he appears to be—a good Christian man who puts others before himself. Mark helped turn Deni from her future with Craig and waits for God's timing on their relationship with each other.

Horton, Chris—twenty-two, Deni's best friend from high school, a nurse who works for the only doctor in their area.

Caldwell, Brad—the Brannings' next-door neighbor, an attorney, a good man but not a Christian. He sets up a "neighborhood watch" in Oak Hollow. An African American, he was initially blamed for the murders and robberies in the neighborhood and was beaten up and almost killed. But he has proven to be a good friend to the Brannings and is Doug's most trusted partner in fighting the crime that threatens them. His wife, Judith, is a nurse and the mother of Jeremy and Drew (seven and nine). She's close friends with Kay.

PROLOGUE

ON MAY 24, CIVILIZATION AS WE KNOW IT COMES TO AN END.

Plumbing doesn't work because the water treatment plants run on electricity. Trucks and trains don't run, so stores run out of food. Generators are rendered useless. In this major meltdown of life, people are stranded where they are, with no transportation, no power, and no communication. Crime runs rampant as evil fills the void, and desperation becomes the only moral guide many people recognize.

Eventually, word makes its way to Crockett, Alabama, that the event was caused by a star—a supernova named SN-1999—which is emitting electromagnetic pulses every few seconds. With no assurances of when the star might burn itself out and allow them to rebuild, people are left with a choice: will they hoard what they have until it all runs out, or will they share with those around them who are in need?

The Brannings, an upper middle-class Christian family, struggle to maintain their faith in the midst of the world's new challenges, and learn the lesson of giving of themselves ...

Even when it threatens their survival.

ONE

The buck fell with the first shot, and Zach Emory couldn't help being impressed with himself. From his deer stand, it looked like an eight- or ten-pointer. If the weather stayed cold, he'd be able to make it last for several weeks' worth of meals.

He climbed down from his deer stand and pulled up the collar of his jacket. It was so cold his ears were numb, and his fingers had begun to ache. But it was worth it. Even in the pre-outage days, Zach had spent many mornings sitting in a deer stand freezing to death, just for sport. Now it was a matter of survival.

He jogged toward the animal that lay dead twenty yards away. His brother Gary would be crazy with envy. They had a competition going, and Gary was two up on him. Zach hoped Gary had heard the gunshot and would come to help him move the deer. It would take both of them to lift it into their rickshaw.

He bent over the buck. Ten points. And a perfect shot right through the heart. His dad would finally be proud, and if he was lucky, his mother would drag herself out of bed to get a look.

He heard footsteps behind him and turned to see a man emerging from the trees, walking toward him. Zach squinted, trying to place him. He'd seen him before, but he couldn't remember where.

"Did I score or what?" he asked as the man came closer. "He's a ten-pointer. Got him in one shot, right through the ticker!"

The man didn't look like he'd come to celebrate. He stopped about thirty feet away … and raised his rifle.

Was he going to shoot? Zach's hands came up, as if that would stop him.

The gun fired—its impact propelling Zach backward, bouncing him onto the dirt.

TWO

THE BUILDING SMELLED OF MOTOR OIL AND GREASE—A scent Deni Branning associated with progress. A symphony of roaring engines brought a smile to her face as she rolled her bike inside. Oh, for the days of noise pollution and hurry—of bumper-to-bumper traffic, honking horns, blaring radios, and twenty-four-hour TV.

All over the large warehouse, mechanics and engineers with black-stained fingers worked at converting engines. The building had been purchased by the feds a few months ago, when they instituted the draft. Instead of drafting soldiers, the government had conscripted all of those with experience as mechanics. Later, they'd added others to the conscription list: electricians, scientists, and engineers. Many of them were allowed to live at home and work in the local conversion plants, but others had been sent across the country to serve where they were needed.

Pushing down the kickstand on her bike, she reached into her bag for her notepad and looked around for someone in charge. She saw Ned Emory, from her neighborhood, standing nearby with a clipboard, instructing a group of mechanics with a disassembled engine laid out in front of them. She headed toward him.

"Excuse me," she yelled over the noise. "Mr. Emory?"

He turned. "Yeah?"

She could see that he didn't recognize her, even though his son Zach had been close friends with her brother for years. "Deni Branning. Jeff's sister?"

Recognition dawned in his eyes. She reached out to shake hands with him, but he showed her his greasy hands. "Better not shake. What brings you here?"

"I'm writing an article about your work here. Do you have time for an interview?"

As if he hadn't heard her, he turned back to the men, barked out some orders that she couldn't hear, and started walking away. Glancing back over his shoulder, he said, "I heard the newspaper is back up and running. They hired you, did they?"

She caught up to him and tried to match his steps. "That's right. the *Crockett Times*. They liked what I'd been doing on the message boards around town. This'll be the cover story for next week's issue."

He didn't seem impressed, so she pulled out her big guns. "You guys are like rock stars. Everybody wants to know what you're up to."

Pride pulled at the corners of his mouth, and she knew she'd struck a chord. "Sure, I can give you a few minutes. What do you want to know?"

He started up a staircase, and she blew out her frustration as she followed him. "Is there someplace we can sit down?"

"I don't have time to sit down." He reached the top of the stairs and headed across the concrete floor to an area where a dozen mopeds sat in various stages of completion. "Hey, Stark! I need at least four of these done by the end of the day. Get Bennett over here to help you."

Deni's gaze swept over the bikes. "Wow. How can I get one of those?"

"You can't. They're not for the private sector." He was walking again, but she hung back, unable to tear herself away from the coveted mopeds. She stepped toward one and touched the seat.

He turned back and gave her an impatient look. "Do you want to do the interview or not?"

She shook off her longing and forced herself to focus. "Of course."

He led her past a table filled with generators, and again, her longing kicked in. "Do those work?"

"They do after we harden them against the Pulses."

Her heart quickened. If they were making hardened generators here, it wouldn't be long until they actually had electricity. Could there really be lightbulbs at the end of the tunnel?

"When will those be available for the public?" she asked, catching up to him again.

"Our illustrious supernova will burn out before we can finish supplying the hospitals. They're priority number one for the generators right now. Without robotics, assembly lines—electricity, for that matter—we have to do everything by hand, one at a time. And even if we could produce enough for the public, there's one missing ingredient."

"Gasoline," she said.

"You got it." He reached a series of offices with glass walls, overlooking the work on the floor below them. "We can't get enough gas without operating tanker trucks, and once we get it here, we don't have electricity to work the pumps."

She was well aware of the chain of problems. "But aren't you guys all about creating work-arounds?"

"Right now we're just trying to help critical services operate. Like I said, the star will likely burn out before we get caught up with that. Then we'll shift our objectives from sustaining to rebuilding." He headed into one of the offices, dropped his clipboard on his desk, and motioned for her to take a seat.

As Deni sat down, something outside the glass caught Ned's eye, and Deni turned to follow his gaze. Someone was running up the stairs.

Ned frowned as his son Gary came running toward his door. "Dad, Zach's been shot!"

"What?"

Deni caught her breath and got to her feet.

"We were hunting at the Jenkins's place. I heard some gunshots and ... when I found him ..."

"Is he dead?" Ned blurted out.

"I don't think so. I got help and somebody went to get an ambulance. They're taking him to University Hospital."

Ned grabbed his son's shoulders. "What condition was he in when they took him?"

Gary trembled as he raked his hands through his hair. "There was blood all over his shirt ... front and back."

Deni's heart stopped. Her brother's best friend ...

Ned raced out of the office and hurried down the stairs, Gary on his heels. Deni followed them as far as the top of the stairs, then waited there as they hurried through the building. All the engines went quiet, and everyone stared as Ned ran to a beat-up Buick. "The keys!" he shouted. "Where are the keys?"

Someone tossed them to him, and he got in and started the engine. Gary jumped in beside him. Two guys pulled up the garage door and the Buick rumbled out.

Deni muttered a prayer for Zach as they drove off—and then a thought struck her. Jeff, Deni's brother, sometimes hunted with Zach. Could they have been together? What if he'd been hurt too?

She had to get to the scene of the shooting. She ran downstairs, grabbed her bike, and pedaled out behind them.

THREE

"ZACH? ZACH, CAN YOU HEAR ME?"

Zach tried to open his eyes, but they were glued shut. Something was shaking and bumping him—and with each jolt, pain exploded through him.

"Zach, we're getting you to the hospital, okay, buddy? Stay with me."

Was he in an ambulance? How long had it been since he'd been in a running car? Weeks? Months? Years? His brain couldn't find the answer.

He tried to breathe, but something was crushing his chest. Drowning … choking … gurgling.

Something sliced through his throat. "We're gonna help you breathe, buddy. Hang on, we're almost there."

He couldn't breathe. Gagging. Smothering. Gasping.

The ambulance jerked to a stop, people all around him yelling, probing, pushing.

As they rolled him into the building, Zach knew he was dying.

FOUR

THE MEETING HAD BEEN DRAGGING ON FOR HOURS. DOUG Branning shifted in his seat and wished they would take a break, so the attendees could dash outside to the Porta-Johns lined up around the Birmingham Jefferson Convention Complex. For weeks, he'd looked forward to the symposium of economic leaders in the area. His success as a stockbroker had gotten him an invitation, and he hoped to hear about when the banks would open and what the plan would be for infusing money into the economy.

Because the big complex was without electricity, chairs had been set up in the multileveled lobby of the big building, so they could take advantage of the light from the windows. He'd sat riveted for most of the day as financial leaders argued that opening the banks would have a destructive effect on the economy. Others countered that opening them would help. Doug wasn't sure which side of the fence he landed on, professionally. But as a victim of this disaster, he wanted his cash.

The government leaders who'd come in for the symposium and who had been conducting meetings like this in several major cities, were here to gather advice from local leaders and update them on the state of the economy. So far, all Doug had done today was listen.

"The banking systems lacked sufficient records of their account balances to open the banks a few months ago," Edward Freelord, Federal Reserve Chairman, said, his voice carrying over the crowd. "When the computers crashed, most of the banks had only a few current hard copies, and those have had to be reproduced by hand. Local banks now have the information they need for their local account holders, so it is feasible for them to open. We're considering instructing them to give account holders no more than 2 percent per month of their balance, to avoid a run on the banks."

They'd already established that the law would prohibit foreclosures on property during the Pulses, since no one was able to make payments right now, and the banks would not be allowed to loan money except to those involved in rebuilding the infrastructure and helping the government function.

Several of the audience members weighed in on Freelord's idea, offering pros and cons that Doug was sure the leaders had already considered. But Doug's mind was busy calculating the scenario's direct benefit to his family. He'd had about 15,000 dollars in his checking account at the time of the outage, and another 30,000 dollars in savings. His stocks and bonds and other investments totaled over a million dollars, but those were worthless right now.

He jotted the figures in the margin of his legal pad. With the government's suggested plan, his family would be entitled to 900 dollars a month. With the new rock-bottom prices, they would be in great shape.

Once again, the world would be separated into the haves and have-nots, and his family would rise to the top. It wouldn't help his friends in the Sandwood Place Apartments, most of whom hadn't had any money even before the outage. But maybe it would help them indirectly, as money spent in the economy trickled down to make their lives better.

Would it? That was a pipe dream, he feared. But he'd deal with it later.

Someone tapped on his shoulder, and he glanced up to see Jeff, his sixteen-year-old, standing over him. "What are you doing here?" Doug asked in a whisper.

"Sorry, Dad." Jeff looked upset, and Doug knew something was wrong. "I have to talk to you."

Doug got up and followed Jeff back up the aisle, to the front door. They stepped out into the cold. "What is it?"

"Dad, Zach Emory was shot this morning!"

"What? How?"

Jeff told him the little he knew.

"You weren't with him?"

"No, I was helping Mom set up at the swap meet. They said he was really bad, that he lost a lot of blood. Some people who were there when the ambulance came weren't even sure he was alive." His chin trembled, and he settled his misting eyes on Doug. "Dad, I want to go see if he's all right, but Mom told me to come by and get you first."

"Of course," Doug said, glancing through the glass back up at the podium.

"You don't have to leave," Jeff said. "I can go by myself. It's just that Mom thinks I'm a kid who can't be alone in the city."

"I can leave now. Don't worry about it."

"But what if you miss something important? Like when they're opening the banks?"

Doug shook his head. "This is just a fact-finding mission. They haven't made any decisions yet."

They headed to the bike rack and unchained their bicycles. Getting onto his bike and pumping out into the street, Doug couldn't imagine what Zach's parents were going through. He looked over at Jeff as they rode. The boy's gaze was fixed on the road, but Doug could see the pain behind his eyes. Zach was one of Jeff's closest friends.

He prayed as they rode, but his prayers were selfish. As much as he wanted Zach to be alive when they got to the hospital, he wanted even more to protect his son from the pain of sudden and unjustified loss.

Only God could control that now.

FIVE

The clouds were threatening snow by the time Deni found a hunter who could lead her to Zach's deer stand. They tromped through the barren trees to the place where Zach had been found. The sheriff's department had cordoned off the area, keeping everyone a hundred feet away. Deni joined the crowd standing at the yellow tape. In the distance, she could make out two broad, dark stains on the ground.

Her heart jolted. Was all of that Zach's blood, or had someone else been shot too?

Deputy Jones, who was usually more open with her than the others in the department, was keeping the crowd back. She pushed her way to him. "Gordon, what happened?"

He gave her a cursory glance. "Kid got shot."

"I know that." She started to respond sarcastically but stopped herself in time, not wanting to anger him. "But was it an accident?"

"Doesn't look like one to me," he said.

"Then someone shot Zach on purpose?"

The deputy squinted as he turned to her. "Is this on or off the record?"

He knew her too well. "Depends."

"If it's on the record, all I can tell you is that an investigation is underway."

Again, sarcasm sprang to mind: *Now there's a scoop!* But she squelched it. "Come on, Gordon, you can give me more than that."

"Off the record?"

"Okay, we can start with that."

He hesitated, glanced at the sheriff who was kneeling at the blood spots. He stepped closer to her. "I don't know ..."

"Come on," she said in a low voice. "He's one of my brother's best friends. I want to know what happened."

Jones turned back to her. "See that second blood spot?"

Deni nodded.

"We're not sure yet, but we suspect Zach had killed himself a deer and somebody wanted it."

She stared for a moment, trying to picture it. "Are you saying someone shot him to get his deer?"

"I'm not saying it for sure. Just that we suspect it. Off the record, until the sheriff confirms it."

She looked at the sheriff, talking quietly to one of his detectives. If only she could talk to him ...

"Deni!" She turned; it was Brian, another of her brother's friends, looking shaken as he made his way to her. "Jeff told me what happened. Do you know who did it yet?"

She breathed relief that her brother was safe. "No. I can't get any information. What did Jeff say?"

"Just that Zach had been shot and taken to the hospital. He was headed to town to see how he was."

Deni turned back to the crime scene, hoping she could catch the sheriff's eye. Scarbrough was usually pretty up-front with her, since her reporting was always fair and accurate and sometimes helped move the case along. She hoped he would talk to her soon, so she could go from off the record to on the record and confirm the reason for the shooting. "Local Boy Shot for Deer" would make an eye-catching headline. The reality of it made her sick.

SIX

Beth Branning had learned to live in fear of the Next Terrible Thing. First there had been the outage, then the total shock to civilization. No more Facebook or IMs, no more *That's So Raven* episodes. But life had gone from bad to horrible when she'd discovered her teacher and her husband murdered. And Beth had grown up from twelve to about a hundred and eighty when her sister was kidnapped by the same killer.

When Deni had come home alive, the world still wasn't safe—the Next Terrible Thing had begun. Beth's family had found four abandoned kids and wound up with another maniac after them. Now Beth felt as if there were killers everywhere she looked—in crowds, on the streets, in the homes in her neighborhood ... now even in the woods where her dad and brothers hunted.

"Beth, are you all right?"

She looked up at Mrs. Carroll, who taught all eight of the Oak Hollow junior high schoolers in her kitchen each afternoon. "Ma'am?"

"I said, are you okay?"

"Yes, ma'am, I'm fine."

"You can go home if you want. I don't think you're focusing."

"She's just trying to get out of working," Jordan Miller said. "It's not like Zach Emory's her best friend."

Beth ignored the class loudmouth and looked at Cole Hampton, who'd told her about Zach. "Are you sure he wasn't dead?"

"No. Nobody was sure. And if he was alive, they probably didn't get him to the hospital on time. I heard there was blood everywhere."

She hoped he'd heard wrong. Tears came to her eyes again as she prayed that they wouldn't have to bury her brother's best friend.

A year ago, she'd been to only one funeral in her whole life and that had been for some aunt she'd never met. Since then, she'd found a murdered couple, seen violent people shot dead in their tracks, and been to countless other funerals. Now the number of dead she'd seen was somewhere in the teens. Probably more than the twelve years she'd been alive.

But sixteen-year-old boys were not supposed to die when all they were doing was hunting to feed their families. And a guy who'd been to her house with her older brother Jeff, a guy who'd teased her and flirted with her and ignored her, wasn't supposed to be there one morning and gone the next.

She looked down at the paper she was working on. In the dim indoor light, she had trouble seeing the numbers on the page. "Can I go sit by the window in the den?"

Mrs. Carroll shook her head. "No, Beth. I want you all in the same room."

It had been nice when the little neighborhood home schools had first started up back in September. Since May 24 of last year, they'd worked themselves to death trying to survive. Some of the poor people starved to death; many people got sick with viruses or infections they couldn't fight off, since medications were hard to come by. Those who did survive were almost as likely to get gunned down by someone who wanted what they'd worked for.

The children had become workers in their families' struggle for survival, so school, which started at one in the afternoon and went until four, had been something to celebrate. Three hours doing math and history were way better than scaling fish or skinning the animals her dad and brothers killed. They had enough of that to do in the mornings; in the afternoons, it felt good to settle into the routine of learning. When the Pulses eventually ended and the real schools were open again, most of the Crockett kids would be way behind. But not the ones in Oak Hollow.

But today, Beth didn't want to be here. She couldn't concentrate.

Tears came to her eyes again. Maybe she should take Mrs. Carroll up on her offer to go home. She could find out if they'd caught the shooter, and whether her family had any word on Zach's condition. After all—if he could just wake up, he could tell them who had shot him.

By now, Deni may have found out something as she snooped around for the *Crockett Times*.

Beth grabbed her backpack from under her folding chair and started to load her books in. "I changed my mind."

Her teacher looked up from her stool at the kitchen bar. Beth hated to disturb her. As teachers went, she was a little scattered, and she wasn't used to dealing with kids this age. She'd taught second grade before the outage, but they already had enough elementary school teachers in the neighborhood, so she'd taken this group. She had a nervous tic that continuously jerked her lip up at the corner, and a mild personality that invited the worst kids in the class to walk all over her. She hoped Mrs. Carroll didn't think Beth was taking advantage.

"Changed your mind about what, honey?"

"I think I will go home."

"What a drama queen!" Jordan wiped his paper where he'd erased a hole in it, and set his jaw on his fist. "She didn't hardly even know that guy."

"I did too. He was my brother's best friend."

"Was not. Your parents wouldn't even let Jeff hang out with him!"

She wished she had a sock to shove into his mouth. "That was before. Jeff's allowed to hang out with him now."

"Stop it, Jordan," Mrs. Carroll said. "Don't be so cruel. Beth, it's fine if you go home. Just bundle up. It's cold."

Beth blinked back tears of indignation and pulled her coat on. It was just a lightweight denim jacket. After all, it never stayed cold in Birmingham for long. But today it was in the twenties, and people who knew clouds were saying it was going to snow. She'd worn several layers of clothes under her jacket, but even with the corduroy lining zipped in, it still wasn't quite enough. She hoped someone at home had kept some logs on the fire.

Jordan made a face at her as she packed up her book bag. The idiot acted like he was in fourth grade instead of seventh. He gave all of them a bad name. He didn't know anything about her brother or his friends. It was true that her parents hadn't approved of Zach, but over the last several months, Jeff had become so responsible—helping protect the family and making good decisions—that they'd given him a little more slack with the Emorys. He still wasn't allowed to go to their house at night. Ever since he'd been caught sneaking out to party with Zach and his brother a few months ago, right after the Pulses began, he'd been forbidden to go there after dark. But he was allowed to hang out with him during the day and early evening.

She pictured Zach going out in the twenty-eight degree cold that morning, watching his breath fog in the icy air. She imagined him walking through the woods to his deer stand with his rifle, climbing into the tree, waiting there in the chill for a deer to come along.

One thing had become clear to her over the last eight months. Since the Pulses, there didn't have to be a good reason for killing.

As she turned off Mrs. Carroll's street, she saw Mark Green in his driveway, holding a dead bobcat by its back legs. He opened the door to his mother's stranded Caravan and leaned inside.

"Hey, Mark," she called.

He turned and grinned at her. "Hey, Sparky. Where'd you come from?"

"School."

Mark was the only one who ever called her Sparky. He'd made up the name because he said she'd sparkled on the stage when she'd played Mary in the neighborhood Christmas play, which she had also written and directed.

She came up his driveway and looked into the van. Several slabs of meat hung upside-down from hooks in the roof.

Mark hung the bobcat up. "Did Mrs. Carroll let you guys out early because it's gonna snow?"

"No, she let me go because I wasn't feeling well." She shivered. "Mark, what are you doing?"

He grinned in that way he had. "Check out my new meat locker."

"A van? No offense, but that's crazy."

"Why? It's below freezing out. When I trap animals, I need somewhere to put them. And in the van I can close them in and keep other animals out."

She made a disgusted face. "What are you gonna do when it gets warm again? It'll be all gross."

He shrugged. "Stop using it."

"Your mom'll never want to drive this again."

"Let's be honest," he said, closing the door. "This van's engine is fried. It's not like it's going anywhere unless it's chained to a tow truck."

"But Dad says the body will still be good. And the engine and electronics can be replaced."

"By the time you do that, it'd be just as easy to replace the whole van. But don't criticize. I'm feeding your family tonight. I killed a deer this morning too."

She was glad he was a friend of her family. They never went hungry when Mark was hunting. In fact, most of the people who knew Mark were better for it. Mark had figured out how to make solar ovens out of ruined refrigerators, and the Brannings were just one of many families who were now able to cook so much easier. Beth's mother had been a bread-baking maniac lately, and was helping the family by selling the loaves.

"So have you got any new inventions?" she asked.

He walked her back to his garage. "I'm no inventor. These aren't my ideas."

"But you're the only one who knows how to pull them off." She looked at the things he was working on in his garage. There were two sliding glass doors from a shower leaning against the wall. Each had a crack. "What's this gonna be?"

"I'm working on a solar water heater. I got these doors from Sam Tobias, who has that bathroom renovating company. He let me have them free because they're cracked. I had to promise that if I made it work, I'd give the first one to him."

His flat-screen television sat on the floor. "What are you doing with that? Are you going to use the sun to make the TV work?"

He laughed. "Nope, can't do that. But I'm going to use the TV screen for some of my solar projects. You ever heard of a Fresnel lens?"

She giggled. "What do you think?"

"The screen is a sheet of clear plastic, and its surface has tiny little grooves in it. If I use it in the sun, that'll have the effect of magnification, so you'll be able to concentrate the heat where you want to create energy."

"But you have to tear up your nice TV to do it? No way my mom would agree to that."

"Why not? They're fried too. They're absolutely worthless, even when the power comes back on. If we can use them for something else, especially something that'll heat or cool our houses, then why not do it?"

She let out a heavy sigh. "I guess so. It's just all so sad."

"What? That all our stuff is ruined?"

"Yeah. Sometimes I get really depressed."

He sat down on a table and smiled. "It's just stuff, Sparky."

"Yeah, I know." She shoved her fists deeper into her pockets. "We're lucky just to be alive. Especially after what happened to Zach today."

"Yeah, I heard he was shot. But he's okay, right?"

"I don't think so. It sounds really bad. They said he might have been dead by the time the ambulance came."

"But he was still alive when they drove him off, right? Zach's tough. He'll pull through. A lot of people are praying for him." He looked down into her face and messed up her hair. "Don't let this get you down in the dumps, now. Everybody depends on your smile."

A grin pulled at her lips.

He slid off the table. "Come on, I'll walk you home."

"Deni's not home, you know. She's out snooping."

He chuckled. "I think they call that reporting. And I'm not doing it for Deni. What do you think? That I'm some kid with a crush, trying to find excuses to see her?"

She grinned. "Yep."

He laughed and messed up her hair. "Okay. But I'm walking you home, anyway."

She didn't really know why Deni and Mark weren't together. It was a romance waiting to happen—it just hadn't quite happened yet. Late last September, Deni had broken off her engagement with Craig, her pompous boyfriend from Washington. Since then, Mark had been around a lot. The chemistry between them almost crackled on the air. Whether it was just plain busy-ness, or something deeper, something had kept them apart so far. For the life of her, Beth didn't understand it.

If *she* were older, she would have snapped Mark up and made sure everyone knew he was hers. And if Deni didn't do something soon, Beth might do it, anyway. She was almost a teenager, after all. And Mark was only twenty-two.

But she'd rather have him as a brother-in-law.

They walked quietly for a moment, and as they reached her street, she glanced up at her tall friend. "Mark, do you think Zach got up this morning with some kind of premonition about dying?"

He looked down at her. "I don't know."

"I mean, like, was there a dream last night to warn him? Or did he look in the mirror and just ... know?" She knew Mark couldn't answer that. "I mean, sometimes you hear about teenagers dying, and you find out later they blogged about it, or wrote a poem or a song. Or they talked to their friends about death just the day before."

"Beth, he's not gonna die."

"But what if he does? Do you think he knew?"

Mark sighed. "Maybe you should ask Jeff. He's the one Zach would have talked to."

She looked at her feet. "I doubt he'll talk about it."

Mark set his hand on her shoulder. "Why does it matter, Beth? What difference would it make?"

She thought about that. "I guess … it would make me feel better. Like maybe I won't wind up dead all of a sudden … that God would give me warning before somebody came along and shot me."

He stopped walking and touched her chin, pulling her face up. "You're not afraid of death, are you?"

"I don't think so … I mean, not the heaven part of death. But I don't much want to be gunned down like Zach was."

"Don't worry. You won't be."

"It's not a stupid fear," she said. "We've had people break into our house before, and Dad's been shot once."

"I didn't say it was stupid. But you have a lot of protectors, Sparky. And God has watched over you all this time. Remember the verses your dad had the church learn a few months ago? 'The Lord is my light and my salvation; whom shall I fear?' "

Beth finished the verse. " 'The Lord is the defense of my life; whom shall I dread?' Psalm 27:1."

"It's true, Beth."

"Then why wasn't he watching over Zach?"

She had him there. "We don't know that he wasn't. But living in fear is no kind of life. We have to trust God. That doesn't mean bad things won't happen. But we know he's in charge."

She wished she could believe him. She almost did. Mark always told the truth, and he seemed, to her, almost as wise as her father. Slowly, he started walking again, and she followed, quietly letting his assurances sink in.

"Tell me something, Sparky. When have you felt closest to God?"

She thought for a moment. "When Deni was missing. When little Sarah was in trouble. I prayed more then."

"So could it be that good can come out of suffering? That God uses it to build things into us? Things we might need?"

"Yeah," she said, "I guess he does."

"So just because some evil person shot Zach, or your dad, or kidnapped people we care about ... it doesn't mean that God has lost control. He's allowed it for reasons we don't know, and he's still watching over us, guarding us, protecting us. He loves us, Beth. We have to trust that about him."

She knew that was true, but still her fears remained. "I wish we could control God with our prayers."

He chuckled. "Thank goodness we can't. I've prayed for some pretty stupid things. But our prayers can influence him. He listens to them."

She thought of the time she'd prayed for Jordan Miller to flunk an English test. She'd almost flunked it herself. She sure hoped God took her more seriously when she prayed for Zach.

They got to her house, and Mark hung back on the sidewalk. "Lock the door, Beth," he said. "And when Deni gets home, tell her to come see me. I want to know what she found out about Zach."

"Okay. Thanks for walking me home."

She went into the house and locked the door behind her. The fire had almost died out. The house was almost as cold inside as outside. She stirred the embers in the fireplace and put the last two logs on the fire, then went outside to get more. In the backyard, the cold air slapped her in the face again, making her wish she had stayed inside. Even so, she crossed the yard to the chicken coop. Since her family had gotten the chickens, she'd considered them her pets. Beth's dad had ordered them as little chicks after the first FEMA disbursement. She'd taken care of them herself when they'd kept them in a box inside the house, to keep them from getting plucked up by a ravenous hawk or other predator. The Brannings had learned a lot about raising chickens since then. They'd had to remodel their original coop so the chickens had room to roam and feed on the ground. The yard was mostly dirt now that winter was here, but they maintained a patch of grass at the back of the yard, surrounded the coop with chicken wire, and covered it to keep out birds of prey. Since they'd used the fencing boards to build the coop, there was nothing to keep dogs out of their yard. The Brannings had to keep a close eye on their flock.

Beth supposed that was how it was with human killers too. If someone wanted to do evil, a fence wouldn't keep them out. And if they wanted something of yours, not much would keep them from taking it. Life wasn't worth all that much to some people these days.

Today, because it was cold, the chickens mostly stayed inside, warming each other in a little huddle. As she stepped inside the coop, the rooster cackled and the hens fluttered around as if glad to see her.

"Cold, huh?" she said to her little friends. She reached for the bag of feed sitting on the top shelf and scattered it around the area outside the door. Then she got a handful of fine sand and scattered it on top, to help them grind their food.

"They say it's going to snow. If it does, maybe Dad will let me bring you into the garage. It's dark in there and not much warmer. But at least the wind doesn't blow through."

She checked the nest; a few more eggs had been laid. She put them in her basket. The eggs their chickens produced made it possible for the Brannings to eat even when her father's and brothers' hunting didn't pay off. And there were plenty of eggs to share with neighbors like Amber Rowe, the single woman with three kids who lived next door. They could even sell or trade a few when the need arose.

But there were two things about raising chickens that Beth hated. She threw a fit whenever they slaughtered one. And even if chicken poop was a magic ingredient her father loved for composting, it was still nasty and smelly, and Beth was sick of wiping it off her shoes.

She ducked and stepped out of the little gate again, closed it, and made sure the enclosure was tight. As she wiped her feet on the grass, she looked around, making sure there was nothing around to hurt the chickens. She shivered at the thought of Zach's killer being out there somewhere. Maybe he didn't live in Oak Hollow, or even in Crockett. Maybe he'd gotten what he wanted and hopped a train out of town. Maybe he wasn't a danger anymore.

Whatever.

She decided she'd better take the firewood in and keep the house locked tight.

She suddenly wished she'd stayed at school.

She went back in, leaving her chicken-soiled shoes by the door, and stirred the fire. Then she curled up in the chair close to the hearth and prayed that someone in her family would get home soon.

SEVEN

DOUG AND JEFF LOCKED UP THEIR BIKES AND WENT INTO University Hospital. Dim lightbulbs shone from the ceiling in the lobby. "Hey, Dad, look. They've got electricity."

"Yeah. The conversion plants have hardened enough generators to get the hospitals operational. Otherwise, a lot more people would die."

They pushed through the people crowded into the waiting room, in various stages of illness or injury. They saw a nurse in purple scrubs; Doug headed toward her. "Ma'am, we're looking for a shooting victim who was brought in a little while ago. Where would they have taken him?"

The woman looked tired and overworked. "The surgical ICU is up on the fourth floor." She pointed to the stairwell, then hurried away.

They stepped into the darkness of the stairwell. "Why aren't there lights in here?" Jeff asked, his voice echoing.

"They probably only use the generators for high-priority areas." His voice echoed as they went up the stairs. "Like the operating rooms and monitors and machines."

"Then maybe they can save Zach." Jeff felt for the door to the fourth floor and pushed into the lighted hallway. They saw a sign that said, "Surgical ICU Waiting Room," and went inside.

The room was lit only by its windows, but Doug spotted the Emorys sitting in a corner.

Ellen—Zach's mother—looked as if she'd been in mourning since long before her son was shot. Jeff had occasionally spoken of Zach's mother as if she were crazy. One minute she was screaming at everyone in her family, the next she was so depressed that she couldn't get out of bed. "It's like she's given up," he'd said a week ago. "I really think she's losing it."

She got up when she saw them coming and hugged Jeff as if he were part of the family. "He's alive," she said. "They've got him in surgery."

Gary Emory, Zach's brother, paced back and forth across the waiting room—back and forth, back and forth—as if slowing down or sitting for a moment might mean letting go of his brother. "He was shot right through the chest. They said he couldn't breathe."

Doug's heart sank. He prayed they could still use the equipment they needed to save Zach. Though they could provide electricity to this vital place, X-rays, MRIs, and CT scans would still be out of the question. Any sensitive equipment too high-tech to withstand the frequent gamma-ray pulses emitted from the supernova would still be useless.

"I know why you're here," Ned said, leaning against the wall and looking at Doug. He seemed stunned, shell shocked, as if the news of his boy's injury was still circulating in his head, trying to find a place to rest. "You're here because you think we need a preacher, and the truth is, we do."

Ellen shot him a look. "Speak for yourself, Ned. I don't need one."

"Then who's gonna bury Zach if he dies?" Ned's words whiplashed across the room, and Ellen recoiled as if they had struck her in the face.

"He's not gonna die!" She stuck her chin out, lips tight over her teeth. "Why do you say things like that, like you want it to happen? Are you trying to set me off? Do you *want* me to put my fist through your face?"

Doug hadn't expected to hear such a threat from a woman who weighed about one hundred pounds and looked as delicate as a cracked reed. But there was fire in her eyes, and Doug didn't doubt she would do it.

"I wasn't trying to set you off, Ellen, so stop with the dramatics," Ned returned. "For once it's not about you!"

"It's *never* about me!" she shouted. "I'm surprised you even came."

Doug glanced at Jeff, who looked as if he'd seen this behavior before.

"You'll probably be back at work before Zach even stops bleeding!" Ellen said.

"I'm here, aren't I? Nothing's ever good enough for you!"

"Could you two shut up?" Their son's demand cut through their ire, silencing them.

The others in the waiting room began to applaud. Despite Doug's surprise that Gary had talked to his parents that way, he wanted to join in.

Jeff turned his back to the Emorys and whispered, "Dad, she's crazy. Let me handle this."

Doug couldn't imagine what Jeff could do, but his son turned and approached the feuding parents. "Was Zach awake when they got him here?"

Ellen shot a threatening look to those who had just applauded, then sank back onto a vinyl chair. Her voice was low when she answered. "He was in and out of consciousness, but gasping for breath."

Doug wished Kay were with him so she could comfort Ellen somehow. He'd do it himself, but he feared losing an eye if he reached for her.

"They're able to run ventilators," Ned said. "So he'll have help breathing."

Finally, some good news. "Will you get to stay with him?" Doug asked.

Gary nodded. "One of us at a time."

"I'll help," Jeff said. "I'll tell all the guys. We can take turns sitting with him around the clock. Just say the word."

Ellen's face softened. "Thank you, Jeff. You're a good boy." As if that declaration crushed her, she melted into tears.

For a moment, everyone was awkwardly quiet.

Finally, Gary spoke up. "Is anybody talking about who did this?" he asked Jeff. "Surely *somebody* knows. Somebody saw *something*."

"I haven't heard any rumors," Jeff said. "But we came almost as soon as we heard."

"It shouldn't be that hard to figure out," Doug said. "Whoever it was came home with a deer."

"What?" Ned asked. "What do you mean?"

Doug realized they hadn't been told much yet. He wondered if he should wait and let the sheriff deliver the news.

But Jeff spoke up. "I heard Zach had just shot a deer, and whoever shot him took it."

Ellen gasped, and Ned spun around to Gary. "Did you know this?"

Gary's nostrils flared, and his eyes flashed. "No, Dad. I ran for help as soon as I saw him laying there. There was no deer. They must have already taken it."

"My son was shot for deer meat?" Ellen shrieked, turning to her son. "How long did it take you to get to him?"

Gary looked sick. "I had one in my sights myself, so I waited a few minutes. I figured he'd shot one, but I didn't think it was an emergency. I would've gone if I knew he was shot!" Gary's voice broke and he turned away, hiding tears. Jeff slid his hands into his pockets and looked at the floor. But Doug watched as Ellen took several angry strides toward her son. He braced himself, expecting her to attack Gary. But she surprised him again and took her firstborn into her arms. He clung to her and wept. After a moment, Ned joined their embrace.

Doug set his arm around Jeff's shoulder, feeling his son's struggle to hold his emotions.

"He's gonna make it, Dad," Jeff whispered. "I know he is. He has to."

Doug looked past him to the hallway outside the waiting room, where other wounded or sick people were lined up on gurneys, waiting for the operating room. Thankfully, Zach had been moved to the front of the line. Doug supposed a bullet in the chest warranted emergency treatment.

"It's out of our hands now," he said to the Emorys. "All we can do is pray and wait. But I know from experience that God answers prayer. Will you let us pray with you?"

Ellen tightened again. "I don't believe in God, so do your praying somewhere else."

"Mom ..." Gary said. "You don't have to be a jerk about it."

Ned rubbed his jaw. "I don't know what I believe, but I'll accept your prayers, Doug. They sure can't hurt."

Doug hadn't been in his preaching role for very long—only eight months, since the Pulses began and he'd started a church in their home. He'd never been comfortable in situations like this, especially when the family had shunned his efforts to invite them to church. He wondered if Ellen's and Ned's attitudes toward God had anything to do with the fact that he'd forbidden Jeff to hang around with Zach in the past couple of years. The boy had seemed like a bad influence for Jeff, and Ellen's behavior just now reinforced that.

He was glad that over the last three or four months he had let Zach come around more often. And Doug hadn't tried to stand in the way when Jeff and Zach started a band. The boys needed a diversion, and that was as good as any.

But now he wished he'd been more caring toward the family. He bowed his head and began to pray aloud for Zach, knowing that God heard his prayers whether Zach's family were believers or not. He prayed for miraculous intervention, and for God to give the Emorys peace and comfort. Then he asked God to lead the authorities to the one who'd done this.

When Doug opened his eyes, Ellen's cold eyes were fixed on the wall. "If they find the guy who did this," she said, "I'll make sure he doesn't live to brag about it."

Doug cleared his throat and remembered his own declarations of vengeance when Deni had turned up missing. He couldn't say he blamed her.

EIGHT

It was a terrible day for a swap meet, but Kay couldn't back out now. Despite the snow beginning to blanket the ground and the 28-degree cold—and the terrible news they'd gotten about Zach—she had managed to get a wagonload of goods to the tent. She hoped she'd trade it all, because she sure didn't want to borrow a horse and wagon again to take it back home.

The swap meet was held every month on the playground behind Crockett Elementary. It was a way for people to trade for things they needed. Since anything other than food was considered a luxury, no one had the means to purchase birthday gifts or clothes or shoes ... or anything else.

The swap meet tents were always full of baby furniture, clothes, and toys, and young parents looked for necessities for new babies and growing toddlers. Kay hoped she could trade for some bags of flour and baking soda. She also hoped to find some presents for Doug's birthday tomorrow. She had brought all of her children's outgrown clothes, a tub of shoes that weren't being worn, some blankets she'd made, some old curtains, and a number of other items she hoped someone wanted. She'd also used her makeshift solar oven to bake twenty loaves of bread, with which she hoped to buy food from local farmers in a nearby tent.

Logan, her nine-year-old son, had brought his own box of stuff. She watched as he unloaded it onto their table: there were several action figures, a Rubik's Cube, some soccer shin guards, an old bicycle helmet, and some things she couldn't identify.

He pulled out a wooden ball with sticks coming out of it, each with a smaller ball on the end. She picked it up. "Logan, what's *this*?"

Logan took it from her and grinned. "It's my molecule. I made it for science class last year."

She remembered then—he'd spent hours drilling holes into the wooden ball made for a banister. "And you think somebody'll trade for it?"

"Sure. Look at it. Who *wouldn't* want this?"

It would have been funny on any other day, but her heart was too heavy for amusement now. The news about Zach had made it hard to focus.

Logan spotted something across the tent. "Cool, a parachute! I'm gonna see if I can get it."

"Logan, we need flour, not parachutes. And don't you want to get your dad a present?"

"Dad would *love* a parachute, Mom. Besides, I have plenty of stuff to trade."

"But what would you use it for? I don't want you jumping off anything."

"Mom, get real. You can do a *million* things with it. It's fun just to *have*!"

She sighed and hoped they wouldn't be interested in trading for a molecule.

"Terrible about Zach, huh?"

Kay turned and saw Mark Green's mother Martha setting up next to her.

"Yeah, really terrible. I sure hope he pulls through."

Martha's black hair had grown long enough to wear in a ponytail. With her petite frame, she looked years younger than she was. And Martha didn't have the gray stripe Kay had at her roots. Kay tried not to envy her.

"Have you heard any details?" Martha asked.

"Not really."

"Who would do that?" Martha shook her head and sighed. "I'm telling you, it's a dark world."

Martha knew of what she spoke. She had once been married to a psychopath. He was dead now, but he'd been the bane of her existence for much of her adult life. The trials had made her stronger. Kay supposed she deserved to have great hair, after all she'd been through.

"This is the first one of these I've been to," Martha said as she unloaded her boxes of solar panels Mark had built. "Tell me how it works. If someone wants one of these, but they don't have anything I want, what do I do?"

"You take it to the uneven-trade table, where they'll assign you some tokens for the value of your item. Then you can spend them on other items at that table."

"Sounds complicated."

Kay laughed. "It is. Trade even if you can. But the farmers do set up at those tables, so if you need flour like I do, you have no choice but to go there."

Kay's eyes drifted to Logan, negotiating for the parachute. Thankfully, the owners didn't seem to want his dirty shin guards *or* his science project. Looking discouraged, he started back toward her—but then he spotted a litter of cocker spaniel puppies, and hope filled his eyes again. "Score!" he shouted.

"Logan, no animals!" she called over the crowd.

But he didn't hear her. He made a beeline toward the puppies, brandishing his useless currency. He was going to drive her crazy before the day was over.

NINE

Deni Branning stood over the printing press at the office of the *Crockett Times*, watching Harriet Campbell set the movable type so she could print Deni's story about the shooting for the next issue. "Too bad we can't wait to hear about Zach's prognosis," Harriet said as she worked. Her breath fogged in the dimly lit room. They'd managed to get the press set up, but getting any kind of stove or fireplace into the small building was a luxury they couldn't yet afford.

"Wish we could get the paper out every day instead of just once a week," Deni said.

"Well, with your updates on the message boards around town, we can keep the people informed."

Months ago, when Deni had first decided to be the self-proclaimed journalist for her little community, she'd started the *Crockett Community Journal*, a big name for such a small undertaking. Since she didn't have the benefit of computers and Xerox machines, she'd had to handwrite her stories and stick them up on the literal message boards posted in neighborhoods all over town. Those boards, which were covered with notes, for-sale signs, and other scribbled communications, had become the area's source for all their news.

Then back in November, Harriet Campbell had shown up at Deni's door and asked if she'd like a job. Harriet had bought an old-time printing press that didn't rely on electricity, and she was ready to get the *Crockett Times* up and running again. She'd been impressed by Deni's news items on the message boards and decided she'd be an asset to her little newspaper.

Deni had jumped at the chance. She had dissolved her little journal and merged forces with the *Crockett Times*. This was something she could actually use on a résumé someday, and the printed paper, which could be delivered to homes around town, looked much more professional than what she could produce with a manual typewriter and carbon paper. But it was time-consuming setting each letter by hand. Fortunately, Harriet's husband and children helped so that Deni was able to be a field reporter most of the time.

"I just went by the sheriff's department on the way home from the site of the shooting," Deni told her, "and people are already starting to show up naming men who brought deer home this morning."

Harriet looked up at her. "Can I include them in the article?"

"No, better not," Deni said. "Only one is guilty—and I don't want to smear anyone's reputation if they didn't do anything wrong." She shoved her hands into her pockets and started for the door. "But I'm going now to interview some of them. And I'll let you know as soon as my brother and dad get back with news of Zach's condition."

She pushed out the door into the cold and looked around at the snow already blanketing the street. She'd always loved snow before, but she dreaded it now. This area didn't have snow *every* year—so why did they have to have it *this* year? With no heat, people would die. Not everyone had a fireplace, and many hadn't been able to purchase stoves to help keep their homes warm. She worried about the people in the apartments around town. Many of the residents had died of typhoid, dysentery, and other diseases from the backed-up sewage. Others had left the apartments and migrated to places where living was a little easier—near lakes or farmland. Those who remained were trying to work together to survive. But living without air conditioning in summer was a lot easier than living without heat in freezing weather.

At least the government had used some of their working and revamped car engines to haul tanker trucks full of water to areas where there weren't any wells. This had lowered the mortality rate among the apartment dwellers. Though the tankers were never replaced as soon as the water ran out, still, it had helped the quality of life for so many. News from up north told of thousands dying this winter. The hospitals that were open overflowed with people with contagious diseases and bacterial infections. Deni hoped her dad and Jeff weren't exposed to anything while they were checking on Zach, and that Zach wouldn't develop a staph infection—something that had emerged as a killer of many after serious wounds.

That morning's interviews of the men who'd been first on the scene after Zach's shooting had left Deni feeling, once again, as if life balanced on a thin fulcrum, ready to tip and crash at any moment. Never in her twenty-two years had she been more aware of the fragility of life than she had been these last few months, and Zach's shooting hammered that home.

Sheriff Scarbrough had given her little in the way of comments for the paper, but his suggestion to ask people if they'd seen anyone coming home with a deer this morning had been a good one. She'd had Harriet print up a sheet to put on the message boards around town earlier today. The top half gave the news of Zach's shooting and the known circumstances. Below that, she'd written:

> CAN YOU HELP FIND ZACH EMORY'S SHOOTER?
> If you know of anyone who came home with a deer this morning, February 4, report it to the sheriff immediately.

It hadn't taken long for people to start talking, and before she'd gotten the paper tacked up on all of the boards, she'd started getting names.

But there was one name on the list that she'd rather not see—Mark Green.

She stopped her bike and wrapped her scarf more firmly around her face to keep the bitter wind from chapping her skin. She doubted that Mark knew he was on the list of possible suspects. The idea of his having anything to do with shooting Zach was so preposterous that she couldn't even consider it. Yet the neighbors would. His dead father had been sinister and violent, and no one would forget that. The mere hint that he might be responsible would send the neighborhood into a panic.

Pedaling into Oak Hollow, she bypassed her own house and went straight to his. She found him in his garage, surrounded by the inventions he'd created in the last few months.

"Hey, Mark. What are you doing?"

"Hey." He looked happy to see her. That warm feeling she always got when she was near him swelled in her heart as she parked her bike.

"Any word on Zach?" he asked.

"No, not yet. I'm still gathering facts." She looked at the little box on which he was screwing a hinge. "What's this?"

"I'm working on a birthday present for your dad." He showed her the box he'd built, with a slat at the top.

"What is it?"

"A tool box. I know he has one, but I thought maybe he could use another one." He opened the top. "I carved out this Bible verse inside."

Deni bent over and saw the ornate inscription. " 'Do your best to present yourself to God as one approved, a workman who does not need to be ashamed.' 2 Timothy 2:15."

"He'll love it," she said. Mark was always thoughtful with her family members. But for some reason, he held back when he was with Deni. She couldn't forget the kiss they'd shared last summer. Fireworks had gone off in her chest, and her heart had raced more in Mark's arms than it ever had in Craig's. Then Craig had shown up and messed up everything.

She'd wound up breaking off her engagement once and for all and had sensed afterward that Mark was giving her time to reconsider. And just when he'd finally seemed satisfied that she wasn't pining away for Craig, he'd found a letter she'd been writing to him. He had trouble believing that her letter, far from being a declaration of love for Craig, was simply answering Craig's pleas for her to take him back. But the letter had been unfinished, and what *wasn't* written had done more harm than what was.

So Mark had backed off. Pride had kept her from groveling. But the chemistry remained.

And his friendship had become something she cherished.

He glanced at her face, and she knew he sensed that something was wrong. He set the toolbox down. "What's wrong, Deni?"

She sighed. "Mark, I need to ask you something. Did you kill a deer this morning?"

"Sure did. Eight points. Don't worry, I'm bringing your family some venison tonight."

He clearly had no idea what was being said about him. "Mark, that deer is going to cause you a world of problems."

He frowned. "Why?"

"Because the sheriff is compiling a list of all those who brought home a deer this morning. And you're on it."

Mark set his hands on his hips. "What would my killing a deer today have to do with Zach's shooting?"

"They're saying that whoever shot Zach did it for his deer. They left him for dead and took his game."

Understanding dawned on his face. "And they think *I* did that?"

She sighed. "Mark, you know there are lots of people around here who don't trust you. They'll think—"

"I don't care what they think! I didn't shoot anybody. Zach knows that. And you know it too."

"Of course I do. But I wasn't there. And Zach may not make it. Mark, where were you hunting this morning?"

"Off Tiger Road, on the Carlisle property."

"That's a long way from where Zach was. Did you see anyone? Anybody who can confirm that you were there?"

Mark grunted and gazed down at her. "You don't *believe* me?"

"Of course I believe you. It's not that. It's just that the sheriff is going to question you, Mark. And you need to have someone corroborate your alibi."

"Alibi?" Mark gaped at her in disbelief. "I don't need an alibi, Deni."

"Think," she said. "Anyone. You need a name."

He gave her a look that declared her a traitor. Turning his back, he went across the garage, picked up a screwdriver, and hung it on a hook on the wall. "I didn't see anybody at the Carlisle property. They have a hundred acres, and their house is all the way on the other side. I have a blanket invitation to hunt there ever since I helped them convert their car into a horse-drawn carriage." He turned back around. "But I saw people when I was on my way home with the deer. It was before I'd heard about Zach. Maybe the timing will clear me."

"What time was it?"

"About ten o'clock."

"That doesn't help. They don't really know what time Zach was shot. He wasn't found until a little after ten, and he'd been lying there awhile."

"This is incredible." Mark dropped into a lawn chair and looked at his feet.

Deni sat across from him. "Mark, someone must've seen you, someone who can confirm the time you were at the Carlisle place. We just have to calm down and think."

They heard the rattle of an engine coming up the street, and Mark got to his feet as the sheriff's van came into view. "Oh no, it's happening," he said.

Deni stood back up and made him look at her. "Mark, Sheriff Scarbrough knows you. He'll listen. Just stay calm and tell him the truth."

Mark walked out into the driveway as the sheriff pulled in. Sheriff Scarbrough looked sullen as he got out of his van. "How ya doing, Mark? Deni?"

Deni nodded a greeting.

Mark shook his hand. "Go ahead and cut to the chase, Sheriff. I know why you're here."

Mark was too blunt, Deni thought. Meeting this head-on might make him look guilty. "Sheriff, I heard he was on the list," she said. "I came to tell him."

The sheriff nodded. "Mark, I have to do my job."

"I guess you'll want to see my deer," Mark said, striding toward his mother's Caravan. "I've got it right here. I shot it at the Carlisle place this morning."

He opened the side door, revealing the deer he'd already skinned. But it was still in one piece.

The deer he'd killed weighed two hundred pounds, Deni guessed, and had a bullet through the breastbone.

The sheriff examined the animal for an exit wound. "Looks like the bullet went straight through. Maybe we can find it at the Carlisle place." He glanced up at Mark. "I need to see your guns, Mark."

Mark nodded and led him into the house to get them. He handed them to the sheriff one by one, then brought him back out to the garage where the light was better.

Scarbrough laid the guns out on Mark's work table.

Deni watched him examine them. "He didn't do it, Sheriff. You know he didn't."

Scarbrough just coughed.

"Sheriff Scarbrough, you know him! Mark's not that kind of a person, and he doesn't have to steal someone else's game. He's a good hunter. He's even put food on *your* table."

Scarbrough quit coughing and cleared his throat. "I realize that, Deni."

"Then why don't you leave him alone?"

"The best thing I can do for Mark right now is to find evidence that rules him out."

Hope rose in her. "Then you *do* know that he's innocent."

Scarbrough wouldn't answer.

Mark pointed to his Remington. "This is what I was hunting with this morning, Sheriff. Do you know yet what caliber bullet hit Zach?"

The sheriff opened the action on the gun and took out the cartridges. "I can't talk about the investigation with you, Mark. But I need a list of people you saw when you were bringing your deer home. I'll want to talk to them about the time they saw you. I also want you to take me to where you shot the deer. Show me the bullet. The shell casings. Show me the blood on the ground. Show me your footprints. Prove to me when you were there."

Mark brought his chin up and started toward the sheriff's van. "Let's go right now."

"Can I come?" Deni asked.

Scarbrough shook his head. "No, Deni. I'd rather you didn't."

"Off the record!" she said. "Sheriff, trust me. I won't write anything about it."

"It's a criminal investigation, Deni. You can't come."

Mark turned back to her. "I'll come by your house when I get back." He walked them out, closed and locked the garage door.

Deni hated being left behind.

"Do me a favor and tell my mom," he said as he got in the van. "She's at the swap meet. I don't want her to hear this from someone else."

"I will. Mark, just think. Go over the whole morning in your mind. Someone must have seen you there."

As the old rattletrap of a van pulled out of Mark's driveway, Deni watched as several neighbors came out to see. Lou Grantham crossed his yard and approached her.

"Did he arrest Mark?" he asked her.

"No, of course they didn't." She got on her bike. "He just asked him some questions."

"He did it, didn't he?" Roland Gunn and his wife were crossing the street. "They locking Mark up? I always knew that kid was no good."

She wanted to run over him. "No, you didn't! You thought he was good enough to help you build your greenhouse so you could grow food. And how many times have you eaten things he's provided for you?"

"So he's a good actor."

"Mark is innocent!" she yelled back.

But no one was listening. They already had their minds made up.

TEN

Kay had just made a deal to trade a blanket she'd made out of old clothes for some leather gloves and a knitted scarf for Doug's birthday. She'd also spotted a parka in Beth's size, and now she waited for Logan to come back and man her table so she could go make a deal.

She spotted him in front of a toy table, looking like he'd just hit the jackpot. She dreaded seeing what he had traded for. A few minutes later, he turned with his arms full of badminton equipment and ran back to her. "Mom, look what I got Dad!"

"You got him badminton equipment? Are you sure that's not for you?"

His face fell. "Well ... he can play it with me. But isn't it cool?"

"So what did you trade for it?"

"My molecule," he said. "Told you I'd sell it!"

Something didn't sound right about the deal. She looked across the tent at the people who'd made the trade. Surely they weren't stupid. "So let me get this straight. You told them that was your science project and that it was a molecule, and they traded you?"

He looked away and shrugged. "Sort of."

"Why don't you explain, 'sort of'?"

"Well ... I kinda told them it was a pulsar. A supernova, like SN–1999."

No wonder. There was so much interest in the pulsar that was causing all these problems on earth that it would stand to reason they'd make the trade. But it was still a lie. "Logan, that molecule doesn't look anything like a pulsar and you know it. You made that up. Do you know what a fraud is?"

He narrowed his eyes. "No."

"How about a scam artist?"

"I'm not a scam artist! I'm just a good negotiator."

"It's not called *negotiation* when you start off with a fraudulent product." She took the badminton set from him. "Was this an even trade?"

"Yes."

"Then you're going to take it back and tell them you lied."

"Mom! I can't do that!"

"Oh yes, you can. If they still want it after they know it's a molecule, fine. If they don't, then you'll cancel the trade. And hurry it up, because I need you to man the table while I register my deals."

She marched Logan across the tent. His face was hangdog as he made his confession to the father of the kid he'd scammed. The father looked amused, but the boy was indignant. They traded back without a lecture.

Logan pouted as they headed back to the table. "You've been trying to keep me from selling that all day," he said. "It's like *you* want it or something."

"That's right. I've always loved that molecule."

Logan laughed despite himself. She grinned and messed his hair up. "Wait here. Don't make any deals without me, but you can *start* a negotiation if someone wants something. I'll be over there."

As she went around the table, Martha winked at her, then sidled up to Logan. "Logan, I've actually had my eye on that molecule all day long. Do you think you might like to trade for one of Mark's old track trophies?"

Logan caught his breath. "You bet I would!"

Kay couldn't help laughing. At the table with the girls' clothes, she looked at the ski parka. It was perfect for Beth. Just what she needed. She made a deal to trade them for some of Deni's outgrown ski clothes—the perfect size for their fifteen-year-old daughter—and hurried back to the table with her prize.

"Mom!"

She looked up and saw Deni coming through the crowd. "Hey, honey. Look what I got Dad for his birthday. And I found this parka for Beth! She's gonna love this!"

Deni looked right past her to Martha Green. "Oh, Martha—you're the one I came to talk to."

Martha smiled up at her. "What is it, Deni?"

But Kay could see from Deni's face that something was wrong. "Is there word on Zach?"

"No, not yet," she said. "But Mark wanted me to come and tell you—" Her voice broke, and she cleared her throat. "Sheriff Scarbrough came to question Mark about the shooting."

"*What?*"

"People are saying he did it, since he brought home a deer this morning."

Martha stood up, knocking over her lawn chair. "Was he arrested?"

"No. They just took him to where he was hunting to see if he can prove he was there instead of at the crime scene."

Martha grabbed a box and started throwing things in. "I have to go home. I have to get in touch with my husband."

"Where *is* John?" Kay asked.

"At the conversion plant in Huntsville. They drafted him and sent him there. I don't know if they'll let him come home."

"Martha, what can I do?"

Martha threw up her hands. "I don't know."

"You go on. I'll box your stuff and bring it to you later."

They watched as she walked her bike through the crowd and out of the tent. Deni was shaking. Kay hugged her. "Honey, it's going to be all right. Mark just has to prove he wasn't near where Zach was shot."

"He can't think of anyone who saw him, Mom. And with this snow … what if he can't find proof?"

"Sheriff Scarbrough knows Mark's character. Besides, Zach will wake up. Maybe he has already. He'll tell them who it really was." Kay could see that her words weren't calming Deni.

"I have to go," Deni said, starting abruptly away. "I have more people to interview about the shooting."

ELEVEN

MARK LED THE SHERIFF AND DEPUTY JONES THROUGH THE woods behind the Carlisle property. The sheriff had a nasty cough, and Mark knew the icy air wasn't helping. He hoped he could quickly find evidence that he'd been here and be done with it.

The snow was coming down hard now, blanketing the ground and collecting on the naked branches. They trudged up over the frosty earth and through the barren trees and reached the deer stand where Mark had spent much of the morning. He showed them where his deer had fallen, but the ground was covered with snow.

Dropping to his knees, he raked the snow away with his hands until he found a small spot of blood. "There it is," he said. "This is the spot where he fell." He hurried to his deer stand and looked for a shell casing or discharged cartridge on the ground below. Kicking away the snow, he realized it might be hard to find. Jones climbed up onto the stand. "Here's a shell, boss."

Mark felt a surge of relief. "See? I told you."

Deputy Jones brought it down, and Scarbrough examined it. "Mark, this could have been fired today or two weeks ago. It doesn't prove anything."

"Sure, it does. Sheriff, I told you what you'd find. It's right here, where I said. It proves I was here."

"It doesn't prove *when* you were here."

"Then why did you come out here? Did you expect the casing to have a date stamp on it? I told you I shot a deer, that I shot it here, and I've shown you evidence that I'm not lying. What more can I do?"

"Show me someone who saw you here *today*. Give me something I can work with. I need a time."

"And what if I can't?"

The sheriff just looked at him. "Mark, you see the dilemma I'm in."

"I didn't do it, Sheriff." Mark opened his arms. "I got here while it was still dark. Unless someone saw me without my realizing it, I was alone until I started home. It can't be a big surprise that I wouldn't bring a crowd with me."

Scarbrough rubbed his tired face. "Mark, witnesses who saw you bringing the deer home said you were carrying it in a bike trailer with car tires—like the one your dad designed."

Mark nodded. "That's right. You've seen my bike trailer."

"There were the same kind of tracks at the crime scene."

"Sheriff, you can look at my tires, compare the tread. Check to see if it's the same dirt! You know I'm not the only one with that kind of wagon! People around here have copied that design since my dad came up with it."

Jones buried his hands in his pockets. "Want me to get some dirt samples, Sheriff?"

Scarbrough coughed. "Yeah, go ahead. We'll need them from both sites and from Mark's tires. And compare the shell casings at the crime scene with Mark's guns."

Mark couldn't believe they were treating him as a suspect. "So are you going to arrest me?"

"That depends on what we find, Mark."

Mark threw up his hands. "Sheriff, you know me! You know I'm not the kind of man who would do that!"

"Right now I'm only interested in the facts, son."

Mark decided to keep his mouth shut so he wouldn't make things worse. But that old bitterness burned inside him.

Blame Vic's kid. His dad was a killer, so he must be one too. Anger at his dead father seethed inside him. Even from the grave, he was still jerking him around.

The sheriff took Mark home where his hysterical mother waited. Mark tried to calm her down while Scarbrough and Jones made prints of the tire tracks on his bike wagon and scraped dirt from the treads. When they finally left, Mark tried to believe that the evidence would clear him. But something in the pit of his stomach told him there would be more to come.

TWELVE

Sherriff Ralph Scarbrough's lungs felt full of fluid. He coughed as he drove down the streets dodging bicyclers, horse-drawn buggies, and pedestrians who walked like there were no rules. That weary sense of dread he'd been battling for the last few weeks fell over him again. Another shooting, another killer on the loose, and he didn't know if he had the energy to track this crime to its final conclusion. For the last eight months since the outage began, Scarbrough had been racing from one emergency to another. His job had been busy enough before the outage, when he had radios and telephones, computer databases, functional forensic labs, and a complete, reliable staff.

But everything had changed on May 24, and since that time, the number of crimes reported to his county offices had gone up by about 50 percent. He felt certain that half as many more went unreported, since people had figured out that minor, nonviolent crimes were hardly ever solved these days. The sheriff and his shrinking band of deputies spent all their time chasing down threats, solving crimes without the benefit of modern technology, and trying to keep the county safe.

And Crockett wasn't his only problem. He had all of Jefferson County—including the entire Birmingham area—to worry about, plus the prison and the holding jails in each of the county's regions. Though his main station was in the city, he lived in Crockett, so he worked mostly at the Crockett substation since the outage. It was too expensive and time-consuming going into Birmingham every day. But he'd stationed capable deputy chiefs over all of his substations.

He only hoped he could keep them. Each payday he lost a few more deputies who decided the job wasn't worth it. He couldn't say he blamed them. They were all exhausted and demoralized. And they didn't even make a living wage.

It was past lunchtime and he hadn't eaten breakfast, so he drove to his own house on a rural road where the houses were spaced far apart. He had about three acres with a small house planted right in the center of it. He pulled onto the dirt driveway and rumbled up to his house. He hoped his wife had been able to put a lunch together. Since last summer, they'd been raising rabbits for meat, and when he left this morning she had been planning to slaughter one today.

He pulled his van into the open garage, thankful to be out of the snow, and went into the house. It was warm from the fire crackling in the den. His wife was kneading bread at the counter, a spot of flour on her chin. "Do you believe that snow?" she asked as she took off his hat and shook it out over the sink.

"Wouldn't you know it?" he said. "Where's Jimmy?"

She glanced out the window. "Trying to fish a dead cat out of the well."

What next? He went to the window and saw the pump-style well disassembled. "Who took the pump off?"

"Jimmy was cleaning it," she said. "That cat must have gone in while we had it open. All I know is it's down there polluting our drinking water and we've got to get it out."

He closed his eyes. Somebody would have to scoop the cat out, and then they'd have to cleanse the water. He didn't even know what was involved in that. He supposed he could go find the hydrologist who'd been inspecting the wells around town and ask what he recommended.

He didn't have time for this.

"We'll just have to get water from the Keaton farm until I can get to it," Scarbrough said. "It's too cold to get down in the well."

"Tell that to Jimmy," she said. "He's trying to get down in there this very minute."

Scarbrough groaned again. That was the last thing he needed. The well they'd had in the yard since they had built the house had been altered to include the pump. But the shaft was barely wide enough for a small body to fit through. With his luck, his thirteen-year-old would get stuck like that Jessica baby had back in the eighties.

"Tell him to get out of there before he gets killed. There's a better way to do it."

"Then tell him yourself," Mary said. "He's trying to step up to the plate and take care of things."

Scarbrough stepped outside. His teenaged son was trying to grow up too fast. But what was the alternative? Someone had to take care of things at home. As sheriff, he couldn't let crime blossom while he took time off. Desperate times called for desperate decisions, and staying home was not much of an option when an emergency happened almost hourly.

"Jimmy!" he called as he approached the well. His son was lying on his stomach on the ground, leaning his head into the hole.

Jimmy looked up. "Yeah, Pop? Good thing you're home. You can help me with this."

"You can't go in there, Jimmy. Get out now."

"But, Pop, listen. We can tie a rope around my waist and attach it to your van's bumper."

"And what? Stuff you in? Those walls are icy and you're too big."

"But I've given it a lot of thought. I've measured myself, and I think I'll fit."

"And if you're wrong?"

"Well, you got any better ideas?"

"Not yet, I don't. But we'll think of something. I don't have time to deal with it now," he said. "There was a shooting this morning. I'm in the middle of an investigation."

Jimmy got to his feet and dusted the dirt and snow off of his jeans. "You're always in the middle of an investigation," he said. "But this is an emergency too."

"Just go to the Keatons' place and get some water. They'll let you use their well if you tell them what happened."

"I hate the Keatons," Jimmy muttered. "I'd rather go without than go over there."

Scarbrough grunted, wondering where that had come from. Probably had something to do with one of the Keatons' daughters, but he didn't have time to delve into that. "Just do it, Jimmy. We don't have the luxury of grudges right now."

"But, Dad—"

"Don't make me say it again, Jimmy. Stay out of the well until I have time to do something about it."

"All right, but that Amy better not give me a hard time."

"Treat that family with respect when they're doing you a favor."

"A favor? They used our well for months before they dug their own!"

"And they treated *us* with respect."

"Not me. Amy treats me like pond scum. She's probably the one who threw the cat in there. She's probably laughing her head off." Jimmy huffed a sigh and started off toward the Keatons'. Scarbrough watched him march across the lawn. He knew the boy needed more guidance than he got—and having no school to attend left him with too much time on his hands. He should be spending more time with his son. He was a disappointment as a father. And his confidence as a law enforcement officer was fading.

He went back into the house, thankful for the fireplace in the living room. He warmed his hands over it. His head had begun to hurt.

"I'm roasting a rabbit for supper," Mary said. "For now, I'll cook you up a couple of eggs."

"That'll be fine," he said. "I don't have much time."

While he waited for his eggs, he went back out to the well and looked in. Sure enough, a dead cat floated on the water. He lowered the bucket that Jimmy had rigged up, and tried to maneuver the rope until the bucket got under the cat. It wouldn't quite catch. He started to cough again, each hack ripping through his chest.

Mary called him, so he gave up and went back inside, and scarfed down the eggs. "Mary, keep an eye on Jimmy. If he tries to go into that well, he may not come back out."

He ventured back out into the cold. His old van was on its last leg. He didn't know how much longer he could keep it running. He supposed he could take it to the mechanics, but they stayed so busy at the conversion plants that there was usually a long wait. And he couldn't afford to be without a vehicle.

He got back on the main road toward the Crockett city limits and realized he was low on gas. Now what? The cars that had been stalled along the main drags since May had all been siphoned. If he made it back to the sheriff's department, they had several gallons on reserve—unless anyone else had filled up their vehicles this morning. He prayed he wouldn't have to siphon another car, not with this cough. The burn of gas in his throat was something he wasn't up for today.

The van was just about to die when he got to the sheriff's department. In the garage behind it he found a three-gallon container of gas. That was all he could get for now. It would have to do. He had to get to the hydrologist's house and find out what to do about the well, and then he would start questioning the other people who had killed deer that morning. One of them may have shot Zach Emory.

"Sheriff?"

He turned, still pouring the gas into his tank. His deputy, Milton Asher, stood in the doorway. "Yeah, Milt? What you got?"

"One of the prisoners is sick. I don't know what to do with him. He's got a fever and all the other inmates are afraid they're gonna get it."

Scarbrough shivered and massaged his temple. "Which prisoner?"

"Blatt."

It was probably a trick. That guy had gunned down a family of three at the last Disbursement. No way was he letting Blatt out because he was sick. "I'll see if I can get the doctor to come check on him," he said.

"Well, should we quarantine him or something?"

He shook his head. "Milt, half our prison population is sick as it is. There's so much coughing and puking in there, it's a wonder any of them live through it. But that's all I've got to work with. I don't have an infirmary, I don't have sick rooms, I don't have a place to quarantine them, and I'm sure not going to let him out on the streets. I can't transfer him to the prison until we clear some others out of there."

"But Sheriff, we're just supposed to have holding cells. We're not set up for this many prisoners. We got thirty men in there."

"The prison is packed even tighter. I can't put one more person in there. Until I find another place to convert into jail cells, we're going to have to keep holding them here. And until things settle down and I get some more funding, that's not going to happen."

The force of his words started a coughing spell again, and he bent over, trying to clear his lungs so he could breathe again. Finally, the coughing settled.

"You okay, Sheriff?"

He nodded and wiped his nose. "Milt, did you get the samples from Mark Green to the lab?"

"Yes, sir. And I have a list of six other leads—men who shot deer or have automobile tires on their trailers."

"Any who have both?"

"Still checking on that, boss."

He asked Milt to stay at the department to hold down the fort. He felt sorry for the guy—the department was freezing. He'd been trying to get funding for a stove to put in the building so they could keep it warm, but by the time his requisition was approved, it would be summer again and they wouldn't need it. The cold had a calming influence on the prisoners, though. They were so busy trying to stay warm that they weren't starting fights and causing trouble. At least that's how it had seemed for the last few days.

"Sheriff!"

Another deputy, Curt Lawrence, rode toward him on his horse. He closed his gas cap.

"What is it, Curt?"

"Any word about payroll?"

"No. I've been kind of busy and haven't had enough gas to get to Birmingham to pick it up."

"I gotta be paid, Sheriff. I can't keep coming to work every day if I'm not. They're already paying us peanuts. My family has to eat."

"I'm going to get there today, Curt, but right now I have to deal with the shooting."

"If I'm not paid in twenty-four hours, I'm out of here," Curt said. "If you can't pay me, I can at least go hunt to feed my kids, like everybody else is doing."

"Payday isn't officially until tomorrow, anyway." The sheriff got back into the van and pulled out before anybody else could stop him. He couldn't say he blamed Curt. Curt was right. They weren't paying them enough to keep food on the table. What good was it for them to have jobs, when those who didn't had time to hunt and plant and do the things that kept their families afloat? The load their wives were bearing was much too much. Scarbrough did it because he felt a sense of duty to keep his community safe. But not all of his men felt that duty.

And his own calling was growing more faint with each passing day.

THIRTEEN

"DAD, I HAD YOU A GREAT BADMINTON SET, BUT MOM made me give it back."

From the sincerity on Logan's face, Deni would have believed that her little brother had had nothing but their dad's birthday on his mind for days. But her mother had told them about Logan's wild trading spree, so none of them was fooled.

"I'm not much into badminton," Doug said, "but I sure would have liked a parachute."

Logan gasped. "I almost got one—" Everyone started laughing, and he realized he was being teased. Slamming his hand on the table, he said, "Man! You know you woulda loved that. But *no*, Mom had to get flour, yeast, and baking soda."

"Don't look now," Beth said, "but you happen to be eating what she made of it."

For breakfast, Kay had given them each two slices of the bread she'd baked, and she'd put a birthday candle in Doug's.

"Besides," Doug said. "I've had my eye on your molecule."

Logan made a face. "Very funny."

"The scarf and gloves were from all of us, honey," Kay said. "I hope they'll help keep you warm. Happy forty-eighth birthday."

Doug wrapped the scarf around his neck and pulled on the gloves. "Thanks, I can really use these."

Someone knocked at the door, and Deni ran to answer it. Mark stood there with a wrapped present in his hand. "Hey, is your dad up yet?"

She pulled him in. "Sure is. We were celebrating his birthday over breakfast."

"I wanted to get here before everybody scattered."

"Any word on Zach?" she asked as she led him in.

"Nope. I hear he's still unconscious. I'm still the pariah of Oak Hollow."

"Everybody's praying, Mark."

"Yeah, but most of them are praying I'll be locked up."

Deni knew that was true. But as they went into the kitchen, Mark's melancholy look gave way to a celebratory smile. "Happy birthday, Doug! You don't look a day over sixty."

AFTER THEY FINISHED BREAKFAST, DENI ANNOUNCED THAT SHE was going to the hospital for an update on Zach.

"It's too dangerous for you to go alone," Mark said. "I'll go with you."

Mark's concern for Deni always fell on a soft place in her heart. "I'll take my dad's rifle," she said. "You stay here and figure out how to clear yourself."

"Zach is the only one who can clear me," Mark said. "Maybe he's awake by now and can tell them I didn't do it."

She finally agreed to let him go with her, secretly glad that he'd be by her side. She felt safe with him. At six-foot-three and a hundred-ninety pounds, most of it pure muscle, he was a deterrent to anyone who might hurt her.

Bundling up in gloves and scarves and several layers of clothes under their winter jackets, they set out in the snow and freezing wind, their faces chapping against the cold.

Though her legs were much stronger than they'd been last May, the cold searing through her lungs and numbing her face made her wonder if she could make it. There were still another fifteen miles to the hospital. Oh, how she longed for her Maxima, parked in the airport garage where she'd left it in Washington.

"I'm not sure this is worth it, Mark. I'm freezing to death. They'll have to thaw me out and treat me for frostbite before I can climb the stairs." She wished he hadn't sold his horses and the little VW he'd converted into a horse-drawn wagon. It wouldn't have made the trip faster, but it would have been warmer.

"You want to go back?"

She considered it for a moment, but she couldn't stand leaving anything unfinished. "No, we have to see about Zach. Man, I'd kill for a telephone."

"You know, when the Pulses stop, the telephones will probably be the first things back in service. And even if the star doesn't burn itself out, they might be able to get the phones working using an old-time operator and switchboard. The fiber-optic lines are underground, so they weren't damaged."

"Imagine reporting with phones," she said. "Not having to brave the elements to get one story. It seems like a dream, looking back."

"It'll all be restored before we know it. The Pulses will end and we can start rebuilding."

She knew he was trying to get her mind off the miserable ride, and it worked. The thought of technology kicking back in made her pedal a little faster. By the time they reached the hospital, her lips were cracked and her lungs felt bruised by the icy wind. She hoped it was warm inside.

They chained their bikes to icy bicycle bars, then went inside. She felt as if she should leave the scarf up over her face to block out germs wafting on the air. People who looked gravely ill lined up on gurneys in the lobby and down the halls, or sat on the floors waiting for treatment, their family members pacing back and forth, looking for a doctor or nurse who could help. The building was cold, but the crowd warmed it slightly, and Deni was thankful to be out of the wind.

Mark decided to wait in the lobby, to keep from upsetting Zach's family in case they'd heard the rumors that he'd been involved. Deni started up the stairs, but halfway up, she saw Ellen Emory descending. “Mrs. Emory?” she asked, hoping there wouldn’t be a repeat of what her dad had experienced yesterday. He had warned Deni to speak softly and not make any sudden moves. This woman had a hair trigger, he had said.

Ellen’s face slowly showed recognition, but she didn’t slow down. “Yeah?”

“I’m Deni Branning. Jeff’s sister.”

“I know.” Ellen kept walking and pushed through the door into the first-floor lobby.

Deni hoped she didn’t spot Mark standing beside the door. “Is there any change in Zach?”

“No, he’s still unconscious. I’m just going out for some air. This place smells terrible. It’s making me sick. I don’t know how anybody can get well here. If Zach were awake he’d be fighting to get out.”

“A lot of people are praying for him. We’re so hoping—” Deni saw Ellen’s gaze connect with Mark, and her words trailed off.

Slowly, Ellen’s teeth came together in a tight clench.

Uh-oh. Here we go.

“What are you doing here?” Ellen shouted.

Mark stiffened. “I just came with Deni.”

“To do what?” Ellen roared. “To finish what you started?”

A vein in Mark’s temple began to swell. “Mrs. Emory, I didn’t have anything to do with—”

“Get out of here!” Ellen cried. “Security! Someone call security!”

Mark started to back out of the building, but rage shot through Deni, and she stepped in front of the crazed woman. “Look, I know you’re upset, but it won’t do any good to accuse Mark. You don’t want them to arrest him just to lock somebody up. You want them to find the person who really did it, and I’m telling you, it wasn’t Mark.”

“You go with him,” Ellen bit out. “And don’t you come back here!”

All eyes in the waiting room watched them, frightened, as if they were armed killers. Deni decided the best response was to make a quiet exit.

"All right," she said quietly, "we're going."

"They should lock you up, Mark Green!" Ellen shouted as he and Deni went out the door. "They should put you in jail with the other criminals and show you what it's like to suffer!"

Mark was familiar with suffering, Deni knew, but it wouldn't help to tell Zach's mother. The wind assaulted them as they hurried back to their bikes. Some key part of Ellen's brain must have snapped with the news of Zach's shooting, Deni decided. She'd always had a reputation for being volatile and angry, but right now she seemed beyond that.

"She's crazy, Mark!" Deni said as he unlocked their chains. "I can't believe she did that in front of all those people."

Mark's face was pink, but he didn't look angry. "Her son is struggling for his life, Deni. She has every right to be upset, especially when she thinks I did it."

"But she's wrong! She slandered you in public!"

Mark got up. "I appreciate your indignation, Deni, but this isn't about me. God knows I didn't do it, and when Zach wakes up—"

"What if he doesn't, Mark?"

He was quiet for a moment, his breath clouding in front of him. "We'll deal with that then."

She wished she could be more like him. "Mark, aren't you scared?" Her voice shook with the question.

"Yes."

She hated that pain in his eyes. It wasn't fair. Ellen Emory had no right to say what she'd said, even if her son *was* dying.

They were quiet as they pedaled home, and Deni's mind buzzed, compiling a list of people she could talk to to help clear Mark's name. Time was running out. The people of Oak Hollow would take matters into their own hands if they thought the law wasn't handling it.

Innocent or not, that could cost Mark his life.

FOURTEEN

Zach heard voices, muffled and garbled, like the teacher's voice in Charlie Brown. *Waaaw-waw-waw. Waaaw-waw.*

His chest was on fire, and his throat was tight around some object in his mouth. He opened his eyes.

"*Waaaw-waw-waw* … He's waking up … *Waw-waw* … Can you hear me, Zach?"

He tried to focus through the haze. His mother's face moved closer. She'd been crying again. At least she was out of bed. He tried to whisper *Mama*, but that thing in his mouth choked him.

Something was clamped to his face …

"Hey buddy, you're in the hospital. You're gonna be okay."

It was Jeff, standing over him, looking worried.

"Zach, you were shot." His dad now. "Wake up, son."

He clawed at the thing on his face, pulled it away … gagged. His chest felt shredded, lungs ripped apart. *Fire. Help—*

"Honey, you can't breathe on your own." His mother sounded sane; he must be dreaming. "Leave the mask alone. The tube in your throat is helping you breathe."

He swung his arms, pushing her back, fighting.

His father wrestled him, and they were all pulling him down, fighting him … shoving the tube deeper …

Smothering him until he slept again.

FIFTEEN

SHERIFF SCARBROUGH'S THROAT HURT. HIS HEAD FELT as if it had been slammed with a sledgehammer, and he couldn't stop coughing. He must have the flu, but he had to keep going. His staff needed payroll, and somehow he had to get to Birmingham to pick it up. Thankfully, his old van did have heat, but it was almost out of gas again. The three gallons he'd put in earlier had already been used up. Though he was thankful for the working van, it was a 1964 gas guzzler and gulped fuel almost as fast as he could put it in. Now he had to figure out where to get more. If he could make it twenty more miles, he'd be able to pump it from the state police's filling station, where an early twentieth-century gas pump had been installed. It operated much like a hand water pump. It pumped fuel into a glass globe, then discharged it directly out of a nickel-plated spigot. State engineers had copied the design from the exhibit at their local agricultural museum and were trying to reproduce it across the state. But getting gas to the pumps was another thing altogether. Mechanics were working on converting fuel trucks, but without electricity, oil refineries were still shut down. Half the time, if he did make it to the pumps, he found them empty.

But today, he knew he'd run out long before he reached it.

No, he would have to find gas some other way, and quickly. He pulled into a parking lot in front of a manufacturing plant, hoping to find an abandoned vehicle that still contained some fuel. Most of the cars that had stalled on the roads on May 24 had been towed away by now. The government had cleared the roads to make it easier for their own vehicles, as well as horse-drawn carriages, wagons, and bicycles to get through.

But the cars that weren't blocking the roads had been left where they were, so many of the parking lots were still full.

Getting his gas can, he lay down on the snow-covered pavement and slid under a Lincoln Town Car. Pulling the knife out of his pocket, he stabbed the fuel tank and quickly slid out of the way. Only a trickle came dribbling out, but he caught it in his container. Either the car had been low on gasoline when the Pulses hit, or it had already been siphoned empty.

He slid under the next car, a Chevy Malibu, and stabbed the tank. A healthy flow streamed out, and he knew he'd hit pay dirt. Lying on his back, trying not to breathe too deeply because he would cough if he did, he waited, shivering in the icy wind sweeping under the car, until the stream of gasoline filled up the three-gallon container. Then he slid out, got another can, and pushed it under the flow, trying to waste as little as possible. By the time the fuel tank finished trickling, he had about eight gallons.

When someone had first suggested stabbing a hole in the tanks to drain them, he'd balked at the idea. He wouldn't do it if he thought he could siphon the fuel out. But the fact was, these cars were never again going to run—not without a lot of work. All modern internal combustion engines, which relied so heavily on electronics, had been fatally damaged. And what the pulsar's gamma rays hadn't destroyed, vandals had. Many of the cars had been stripped of their radios and stereos, their navigational equipment, their radar detectors, their tires, and sometimes their seats. There were people who had entire warehouses full of useless stolen equipment from these cars. He supposed they thought they'd be able to sell them after the Pulses stopped.

Maybe one day the thieves would be rounded up and locked away, but meanwhile he had to do his own share of vandalism to get the gas out.

Finally able to fill his tank, he got back in and started the engine. The motor rumbled and died, rumbled and died, then finally, caught and started. One of these days it wouldn't. Then he supposed the government would give him another clunker, and he'd spend his days coaxing it along.

When he'd first been elected sheriff of Jefferson County, he'd signed up a volunteer force of reserve deputies, and there had been a few times over the years when he'd been able to call them into service. But now communication was the major problem. It wasn't like he could pick up the phone and ask the volunteers to report for duty. Besides, people were willing to volunteer their services when they had another source of income and extra time on their hands. Right now, very few had an income, and survival was such a struggle that there was no extra time.

He made his way into Birmingham, dodging the horses and wagons and bicycles and pedestrians walking on the interstate even in the snow. Now and then he saw another vehicle from one of the police forces or ambulance services, or a government employee. But motorized vehicles were few, and most of the slower traffic had gotten out of the habit of yielding right of way. Getting from one place to another without killing someone was quite a challenge.

He decided to swing by the hospital to check on Zach Emory on the way to his downtown office. If the young man would wake up and tell him who had shot him, he could make an arrest and call it a day. Plus, he would love to take the heat off Mark Green.

The ground seemed to tip as he got out of the van, and he closed his eyes, fighting the sudden rush of vertigo. He touched the hood to steady himself. The snow was coming down harder, and bitter wind blew through his coat. He shivered and shoved his hands into his pockets.

Trudging through the powder, he made his way through the emergency entrance. A coughing fit overcame him as he got inside, but no one noticed. The lobby was full of moaning, bleeding, injured patients. Doctors in scrubs went from patient to patient, assessing their condition.

He hesitated at the door and tried to cough his lungs clear. A nurse hurried toward him. "Afternoon, Sheriff. Respiratory infections go down that hall and to the right."

He sucked in a searing breath. "I'm not here for me."

"You sure? You should get that checked."

"It's probably just an allergy."

She snickered. "Yeah, there's a lot of ragweed growing up through that snow." She grabbed a box from a nearby table and pulled out a pair of gloves. "Put these on, and get a mask from that table over there."

"Thanks." He pulled the gloves on then went to the table and looped the surgical mask around his ears. Not certain whether it was to keep germs in or out, he started up the stairs.

As he went up, he stopped and caught his breath at every landing. Stopping on the third floor, he leaned against the wall.

He'd never had a cold do such a number on him. He wanted to sit down, right here on the floor. But there was too much to do. Steadying himself, he launched out again and made it to the fourth floor.

He found the waiting room and looked in. The Emorys weren't there, but he saw Jeff Branning and his friend Brian sitting on the windowsill.

They saw him as he came in and shot toward him. "Sheriff, Zach woke up!"

Scarbrough would have celebrated if he could have worked up a smile. "He did?"

"Yeah. Came to long enough to wrestle the ventilator off. But they finally settled him back down."

"Did he talk?"

"Not yet. He was out again before we could really communicate."

Just his luck, Scarbrough thought. "Is he still in ICU?"

"No, they moved him to 412. His parents are in there with him."

"Good. I'll go talk to them." He started down the hallway.

"Hey, Sheriff, you think you could give us a ride home? It's really cold out there."

"Sure," Scarbrough said. "You'll have to wait while I make a stop on the way home."

"No problem."

Sheriff Scarbrough found the room, but it was a little crowded. They'd moved Zach into a small room with a roommate, and his parents and brother had squeezed in and were standing over his bed, among the family members of the other patient. A nurse swept in past him. "Okay, this crowd has to go. Two visitors at a time! That's it."

Scarbrough waited outside as Zach's parents came into the hall. They too were wearing masks. "I heard the good news," he told Ned and Ellen.

Ned's face looked much less tense than it had yesterday. Ellen's eyes were swollen from crying, but she was smiling now. "He's still in critical condition, and he can't breathe on his own. But the doctors think he'll survive."

So it wasn't going to be a homicide he was investigating, and chances were Zach would name the perpetrator soon. "I want to talk to him as soon as he's able."

Ned nodded. "He's in and out of consciousness. I'm not sure he even knows his own name."

"Meanwhile, you'd better get Mark Green off the street," Ellen said. "He's already been here this morning, if you can imagine the gall."

Something about that didn't sound right. "Really? He came here?"

"Yeah," she said. "With Deni Branning. Probably intended to finish the job."

"What did he say?"

"He didn't get to say anything. The minute I saw him I lost it, and he ran out."

He didn't want to set her off by interrogating her, but he made a mental note to get to the bottom of it as soon as he got back to Crockett. "Look, I don't know why he was here, but there's no solid evidence that he shot Zach."

"You got the deer, don't you?" Ellen demanded loudly.

"Yeah, but Mark's not the only one who came home with a deer yesterday."

"Oh, I see what we're dealing with here," Ned said. "You're one of his buddies, aren't you? What did he do, bring you food? Build you a wagon? Did he butter you up so you wouldn't arrest him when his true nature was exposed?"

Scarbrough didn't have the fight left in him for this. "That's not how I work, Ned. If I get a case against Mark Green, I'll take him into custody. Not before."

He was glad to finally leave the hospital with Jeff and Brian, and he headed over to his downtown office. Leaving the boys in the van, he went in. Like every other building in town, the place was freezing, and he trudged up the stairs to the second floor where the county's comptroller worked. Thankfully, Andy Truett had stayed on board, but he had a thankless job. Scarbrough tried not to give him too much flack when things didn't go the way he wanted.

Andy sat behind his desk, papers covering its surface. He wore a big parka with the hood up. He was blowing on his hands when Scarbrough came in.

"How's it going, Andy? You got the payroll ready?"

"Yeah, such as it is, Sheriff." He turned his desk chair around, pulled out a big envelope, and thrust it at Scarbrough. "They've cut everybody's pay again."

"No way." Scarbrough snatched the envelope. "Nobody told me."

"They said they were going to tell you but they hadn't been able to get over to Crockett. They were waiting until you came in."

They'd already cut their pay by 90 percent, Scarbrough thought. How would he keep anybody working if they lowered it any more?

"We're now officially at 2 percent of our pay scale, and the county supervisor said you should take it up with them if you don't like it. Seems *they're* not getting paid a thing."

"Yeah, well, they're not out risking their lives chasing bad guys, either." He opened the envelope and looked inside. "Just make sure you get what you've got over to the substations, even if you have to take it yourself. We've got to pay them something to keep them from walking off the job. I've got hundreds of prisoners in jail that I can't keep if I can't pay people to guard them and feed them."

He stormed out of the office and up the stairs again, hoping someone in the county supervisor's office was still around today. He had to stop on one of the landings and catch his breath. Lightheaded, he tried to regain his equilibrium, but he feared he would pass out. The coughing started again.

He tried to pull himself together, wishing for a drink of water, but he'd have to wait. He finally reached the county supervisor's office. Joe Hamilton sat behind his desk, looking as haggard as Andy.

"Joe, what do you think you're doing?" Scarbrough demanded in a raspy voice.

Joe looked up at him, unsurprised. "I was waiting for you, Sheriff."

"Well, you *should* have been waiting for me. How did you think I was going to react?"

"Sheriff, you're lucky you got anything. It's not like I can reach into my own pockets and pull out the cash. We take what the feds give us, and even then it has to trickle down through the state agencies."

"I don't care about the state agencies," Scarbrough said. "I have to uphold the law and keep prisoners locked up. In case you haven't noticed, crime's at an all-time high and you need me and my force. I already have enough problems keeping a staff as it is. Now you're doing this?"

"I'm sorry, Ralph. It's the best I can do." He rubbed his unshaven jaw and raked his hand through his unkempt hair. "Believe me, I know how you feel. I'm working for free, just trying to hold things around here together. I'm doing everything I know to do—" His voice broke off, and his mouth trembled. Scarbrough knew he was about to lose it. They all were.

There was no point in chewing him out. It wouldn't do any good.

He looked down at the envelope in his hands. "So this is the best we've got?"

"That's it," Joe said. "Ralph, I promise you, if any other funds come up, I'll be sure and direct them to your department. You just can't get blood out of a turnip. The country's in a crisis."

"If they would just open the banks, it wouldn't be so bad."

"Tell that to the feds," he said. "They must have their reasons for keeping them closed."

SIXTEEN

MARK HAD BEEN QUIET FOR MOST OF THE RIDE HOME, AND Deni knew Ellen Emory's hysteria had shaken him. She'd tried to make comments along the way to lighten his mood, but eventually the cold numbed her lips into silence. As they rounded the corner into Oak Hollow, she saw the welcoming plume of smoke from her chimney.

She coasted toward her driveway. "Come on, let's go in."

Mark hung back. "No, I have to get home. I have things to do."

"Deni! Mark!"

Deni turned to see her next-door neighbor, Amber Rowe, sliding toward them through the snow in some kind of snowshoe. "Hi, Amber."

As she and her children got closer, she saw that Amber had cut two-liter bottles in half and tied them to her feet. Behind her, she pulled her children on a car door that doubled as a sled. "Mark, I'm so glad I caught you. The kids and I just got back from the well, and we saw a bunch of angry men at your house."

He set his foot down to balance his bike. "What men?"

"Sam Ellington, Lou Grantham, and about half a dozen others. They had guns, Mark, and they're waiting for you. I wouldn't go home if I were you."

Deni's heart sank, and she turned back to Mark. "Mark, let's get in the house. I don't want them to see you."

"No, I have to go home. My mother's there alone."

"Mark, you *can't*!"

"She's right, Mark," Amber said. "It's you they're looking for. They think you shot Zach."

Deni jumped off her bike and pulled the garage door up. "Come on, Mark. Please come in."

The sound of a car engine turned them all to the neighborhood entrance, and they saw the sheriff's van turning in. "Thank goodness," Deni said. "The sheriff can help us."

Surprisingly, the van rumbled up in front of her house, and Jeff jumped out. "Zach woke up!"

Mark gasped. "He did? Has he told them who shot him?"

"Not yet." Jeff opened the back door and lifted his bike out, then reached for his shotgun. "He's still hooked up to that breathing thing."

Deni went to the passenger door and leaned in. "Sheriff, Lou Grantham and his band of vigilantes are waiting for Mark at his house."

Sheriff Scarbrough looked exhausted. Deep circles shadowed his eyes, and she could hear the whistling of his breath. Rolling his eyes at the news, he said, "All right, y'all get into your house. Mark, I'm going to break them up, but I don't recommend going home for a while."

"What about my mother? She's there alone. My stepfather's in Huntsville."

"She'll be all right," he said. "Maybe the good news about Zach will calm them down a little."

Deni pulled on his sleeve. "Come on, Mark. Hurry!"

Mark looked as if he wasn't certain about coming in to hide. Reluctantly, he rolled his bike into the garage as the sheriff's van rattled away. Deni pulled the door closed and locked it. "Jeff, is your shotgun loaded?" she asked as they went into the house.

"You bet."

"Then give it to Mark." Deni looked out back and saw her mother in the chicken coop with Logan. She pulled off her gloves and went to the fire. Mark stood just inside the door, staring at the floor as if trying to think this through. Finally, he looked up at Jeff.

"Jeff, instead of the gun, can I borrow some warm clothes?"

"Warm clothes?" Deni asked. "What for?"

"I need to pack a bag, and I can't go home."

Deni turned from the fireplace. "Pack a bag for what?"

"I have to leave. I obviously can't stay here and endanger the lives of my mother and your family."

"Mark, you're not endangering us. My dad and Jeff won't let those guys— "

"I don't want your dad and Jeff to have to fight for me. They didn't do anything wrong."

"Neither did you!"

He turned back to Jeff. "I'll need a sweatshirt, some socks, a sleeping bag— "

"What are you planning?" Jeff asked. "To sleep outside?"

"I don't know where I'll sleep. I'll be okay."

Jeff hesitated a moment, then said, "I'll get some stuff together."

Deni stood in front of the fire, gaping at him. "Mark, what are you doing?"

"I have no choice but to leave, Deni. I can't stay here or I'll get lynched. Everyone around me will get hurt in the fallout."

"But where will you go? You can't just skip town and run away, especially if you're a suspect."

"I'm not skipping town. I won't go far."

"But Zach is getting better, Mark. What if he clears you and they can't get in touch with you?"

"Then I'll find out tomorrow." He went to the window and looked beyond the backyard toward his own street. "Why would I kill Zach Emory over a stinking deer? My family's not starving. I'm a good hunter. How could they think I would do such a thing?"

She came up behind him and touched his arm. "Just wait here until Zach can talk. He'll tell them, Mark. He'll clear your name. We just have to wait a little longer."

"I don't have time to wait. The vultures are circling."

She stared up at him, stricken by the pain in his eyes. Those eyes always killed her. They were so blue and clear and represented him so well. Deep with layers of pain and heartache, but usually bright with hope. Right now they were framed in defeat.

He looked down at her, a million unspoken words poised on his lips. She touched his face. He took her hand and held it against his cheek. "It'll be okay, Deni."

Their eyes locked and held for a long moment, and finally, Deni rose up on her toes and kissed him.

She felt the tension in him relaxing into the kiss. Her heart slammed with unforgettable pain, as if she stood on the brink of a cliff, trying to hold him back. But he was destined to jump.

She pulled back and looked at him, her lips inches from his. "I'm scared, Mark."

"Don't be." He stroked her hair back and swept her face with his gaze. For a moment, she thought he might change his mind and stay.

Then someone banged on her front door. She swung around.

"They're here," Mark said. "I told you."

Jeff ran down the stairs. "The sleeping bag's in the attic and there's no time for me to get it. But there's warm stuff in here." He thrust his duffel bag at Mark. "Go out the back while I hold them off at the door!"

Deni couldn't believe this was happening. They banged again—an angry pounding, as if they were about to kick the door in. She realized fleeing was his only option. "Go," she whispered. "Hurry!"

Mark bolted out the back door. Deni watched as he raced through the yards and disappeared from her sight.

SEVENTEEN

THE SNOW WAS THICK ON THE GROUND BY THE TIME Scarbrough ran the men off Mark Green's doorstep and calmed his mother down. He hoped the men would heed his warnings and leave Mark alone, but he feared they had only dispersed until he left the neighborhood.

Back at the station, he found all of his deputies—on and off duty—waiting for him.

"Did you get it, Sheriff?" Gordon Jones asked him.

He tossed him the envelope.

"Hot dog!" Jones shouted. "Come and get it, everybody!"

Scarbrough wished he could disappear as they tore into the package. The cash was separated into smaller envelopes, and Jones pulled them out. "Anderson. Asher. Black."

Anderson tore into his envelope, and his face fell. "Hey, this is even less than last time!"

"Be glad you got anything at all," Scarbrough muttered.

The others opened their envelopes and looked at him like they'd been betrayed. "Sheriff, what's going on?" Asher yelled.

"You said they were going to pay us!" Jones knocked a framed picture off his desk. "I can't feed my family with this! You got us in here working like dogs and this is the thanks we get?"

"Look, I fought for us, but you can't squeeze quarters out of a banana tree. I'm in the same boat you're in. I don't like it, but it's all we got."

The deputies looked ready to revolt when he heard the front door open. Two teenaged boys came in. The deputies kept grumbling, and Scarbrough called, "Can I help you?"

The men grew quiet.

"Yes, sir. We have some information about Zach Emory's shooting."

He nodded toward his office, and the kids followed him in. His desk was piled high with paperwork he hadn't had time to get to. He sank into his chair and fought the urge to cough again.

"Take a seat and give me your names," he said as he searched for something to write on.

"Randy Kraft."

"Blake Mahaffey."

He found a fresh page on his notepad and wrote the names down. "So what have you got?"

Randy sat straighter, and looked at the legal pad that held his name. "We were hunting yesterday out around the Jenkins place."

Scarbrough's eyebrows shot up. "Did you witness the shooting?"

"No, not that. But we did see someone who claims he wasn't there."

"Yeah? Who?"

"Mark Green."

Scarbrough's heart plunged, and he set his pen down. "Are you sure?"

"Yes, Sheriff. We saw him about an hour before the shooting. He was there with that bike trailer of his with the big car tires."

Scarbrough couldn't hold back the cough any longer. He gave in to it, trying to get a clear breath again. Finally, he said, "Did you talk to him?"

"No, sir. We were in a deer stand, and we saw him hiding his trailer in the trees. I don't think he saw us."

"And you're absolutely positive it was him?"

"Yes, sir," Blake said. "We've known Mark for years. He used to play baseball with my brother."

"We didn't think it was important until we heard that he claimed he wasn't there," Randy said.

Blake nodded. "We aren't saying he shot Zach. Just that he lied about where he was."

"And if he lied about that, then he may have lied about other things."

Scarbrough leaned forward. "Tell me something. Did you happen to tell anybody this before me?"

The boys exchanged looks. "Yes, sir. We told our dads."

He clasped his hands in front of him. "And they didn't by any chance go tell some of the men in Oak Hollow, did they?"

Blake shrugged. "They were pretty hot about it. I wouldn't be surprised."

So that was what had prompted Lou Grantham and his buddies to decide to take matters into their own hands. He leaned on his desk and rubbed his tired face. "All right," he said. "I appreciate you coming by. If you don't mind giving a statement to Deputy Jones, I'll need this in writing."

The boys exchanged looks again. "Do we have to? We don't really want Mark to know we told you this. He might come after us."

Scarbrough was losing patience. "Yes, you have to. The DA is going to need your testimony if this goes to trial."

Randy swallowed hard. "Okay, I guess we will if there's no other choice."

Scarbrough told Jones to get the statement. The deputy was still brooding, but at least he hadn't walked out yet.

The boys signed their statements, then started to leave. Before they opened the door, they looked back. "Sheriff, are you going to arrest Mark Green?"

"I can't discuss an ongoing investigation," he said. "But thank you for coming forward." He watched the boys go out, then stood for a moment, staring through the window.

Why would Mark have lied if he wasn't guilty? And if he was guilty, what motivation would he have had for shooting Zach?

His gut told him this was all a mistake. Mark Green was no killer. But he had to act quickly, because Mark wasn't safe now. At the very least, locking him up would keep anyone from attacking him.

He turned back to the deputies. "You men get back to work now. I need someone to go with me to bring Mark Green in." He'd expected them to balk and walk off the job, but surprisingly, no one did. Not yet. Thankful that disaster seemed averted, at least for now, he headed back out into the cold.

EIGHTEEN

"TELL ME, WHERE IS HE?" LOU GRANTHAM'S VOICE bellowed through the Brannings' open doorway.

Deni tried to look innocent. "Where is who?"

"Mark Green! He was seen coming here with you." They started to push into the house, and Deni couldn't hold them back.

But her mother tried. "Hold on, here! You will not come busting into my house— "

The sound of Jeff chambering a round on his shotgun stopped them. Keeping his gun aimed at the ceiling, Jeff walked in front of them. "Mark is not here, so back off!"

"Put that gun down, son. We don't have a quarrel with you. But harboring a criminal is against the law."

"Mark is not a criminal!" Deni cried. "Why are you doing this?"

"We have witnesses who saw Mark at the scene of the crime yesterday."

"*What?*"

"His alibi was a lie. He's the one who shot Zach Emory, and we're going to make sure he doesn't kill anyone else."

Fearless, Sam Ellington pushed past Jeff and started up the stairs.

"Careful, Sam, he might be armed," Grantham called.

"He's not here!" Kay yelled. "What don't you understand about that?"

Sam marched around upstairs, slamming doors and pounding across the floor.

Paul Burlin brushed past Jeff and began to search the rooms on the first floor. Jeff looked confused, as if he didn't know whether to use his shotgun or not.

"Stop it!" Deni shouted. "You're trespassing on private property!"

Kay grabbed her arm and held her back. "Just let them look, Deni. When they see he's not here, they'll leave."

Deni swallowed her rage as they completed the search of the house. If her father came home while this was going on, he would go ballistic.

Finally, the men came back and reported to the crowd. "They're right. He ain't here. He musta got away."

"Where'd he go?" Grantham demanded. "Deni, tell us where he is."

"I don't know!"

"If you're helping him, Deni, then you're an accomplice. Is that what you want to be? An accomplice to murder?"

"Zach is not dead. He's improving!"

"Get out of my house," Kay said, ushering the men to the door.

"If you see him, Kay, you let us know," Lou Grantham said. "It's in your daughter's best interest to tell us where he is."

Deni gasped. "Is that a threat?"

"It's a warning," Grantham said. "We're trying to help you."

"I said to leave!" Kay shoved them out and slammed the door. Then she turned to Deni. "Where *did* he go, Deni?" she asked quietly.

"I don't know. He wouldn't tell me."

She sighed. "Honey, I know he wouldn't shoot Zach. But a lot of people think he did. I don't want you getting caught in the middle of this."

"I am in the middle, Mom. This is *Mark* we're talking about."

NINETEEN

NOT CERTAIN WHAT DIRECTION TO GO, MARK HEADED into the woods surrounding Oak Hollow. He wouldn't be surprised if they got the dogs out after him, so he couldn't stay here long. Just long enough to make a withdrawal …

The forest changed daily as people cut down trees, and without their leaves the trees remaining provided little cover. Some of his markers were hidden under the snow, but he still managed to find his way. He'd set a trap for small animals near the stump that held his treasure. He counted off the trees from the dry creek bed next to a fat spruce, then found the trap.

And right behind it was the stump.

The hole he'd chiseled out was stuffed with dead leaves. No one had bothered it, thankfully. If they'd known what was in it, it would have been long gone.

He pulled the dead leaves out. They crunched with frost and crumbled in his hands. He let them drop to the snow. Reaching inside, he pulled out the metal lockbox he'd hidden there. It was heavy with the weight of his fortune.

He opened it. The box was filled with gold coins—the ones he'd found in a chest in his father's house. He had thought of taking it home and sharing it with his mother and stepfather, but he knew that if they started spending them, someone would paint a great big bulls-eye at the center of his forehead, and his family would be in danger of being killed and robbed.

Instead, he'd kept it to himself, hidden in this tree. He hadn't used any of them yet—and he had never intended to spend any on himself. His father had been involved in the pornography industry and had been guilty of a long list of criminal activities, including murder. Mark wanted nothing to do with any of his illegal gains. But he'd found a receipt for the gold coins—meaning they'd been bought, not stolen. The U.S. Eagle gold bullion coins weighed an ounce each, and the receipt said they had cost 660 dollars apiece. There were a hundred of them—66,000 dollars worth before the outage. What they were worth now was considerably less, but it was still a fortune by anyone's standards.

Maybe it wouldn't hurt to keep a few of them with him now. He might have to pay for a place to stay. He took three coins out and dropped them into his pocket. Then he closed the box, put it back into its hiding place in the stump, and stuffed the opening with more crunchy dead leaves.

He went back to the creek bed and followed it to the other side of the woods, to the alley behind Kroger. Sitting on an old crate, he waited for daylight to play itself out so he could get away from Crockett without being seen. The cold and snow made him feel more bereft. He'd gotten up yesterday morning with a sense of confidence and purpose that all was as it should be.

Then everything had gone terribly wrong.

Was it some sin he'd committed, or just more of his father's curse being played out? He knew the biblical warnings about the sins of the father being visited on the sons to the third and fourth generations. But didn't it also say that God would bless to the thousandth generation those who loved him?

Yet here he was, hunkering in an alley like a fugitive, trying to decide where he would sleep tonight.

He thought of the area under the bridge, a mile east of the Crockett exit on I–20. There wasn't anything there but woods. It would be easy to walk to, and if he started a fire there, maybe no one would see it. Maybe by morning Zach would tell them the truth and all of this would end.

Mark sat in the alley for hours until darkness fell. As he waited, he looked through the bag Jeff had packed for him. He'd given him a flashlight with extra batteries, some sweatpants and a sweatshirt, a ski cap, some extra socks, and a small Bible. *Way to go, Jeff.* He couldn't have packed better himself.

When he felt covered by darkness, Mark made his way to the street and started walking to I–20.

The interstate was barren and covered with four inches of snow. The moon overhead lit the road ahead of him, uncertain and long.

Cold dried his lips and numbed his face, and he wished for waterproof shoes instead of this worn-out pair of Nikes. Burrowing his hands into his pockets, he trudged toward the bridge, doubting he would find much comfort there.

As he approached, he smelled smoke and saw the light of a fire flickering near the bridge. He slid down the grass embankment before he got to the bridge, and walked under it.

And then he saw it. A community of tents, spread out among the trees and under the bridge …

Who lived here?

Carefully, he approached the fire. People sat around it. A woman, some children, a man … and on the other side of the flames, more people. Skin-and-bones people with dirty, unshaven faces, filthy skin, rotting teeth. Their clothes were not warm enough to brave this cold, and yet this seemed to be their home.

No one seemed to notice him as he walked up to the fire. He got the feeling that transients came and went from this place—strangers sharing a patch of earth, never knowing each other's names. He wondered if they were hiding from the law, or if they were simply here because they had nowhere else to go.

He counted five tents, two fires … Twenty or more people of all ages.

He warmed his hands, then walked between two tents to another fire coming from a hole in the ground. Someone had dug a pit there and filled it with wood, set a fire, then placed an oven rack on top of the hole. They were using it for cooking. He moved closer to see what was on the rack. It was some animal the size of a chipmunk. That wouldn't go far.

"Hey, mister. You got any food?"

The voice came from a little girl about eight years old. Her hair was long and matted, and she looked as if she wore her whole wardrobe layered thick. Pants on top of more pants, a dress on top of that, sweaters and a hooded sweatshirt, all padding the little girl for warmth.

She needed a good coat. And a place to live.

"No, I don't have any food. I'm sorry." He stooped down to look at her. Her face was dirty, and snot crusted under her nose. "Do you live here?"

"Yeah," she said. "I hate snow, don't you?"

Little girls were supposed to love snow. They were supposed to laugh and slide around in it, to make snow angels and snowmen.

"How long have you been here?" he asked her.

"A few weeks," she said. "Ever since our house burned down."

"Ruth, come here." It was a woman's voice in the darkness. The little girl turned and hurried to her mother. "I told you not to talk to people," she whispered harshly.

The girl went into the tent, and came out a few minutes later with two other children. The boy was a little older than she, and the other girl a little younger. A man who must have been her father took the chipmunk—or whatever it was—off the flames and carried it into the tent. The children and mother all hurried in after it.

As the fire warmed him, he looked around, astonished at what he'd found. When he'd learned about the problems in the apartments around town, he had done his best to help them survive. He'd helped dig a well and had altered some of the apartments to add fireplaces and cookstoves for the winter. He'd even taken them food.

But he'd never imagined that, right here in Crockett, there were people who didn't have any roof over their heads at all—who slept with their families under a bridge in twenty-five-degree cold.

The areas around the fire were all occupied by tents or pallets laid out on the ground. Debris sat around all of their areas—discarded items and broken possessions. It looked like most of the people here didn't even have enough blankets to get through the night.

He found a spot away from the fire and leaned back against a tree trunk. Then he got out the Bible Jeff had packed for him.

He pictured Deni's brother running around frantically, trying to think of what Mark might need. He never would have expected the Bible, but it was a godsend.

He opened it and tried to read in the dim light of the fire.

He heard footsteps in the leaves and saw a homeless man staggering toward him. He looked like someone Mark would have avoided if he'd seen him on the street.

"How ya doing?" Mark asked, reaching out to shake his hand.

The man didn't shake. He just looked at the things Mark had pulled out of his bag. Apparently, nothing looked interesting enough, so the man turned and walked away without a word.

Mark hoped Ruth and her siblings stayed away from the man.

The night grew late, and as Mark read, he listened to voices around the fire. Some of the squatters sounded a little crazy or mentally challenged. Others were desperate. A couple were mean and threatening.

And then there were those like him, probably wondering how they'd wound up in a place like this. Longing for morning.

Toward midnight, most of the people settled down on their little squares of earth or in their tents, so he moved closer to the fire to get warm. Since he didn't have a pallet or sleeping bag, Mark found a dry place on the bridge's concrete base and used his bag to pillow his head. He prayed for Zach to be all right, to wake up and tell what happened. He prayed for Deni and her family, and for Sheriff Scarbrough, and for his mother, and his stepfather John. He knew his mother was probably grieving, sick with worry over where he might be. Somehow he had to get word to her tomorrow, let her know that the lynch mob hadn't caught up to him. Sadness washed over him, and he began to wonder what God was doing.

Last Sunday at church, Doug had preached that our trials always had a purpose.

That meant that the thing with his father had been for a reason, though Mark had never seen any good that came from it. The fact that his half-brothers had fled arrest for the shared crimes had had some purpose too. And the legacy of their reputation, which now left him an outcast, had some overriding meaning.

He just couldn't see what it was.

The effort left him defeated.

Lord, I know I'm not alone … but I feel *alone.*

Desperately wanting a word from God, some wisdom, some peace, he flipped through the Bible, wondering what to read. Some people just opened their Bibles to a word from God, flashing out at them like neon, but that had never worked for him. It seemed, instead, that when he needed encouragement the most, he had no idea where to read.

But he'd been doing a read-through for the past few months, and he was up to Isaiah.

He opened the Bible again, and using the flashlight now, he turned to the passage where he'd left off—Isaiah 43.

The Lord was talking to Israel, but as Mark read, the words began to take on life—profound and personal.

When you pass through the waters, I will be with you; and through the rivers, they will not overflow you. When you walk through the fire, you will not be scorched, nor will the flame burn you. For I am the Lord your God, the Holy One of Israel, your Savior; I have given Egypt as your ransom, Cush and Seba in your place. Since you are precious in My sight, since you are honored and I love you, I will give other men in your place and other peoples in exchange for your life.

God was paying attention. None of this had escaped his notice. He had not abandoned Mark as the neighbors had. And Mark had nothing to fear.

You are precious in my sight … you are honored and I love you …

He kept reading until his defeat turned to devotion, and as he lay under the bridge, watching an occasional lonely man feed the fire from a woodpile they had cut, he felt blessed again. Sleep came in snatches, dipping into dreams that mingled with the cold of reality.

When the first lights of morning broke, he gathered his stuff and hurried back to Oak Hollow. Hoping his neighbors would sleep a little longer, he sneaked into his yard and to the van that held all his family's meat. Pulling out the bobcat and some of the venison he'd stored there, he loaded his bike trailer and headed back to the bridge.

Little Ruth was already up when he got back to the campground. Her father had an ax and was chopping wood for the fire.

Mark pulled his bike trailer among the tents and began unloading the meat. "I brought you some breakfast," he told her parents. "There ought to be enough for everybody."

Others came out of their tents, and those on the ground began to stir. They eyed the meat with hungry eyes. Ruth's father got the pit stove lit and began to cook.

As hungry as Mark was, he ate only a little; then he sat by the fire, savoring the smell of roasted game, watching as the homeless filled their bellies.

After they'd cleaned the bones and tossed them into the fire, Ruth approached him again. "Thanks, mister," she said.

"You're welcome." Grief overcame him that this child had to live in a place like this. He reached into his pocket and pulled out the three coins. "Here," he whispered. "Give these to your dad. Maybe he can use them to get your family into an apartment or something."

She took the coins, her eyes widening with the beauty of them. "Wow," she said. "Pretty quarters."

He grinned. "They're worth a lot more than quarters."

She brought her curious gaze up to him. "Are you rich?"

He thought of evading the question, but compared to them, he was. "Yeah, I guess I am."

"Then why were you sleeping outside?"

He smiled. "It's a long story."

"Ruth! Come here! I told you— "

Ruth hesitated, looking up at him.

"You should listen to your mom," he said. "People around here could be dangerous. You really shouldn't talk to strangers."

"You're not a stranger. You brung us food. And money."

"It's not money, exactly. Just give it to your mom and dad, okay? Don't tell anybody else."

"Ruth!" Her mother was getting angry.

"I'll see you later, Ruth," he said. "I have to go." He started to walk his bike back out of the woods. Before he had gotten far, he looked back, and saw Ruth showing the coins to her mother. The woman looked up at him, her mouth open in astonishment.

He hoped it would make a difference.

TWENTY

ZACH HUNG ON THE EDGE OF CONSCIOUSNESS, EMBEDDED in a cloud. Sounds—words, footsteps, the hum of a machine, his mother's crying—floated through the haze, registering in fragments in his brain, but he couldn't find his way out.

He tried to open his eyes or to reach out to his mother to tell her to stop crying, but he couldn't move his hands or his eyelids.

She was always crying. Lying in bed in a dark room, staring at the walls and wishing for brighter days. He never could make her smile.

Voices slammed against each other over his head—Dad condescending, Mama raising her voice. A nurse asking them both to leave.

Yes, Mama. Cry somewhere else.

Silence, then a crash some distance away. Had his mother turned something over?

Calm down, Mama. Calm down.

The clouds thinned, and he managed to slit his eyes open. Tubes tangled over him, something on his face ... in his throat. Someone beside his bed, bent over.

The hum silenced.

He tried to focus on the man rising up, looking down at him. Blurred ... unfocused.

"Doc, you gotta help me."

Whose voice? It came from across the room.

Clouds closed in again ... eyes shut. Swimming through the fog, trying to reach the surface.

"Sorry, I'm not a doctor. I'm just visiting Zach." It was the man above him, strange, unfamiliar.

He couldn't breathe. Forced his eyes open ...

"Then go get one, man." The panicked voice came from the bed next to him. "My IV's come loose."

Zach couldn't catch his breath. Panic tightened his chest.

Help!

Man walking around his bed. Too fast, too blurry. *Help ... can't breathe ...*

Gasping.

"Hey, he can't breathe. Listen to him!"

"I'll go get a doctor."

"Tell him to hurry. That guy's ventilator is off!"

Sucking air through a straw. *Help me!*

"I'm going. If anyone asks you, tell them Mark Green stopped by."

"I don't care who you are! Call him a doctor! Help! Somebody help!"

TWENTY-ONE

THE LAST THING SHERIFF SCARBROUGH WANTED TO DO was arrest Mark Green. But the Emorys' claim that Mark had been in Zach's room and unplugged his ventilator gave him little choice. Thankfully, the event had shown them that Zach was able to breathe on his own, though he'd struggled at first. They'd been able to take the tube out of his throat, and Scarbrough hoped he'd be talking soon. But the exhaustion from the struggle had plunged him back into sleep.

"So you didn't see him?" he asked Ellen and Ned softly as they stood over Zach's bed.

"No. We had stepped outside—something crashed down the hall, some drunk guy was yelling. We went to see what was happening."

Charles Hoyt, the man in the bed next to Zach, looked exhausted. Yesterday, he'd had stomach surgery for a stab wound. "I saw the guy," Hoyt said. "Right after the nurse left the room, he came in here real quiet. I was trying to sleep, didn't even hear him come in. When I woke up, he was standing over Zach's bed, and the ventilator was off."

"What did he look like?" Scarbrough asked.

"What do you mean, what did he look like?" Ellen asked. "He looked like Mark Green!"

"Guy must have been crazy," Charles said. "Walked over and introduced himself."

Scarbrough couldn't make it add up. "Presuming Mark Green wanted to kill Zach to keep him from telling who shot him, why would he leave his name so he could be identified? It doesn't make sense."

"He's insane, like his father," Ned said. "If you don't arrest him, we'll make sure that someone else takes care of him."

"Don't go making threats, Ned. You let me handle this."

"Are you going to? Before he *really* kills Zach?"

Scarbrough evaded that question and looked at the man in the bed again. "Mr. Hoyt, you never did describe the man you saw."

"He was average height, I guess. Five-ten, five-eleven. Light brown hair. Kind of skinny."

Scarbrough frowned. Mark was taller than average—six-two or -three. His hair was dark brown, almost black, and he would never be considered skinny.

He glanced at Ellen and Ned. "That doesn't sound like Mark."

Ellen seemed dumbfounded that he wouldn't just believe them. "Charles, did you have your glasses on?"

Charles shook his head. "I was trying to sleep. They were on my bed table."

Scarbrough stepped closer to him. He was wearing the glasses now. "So you didn't see him clearly?"

The man took his glasses off and handed them to the sheriff. "I'm not *that* nearsighted, but yeah, the man was a little blurry. But I saw him."

Scarbrough looked through the lenses. They were pretty strong. His heart sank. Maybe it *was* Mark, after all. Maybe he didn't really know the kid. Maybe everything he thought about Mark was just a facade to cover his true nature.

He had been wrong before.

TWENTY-TWO

DENI BRANNING PACED ACROSS HER LIVING ROOM, THE heat of her anger warming her face even though the fire had died out an hour ago. "Not Mark!" she cried to her father. "He wouldn't *do* that!"

"Zach's roommate confirmed it. Said Mark told him his name."

This was getting worse and worse. Why would Mark go to the hospital after Ellen Emory's reaction yesterday? Tears burned in her eyes as she tried to sort through it.

"I tried to go talk to him, Deni, but he isn't home and hasn't been seen all day," Doug said.

Deni hadn't heard from Mark since he left yesterday to escape the lynch mob. Where was he? "Dad, I don't know what happened or why he was there. But I know it's not like they're saying. What if something's happened to him? What if Grantham's gang caught him?"

"I think we'd know if that had happened. They would have bragged about it. It's more likely that he's been arrested."

She didn't like that idea any better. She grabbed her coat and started for the door. "I have to go look for him."

"Deni, what if he comes here? We're one of his last safe places."

She sighed and realized he was right. "I'll give him an hour," she said. "Then I'm going out there to find him."

TWENTY-THREE

SCARBROUGH LEFT THE HOSPITAL, A SICK FEELING IN THE pit of his stomach, rivaling the fluid in his lungs. He now had probable cause to arrest Mark Green—three of them, to be exact—and he knew there was no way around it. But for some reason, he couldn't make it compute in his gut.

The DA gave him an arrest warrant, and Scarbrough picked up two deputies to accompany him. But when he got to Mark's house, he found Deni and Doug there, talking to his crying mother. No one knew where Mark was.

He searched a few places that Mark might be, but came up empty. Fatigue washed back over him, and he thought of that cat in his well. He hoped Jimmy hadn't tried again to get it out. He'd forgotten to get a hydrologist to tell him what to do. He supposed they'd have to get water from the Keatons for another day. But there wasn't time to waste taking care of personal business. He had to find Mark and lock him up before someone else found him. If Lou and his buddies got wind of the latest accusations and found him first, Mark might not live through it.

He pulled his van back into the parking lot at the sheriff's department and headed inside, despite his debilitating fatigue. He'd give anything to lie down just for a moment. The coughing had exhausted him. Maybe if he did go to the doctor, he could get some cough medicine to get him through. Maybe it would be worth the time ... *after* he found Mark.

He went up the front steps and into the cold building. Deputy Jones met him at the door. "Sheriff, there's someone here to see you."

What now?

He started to cough outside his office door, doubling over as he tried to clear his lungs. Finally, he heard a familiar voice.

"You really need to see a doctor, Sheriff."

Scarbrough stopped coughing and stepped into his office. Mark Green sat with his elbows on his knees.

"Here I am," he said. "I've come to turn myself in."

TWENTY-FOUR

THE JAIL SMELLED OF PORTA-JOHNS THAT WEREN'T MEANT to be inside. They had been set into each cell, the inmates' only way of relieving themselves. The nauseating stench hit Mark the moment he stepped into the dark room, and he fought back the urge to gag.

The only light came from slits of windows at the tops of the walls, not big enough for anyone to crawl through, and not low enough to illuminate the faces of those crammed into the cells. The inmates were like shadows moving aggressively through a dream, but their voices layered upon each other in a deafening sound—obscenities, accusations, threats echoing off the concrete walls.

The muscles in Mark's neck, shoulders, and arms were on full alert, rigid with dread. Men yelled demands through the bars. Scarbrough walked Mark down the center of the room, just out of their reach. The holding cells in Crockett were not meant to be long term, nor were they meant to hold more than a few prisoners at a time. Before the Pulses, those who were arraigned in the county court were transferred to the county prison or penal farm in Birmingham. But now the substations around the county housed their own inmates until places for them could be found.

As they walked through, Mark wondered whether he'd been wise to turn himself in. He'd tried earlier to come back to Crockett, but as he'd approached one of the community wells for water, he'd seen his name on a message board—WANTED: MARK GREEN. Pulling his ski cap low over his face, he'd moved close enough to read of his alleged attempt to kill Zach yesterday. Someone was setting him up, and they meant business. He'd decided there was no point in running anymore.

Now regret pulsed through him. The sheriff and his deputies didn't buy his innocence, and he had to admit that he *looked* guilty.

The room was freezing, almost as cold as it was outside. Still, perspiration broke out over his lip and beaded on his temples.

He tried not to make eye contact with any of the prisoners, but he could see that there were five cells—two on each side and one at the end of the room. Each had three bunk beds—six beds in all—but there were at least ten men in each of the cells. Where did they all sleep?

Dread seized Mark as the sheriff stopped at the last cell and ordered the inmates to back against the wall. Mark's mind raced for refuge.

Even though I walk through the valley of the shadow of death, I will fear no evil, for you are with me; your rod and your staff, they comfort me. He muttered the words over and over in his mind, a rote prayer, an expectation.

The sheriff stopped to cough before unlocking the door, and Mark took a moment to size up his cellmates. As far as height went, he could hold his own with them. At six-three, he could meet most of them eye to eye. Only one loomed larger. Three or four of them had bulked-up steroid builds and looked like pit bulls waiting to attack. Three of them were small and frightened, beat up and abused. One had clearly lost a fight—he had a busted lip and a twisted, broken nose.

And one lay in bed, curled up and shivering on a bottom bunk.

Scarbrough kept coughing, lost in a fit that he couldn't control.

"Aw, man, you're sick too." The biggest guy in the cell stepped forward. "Man, this place is *full* of disease!"

"And Blatt's ate up with something." One of the pit bulls kicked the metal bedpost, rattling the bed where the sick man lay. "Get him outta here."

"I want my lawyer!" the littlest guy called.

Scarbrough stopped coughing and straightened. "I've been trying to get the doctor to come see him," he rasped out. "I'm still waiting. Now get back!" He put his hand on his firearm. The men drifted back, chins held high. Mark got the feeling they weren't obeying—they were just biding their time.

Even though I walk through the valley of the shadow of death ...

Scarbrough rattled his keys, found the right one, then unlocked the door. The hinges squeaked as he pulled it open.

"I know it's crowded," Scarbrough said, "but it's the best we can do. Go on in, now."

Mark pulled in a deep breath and stepped inside. Scarbrough slammed the door behind him. The noise echoed throughout the room. He wondered if they'd worked on that sound, carefully designing the doors to clang shut and echo. A psychological tactic to freak out the newcomer.

It worked.

The men came away from the back wall and stepped menacingly toward Mark. He pulled his hands from his pockets and held them in fists at his sides.

"You got family?" one of the smaller men asked.

Mark looked into his eyes. The whites of his eyes were yellow, and he was missing his front row of teeth.

"Yeah, I have family," he said. "Why?"

"They close by?" Yellow Eyes asked.

"Not too far."

"Good. Then they can bring you food."

"We provide one meal a day," Scarbrough said through the bars. "That's all we can manage. We bring you water. A lot of the families bring more food up here to supplement. But get ready. You're going to have to fight for it if they do."

The men spread out and went to their bunks, as if making sure that Mark didn't claim one of them. He slid his hands into his pockets and leaned back against a cold wall.

"We'll bring in some mattresses when it gets dark," Scarbrough said. "There's not room for them until then."

Mark nodded and figured it wouldn't pay to lie down now anyway. He was better off standing, warding off those who had something to prove. His eyes were beginning to adjust to the place, and he saw some bean bag chairs scattered around the floor. One of the inmates picked up a pink one and tossed it to him. "Here. This looks like yours."

He didn't much care what color it was. Catching it, he said, "Thanks."

"They can't trust us with real chairs," somebody said. "They figure we could break 'em over each other's heads."

Suddenly, he was thankful for the bean bags. He gripped the vinyl in one hand, but didn't sit just yet.

"What's your name?" the little guy asked him.

"Mark Green."

The little guy held out an ice-cold hand, and Mark shook it. "I'm Sam. You can call me Samuel or Samson or Sambo or Sam-I-Am—whatever you want."

The man seemed simple and defenseless. Mark wondered how he'd survived here. "Thanks. I'll just go with Sam."

"And he's Tree House," Sam said, pointing to the big guy.

Tree House looked like he could mow down a crowd with an AK-47 without blinking an eye. "I'm de one wit' de most upstairs."

The man had an accent Mark couldn't place—Caribbean, maybe. He was taller than Mark and twice as built. He had a smooth bald head and the beginnings of a beard. The sheriff started coughing again as he walked away, letting the steel door clang, its sound echoing through the room. Mark felt abandoned in the very pit of hell.

The noise level rose again as the sheriff closed them in. In another cell, he heard a fight, flesh pounding flesh, vile shouts and a pitiful scream.

Suddenly, Tree House was next to him. Leaning over, he whispered in his ear, "You hear dat, man? I'm de boss in dis cell. You cross me, you wind up like dat dude in dere."

Refusing to show fear, Mark stood taller, straighter, and looked the man in the eye. He could hold his own with him, he thought, if it came down to it. He would do what was necessary to protect himself.

They stared at each other for a long moment, then Tree House took a step back. Walking over to the bunk with the sick man, he grabbed the man's arm and pulled him off the bed.

The man hit the floor with a thud.

Mark lunged forward, but Tree House's hand shot out and clamped Mark's throat. "I tol' you, don't mess wit' me."

Mark jerked free and stooped next to the man, as Tree House stretched out on the sick man's bare mattress. The man's eyes were sunken, dark circles shadowing them. His face had a deathly gray pallor and his lips were blue. His shivers bordered on convulsions. He was burning with fever.

Mark thought of fighting Tree House to get the man's bed back, but he knew it wouldn't be just the two of them. There was a whole crowd of bloodthirsty men just waiting to jump in.

Sam stooped next to him. "We been hoping Blatt would die so we could get him outta here," the little man said. "He's been dyin' for days."

This man might not make it even if the sheriff managed to get him to a hospital, but he would surely die if they kept him in here. Why hadn't Scarbrough gotten him out?

Mark looked up at Tree House as the big man got up from the coveted mattress. He stalked around like a bull looking for the gate. Mark sat down next to Blatt, guarding him with his presence.

Maybe this was why he was here.

TWENTY-FIVE

THE SHERIFF MADE A PRODUCTION OF GETTING BLATT OUT of the cell. Leading the paramedics in with a gurney, he had two deputies stand with guns drawn as the men lined up against the back wall. Then they brought the gurney into the cell, loaded Blatt onto it, and hurried him out.

Mark hoped the man survived the trip to the hospital.

Night had fallen hours before, turning the slits of windows above the cells to black. One of the deputies brought a lantern in and set it beside the door, far out of the reach of any of the prisoners. It gave off little light, only enough to keep those closest to it from tripping over each other.

Mark's cellmates looked like shadows moving around the cell, getting ready for bed, fighting over the territory of the six beds. No attempt was made to disinfect Blatt's mattress, and Tree House continued to claim it as his own. The upper bunk that Tree House had occupied before was quickly taken by one of the other inmates.

The sheriff brought in five small mattresses, thin enough to fit between the bars, and some threadbare blankets. Mark took one of each, found a spot, and tried to settle down for the night.

He was thankful the sheriff had let him keep his jacket. The temperature seemed to have dropped another twenty degrees since nightfall. The cold seemed soul-deep. He turned his collar up and shifted, trying to get comfortable on the thin mattress. The concrete floor beneath him was even colder.

Why hadn't someone put a wood-burning oven in here or altered the room for a fireplace? He'd spent the last four or five months helping people without fireplaces put them in their homes, preparing them for winter. He hadn't even considered the prisoners at the local jail.

A huddle of men had formed in a back corner of the cell. Something was going on. He thought of trying to listen in, but the truth was that he didn't want to know what they were scheming. He was better off not knowing.

He thought back over the last two days—the accusations by Ellen Emory, the furor of the lynch mob. He hoped his mother was all right. And Deni too.

Maybe his being here would cause his arrogant, bloodthirsty neighbors to call off their dogs and leave the people he cared about alone.

He heard laughter from the corner, then someone sang out a line from the old reggae tune, "I Shot the Sheriff," and there was more laughter. He heard Tree House's deep, base voice, adding, "But I also shot de depu-tees." More laughter.

Were they just fantasizing about overthrowing the law, or was there more to it? He sat up and tried to listen. The voices had gone back to whispers.

Slowly, he slid along the wall, moving closer to them. The darkness had its uses, he supposed. Maybe he could get close enough to hear without being noticed.

"They came for the sick dude, didn't dey?" Tree House was saying in a whisper. "So I'm gon' get real sick, myself. Dey gon' come get me outta here. And when dey roll me on de gurney, all limp and weak and dyin', I'm gon' overpower Andy Griffith and dose Barney Fifes o' his, get de closest one's gun, and we gon' stampede outta here over deir dead bodies."

Mark's breath caught in his chest. Was he serious about this? Were these men really going to attempt something so deadly? The others murmured in agreement.

How many of them were in on it? He counted the voices—one, two ... maybe three men.

Sliding back to his mattress, he racked his brain for a way to get word to the sheriff. If they knew he knew, they'd attack him before he could open his mouth. What would they have to lose?

The whispers seemed to stop, and the cell went quiet. He saw a shadow shift in the blackness. Suddenly something was on top of him, knocking him back. His head hit the floor. A man's weight mashed down on him, suffocating, crushing, but Mark gritted his teeth and flipped him over until Mark was on top.

"Get him, Tree House!" one of the men shouted.

Mark's victory was short-lived. The big man's hands came around Mark's throat, cutting off his circulation and his air. He intended to kill him.

But Mark wouldn't die.

His knee came up, knocking his tormenter off balance. He brought his fists up between the man's stiff arms, making him release his hold on Mark's throat. Suddenly it wasn't just Tree House, but at least three other inmates around him, holding him down while Tree House got in his face, his perspiration dripping into Mark's eyes.

"You listen to me, white boy. I'm in charge here, you got dat?"

Mark struggled and kicked against the hands holding him down. "I don't care who's in charge," he said through his teeth. "Be the general, for all I care. The king. The stinking *emperor*."

"You keep your mout' shut about what you hear and stay outta my way, maybe I won't have to kill you."

"I'm not interested in anything I hear in this place," Mark said.

"Oh no? Dat's right. You above it all, aren't you, white boy?"

There were six other white men in this cell alone, and he suspected a couple of them were holding him down.

"You understand what I'm sayin', or do I have to explain it a little more clear?"

Mark struggled against the urge to spit in his face. If he did, he'd probably be dead before his skull cracked on the concrete. And that wouldn't do the sheriff any good.

"I got it," he bit out.

Tree House let him go and got up, and the others backed away. Shivering with rage, Mark sat back down on his mattress, his back against the wall. He didn't want to wait to talk to the sheriff. He wanted to counterattack, knock out Tree House's teeth, listen to bones snap.

Help me, Lord. He didn't know what to do with all this hate pulsing through him. Maybe he was more like Tree House than he thought. Maybe he was even like his dad.

Temptation ignited within him, its heat spreading through his veins.

He could hear Tree House moving to his left, talking to his friends, chuckling under his breath. He could reach him in three steps, have him on the floor face down before he took another breath—

The Lord is my light and my salvation; whom shall I fear? The Lord is the defense of my life; whom shall I dread?

The verse he'd quoted to Beth days ago poured through his mind, unbidden, its power trickling down through his heart, washing out the pride and arrogance that pulsated through him, spraying down the fires of fear and hatred.

He wasn't like Tree House. And the apple *had* fallen far from the tree. He'd wait quietly until he could get word to the sheriff. Somehow, he would warn him.

Despite his fatigue, Mark knew there wasn't going to be any sleep tonight. If he drifted off, someone might ambush him again. Or worse.

What are you doing, God? Why are you letting this happen?

The questions instantly shamed him. Why couldn't he be more stoic, like David, who'd written Psalm 56 when he was in a dark, cold cave somewhere, surrounded by his enemies? Or like Daniel, when they were throwing him into the lions' den? Why couldn't he be like Shadrach, Meshach, and Abednego, when they'd been cast into the fiery furnace?

Our God whom we serve is able to deliver us ... But even if he does not ...

He thought of the three men standing in the flames meant to devour them. They had gone in with courage and bravery, looking not at those flames, but at the God who controlled them. And God had been there with them.

Mark didn't think he had that kind of courage. He'd have been complaining that it was hot in the furnace, ignoring the fact that his hair wasn't singed and his clothes didn't even smell like smoke.

But he would *learn* to be like them, if God could be patient with him. Something told him that God would be—that, in fact, the dissipation of his murderous anger just now had been an act of God.

Eventually, he sensed that the men in his cell had all gone to sleep, so he lay down again. But sleep would not come. And when the first rays of light began to seep into those windows at the tops of the concrete walls, he was thankful that morning had finally come.

TWENTY-SIX

DENI DREADED THE SNOW NOW FALLING IN BIG WHITE flakes. Though it seemed to paint the ground like a clean, white slate, she knew it was only covering the ugliness beneath—and making life cold and soulless. She and her mother, along with Beth and Logan, had all spent the night in the living room where the fireplace kept them warm, because it was too cold in their rooms. Doug and Jeff stayed in their own beds piled high with blankets.

But Deni didn't sleep. Since she'd gotten word that Mark was in jail, fears danced like phantoms through her mind. She couldn't imagine Mark in that place with killers and thieves. She'd been to the sheriff's department before when the jail door was open. The sounds and smells from there had given her a shivering sense of evil—as if the place was full of locked-up demons, looking for innocence to destroy.

Instead of trying to go back to sleep, she went up to the chill of her room and lay face-down on the floor. She couldn't break Mark out of jail, and she couldn't protect him from others' violence. But she could spend her night storming the gates of heaven on his behalf, begging for his safety, and even his comfort.

When morning finally came, Martha showed up at their house, terrorized and trembling.

"My house was robbed last night."

"Oh, Martha!" Kay pulled her into the house and dusted the snow off her shoulder.

"Are you all right?" Deni asked.

"Yes. They didn't find me."

Deni helped Martha shrug out of her coat and led her to the fire. Doug came from the bedroom. "What happened?"

Her words rolled out in rapid fire. "They broke the window on the back door and came in about three a.m. I hid in the back of my bedroom closet while they tore through my house. They came right into the closet, but I was hidden—they didn't see me. I thought they were going to kill me."

Deni got an afghan from the couch and put it around Martha's shoulders. "Martha, come sit down."

Clutching the afghan, she sat down. "I stayed in my hiding place in the closet until just a few minutes ago. The house is ransacked. They pulled out drawers and turned things over, like they were looking for something. They took all the food Mark had in the van."

Deni looked up at her dad. "Dad, do you think it was Lou and his men?"

Doug shook his head. "I know those guys. As bad as they are, they think they're doing the right thing. I don't think they would have taken advantage of a woman at home alone to rob her. Have you told the sheriff, Martha?"

Trembling, she wiped her wet cheeks. "No, I came straight here as soon as I had the courage to come out. But I have to go report the break-in and check on Mark. Whoever it was might have broken in looking for him. I'm afraid to go back there."

"Well, you don't have to," Kay said. "You're staying here until Mark gets out."

"Dad and I will go to the sheriff with you," Deni said. "We'll take some bread for Mark. Mom made twenty loaves in the solar oven yesterday."

"He won't get any," Martha said. "I've heard they fight over every crumb."

"Then we'll take all twenty loaves," Kay said. "Then he'll be sure to get some."

But Logan gasped. "No way we're taking our bread to a bunch of prisoners. Mom, I spent my hard-earned stuff on that flour."

Deni wanted to slap him. "Logan, it's Mark we're talking about. Besides, it's cruel for prisoners to have to starve. Even the ones who are guilty."

"But what are we gonna do when we can't buy seeds or feed for the chickens and rabbits? Mom, you said we had to sell the bread—"

"Logan, that's enough," Kay said. "We thought we were baking them to sell, but clearly, God had other plans."

"I'll skip supper tonight," Beth said. "Mark can have mine."

Martha smiled through her tears. "Thank you, Beth. You're sweet. But I know Mark would rather have you eat."

Doug shook his head. "We have enough for ourselves, Martha. We'll take the loaves to the jail and that's that. Mark's fed us so many times. It's the least we can do for him. Isn't it, Logan?"

His withering look got Logan's attention. "Yes, sir."

TWENTY-SEVEN

Sheriff Scarbrough looked three breaths from collapsing when they found him in his office. His skin was gray, and his eyes cavernous. He hadn't shaved in days, and his lips were cracked and scabbed. He took Martha's statement about the break-in, promising to come and investigate it further the moment he could get away.

"I wouldn't recommend you go back home just yet," he told Martha. "We need to dust for prints and see if we can ID the prowlers. They were probably looking for Mark. No telling what they'd have done if they'd found you."

Martha had a distant, vacant look in her eyes. "I need to get word to my husband."

"Where is John?" Sheriff Scarbrough asked.

"In Huntsville, working at one of the conversion plants. He thought I'd be safe with Mark—no one ever dreamed that any of this would happen." Her voice broke, and she brought her hand to her throat. "How is he, Sheriff? How's Mark?"

He leaned forward on his desk, rubbing his mouth. Not meeting their eyes, he muttered, "He's fine."

Deni had the sense that he wasn't fine at all.

"We want to see him," Doug said.

Deni held up her bag of bread loaves. "We brought food. Can we give it to them?"

His voice was so hoarse he almost couldn't speak. "Yeah, but don't start making trouble, getting the prisoners all riled up. It's all we can do to keep them calm, especially when they've been freezing their tails off all night." He glanced down at the sack in her hand. "Get ready. There'll be a fight for that food."

"We tried to bring enough for everybody to get some."

"We do feed them a meal a day, you know. Some of the older ladies from the Crockett Apostolic Church take turns bringing stuff. We try to pay them for it when we can. Lately, we haven't been able to, and with the snow, I guess they've decided not to come."

Deni was glad someone had made that a ministry. It had never occurred to her that the prisoners were starving.

"Then I guess God provided today," Doug said.

The sheriff nodded. "I guess so."

"Can we see Mark outside his cell?" Deni asked.

He shook his head. "I don't have the manpower to let him out and guard him while he talks to you. You'll have to visit him inside."

He started coughing, doubling over, hacking his heart out. They waited until he could breathe again.

"You're really sick, Sheriff," Doug said.

Scarbrough ignored the comment and got his keys. He led them out of his office and to the door to the jail. He stopped before opening it, and looked back at Deni and Martha. "Ladies, I want you to keep your eyes on the floor until we get to Mark. Don't look around. Don't touch anything. Don't engage with the other prisoners and don't get feisty. Do you understand?"

"What do you mean, feisty?" Deni asked.

"I mean I don't want you to be disruptive. You're a pretty young woman, and these men are going to be making catcalls and yelling lewd things at you. That'll be bad enough, but I don't want you talking back to them."

Her mouth felt suddenly dry. "You act like they're going to come through the bars and attack me."

"They might try. Some of the people locked up here are the worst of the worst, and they don't have a lot to lose right now."

"Mark's not the worst of the worst. Maybe there are other innocent people in there like him."

"Don't count on it, Deni." His breath whistled as he spoke. He opened the door, and they stepped into the rancid-smelling place. There was little light, and the temperature seemed even colder than outside.

The men spotted Deni and Martha as soon as they came in, and catcalls started up just as the sheriff had predicted. Lewd suggestions came pealing across the room, and several of the men came to the bars, making grabbing gestures that made her cringe. She put her hand over her mouth to keep from gagging at the smell, and she strained to see through the dim light coming from the small, barred windows at the top of the wall. Today it was cloudy and overcast—only a faint, gray hue spilled in, just enough for her to see where she was walking.

"Over here!"

She heard Mark's voice over the din, and they headed to the cell where he stood at the end of the room. He looked rough with two days' worth of stubble on his jaw, and his hair was dirty and tangled. His mother burst into tears and grabbed his hands through the bars.

"Mark, are you okay?" Deni asked.

"I'm fine," he said, but she knew he couldn't be—not in a place like this. She got out a loaf of bread and thrust it into his hands. Immediately, the others descended on him, and men from neighboring cells cried out. Doug took the bag from her and began breaking the loaves and passing them out. It kept everyone away from Mark for a moment.

He leaned into the bars, trying to be heard while keeping his voice low. "Mom, Deni, tell the sheriff they're planning something. They're gonna—"

A tall man with a bald head moved closer, and Mark's words fell off.

"What?" Deni asked.

Mark cleared his throat. "Just ... have you talked to the sheriff about my case?"

That wasn't what he'd started to say. Deni took his hand and felt the hard squeeze. He was trying to tell her something.

"Yes," she said, glancing at the big man who seemed to have more than a passing interest in their conversation. Mark wasn't going to talk as long as he was eavesdropping.

He changed the subject and looked at his mother. "Have Grantham and his men harassed you anymore?"

The question brought tears to Martha's eyes. "No, but ... there's something I have to tell you." She brought her hand to her mouth, trying to get the words out.

Deni spoke up. "Mark, your house was broken into last night."

He flinched as though he'd been punched in the gut. "Mom, are you all right?"

Martha nodded and pulled herself together. "I hid. But they took all our food, and turned the house practically upside down."

He clutched the bars, his face twisting. "I can't believe this! What is happening?"

The big man moved away for a moment, and Mark took the opportunity. "Things are getting worse and worse." Lowering his voice so that only his mother and Deni could hear, he said, "We had a sick guy in here last night. He almost died. They came in and got him out."

"What was wrong with him?"

"I don't know." Mark glanced at the big man as he began to step back toward him. "But when they came in to get him ... it was dangerous." The man was in earshot again, but Mark kept talking. "The sheriff ... he should have confirmed it."

Deni frowned. "Confirmed what?"

The big man's arm came around Mark's shoulders—but his expression suggested anything but camaraderie. Mark's chin came up and he stood taller, his muscles rigid and alert. Only then did she notice the bruises on his neck.

Mark grew quiet again. He broke off a piece of the bread she'd given him and put it into his mouth, chewing with his eyes fixed on her.

The big man devoured the rest of his own bread. "You tellin' her 'bout Blatt? 'Bout how he was contagious? Tell her 'bout de human waste festering in dat toilet back dere, breedin' disease."

She didn't doubt it—she could smell the toilet. But somehow, his words sounded like a threat.

Their food devoured, several of Mark's cellmates turned their attention back to her.

Some of the men pushed in around Mark, making lewd comments that made her shiver. One of the inmates who looked like a body builder on steroids pushed in next to Mark. He reached through the bars and grabbed a strand of her hair, using it to tug her closer.

Deni screamed and jumped back.

Mark shoved the man back and pointed in his face. "Back off! Keep your hands off her!"

Doug stepped between Deni and the bars. "Come on, it's time to go."

"But Mark—"

Turning back to Deni, Mark said, "You have to go now, Deni. And don't come back."

Deni let her father pull her away. "Mark—"

"Doug, don't let her come back. You too, Mom. Stay away!"

Martha backed away from the bars.

As the roar rose, Doug pulled Deni back toward the door and forced her through it. Martha stumbled out behind them, sobbing into her hand.

"Dad, he was trying to tell me something!" Deni cried when the door had been shut.

The sheriff sat down on the edge of his desk. "What did he say?"

"Something about a sick man. A plan ..."

"He's talking about Blatt, the prisoner we took to the hospital."

"No, it was something else. That big guy with the bald head made him stop talking. He was threatening him. Mark's neck is bruised. He's not safe, Sheriff!"

"Relax, Deni. I'm about to go back to the hospital. I'll see if Zach's woke up yet. And I have some other leads I'm following. But until I come to any different conclusion, Mark is staying put."

"But you have no right to hold people in those conditions. There's disease festering in those toilets. At least clean them out. And separate the violent prisoners from the civilized ones."

"I'm doing the best I can with what I've got. If you people want to come clean out the Porta-Johns, be my guest. I'm down to a skeleton staff, and last I noticed, crime hadn't taken any commercial breaks."

Deni watched Martha move toward the front door, her shoulders shaking. She was falling apart. Turning from the sheriff, Deni put her arms around Martha and let her cry against her shoulder. Finally, Doug opened the door. "Let's just go."

Casting one final look back at the jail door, Deni helped Martha out into the cold.

TWENTY-EIGHT

MARK WAS SICKENED BY HIS CELLMATES' TREATMENT OF Deni and his mother. He hoped Doug would keep them from returning. His mom was fragile, and Deni, despite her toughness, was small and pristine and naive ... not the kind of woman he wanted to parade in front of men like these. If he couldn't protect her from the verbal assaults, or the groping hands through the bars, then he wanted her to stay away.

He slid down the wall of his cell and sat on the floor, elbows resting on his knees. He thought of his poor attempt to warn Deni of the scheme Tree House was cooking up. He'd meant to give her a message for the sheriff, but it had been so poorly phrased that he knew she hadn't gotten any of it. As astute as she was, his vague words didn't have a shot of hitting home. How could she guess that his mention of the need for sickness to be "confirmed" was a warning to the sheriff? No, she was probably so shaken from her experience here that she was racing home, glad to get away from this place.

His gaze drifted up to the huddle in the corner. He didn't know when Tree House would set his plan into action, but he knew it would be soon. Somehow, he had to figure out a way to stop it.

Even if it meant he got beaten to a pulp.

"She's purty, that girl o' yours."

Mark glanced at Pete, the little guy who'd slept next to him on the floor last night. Pete was no more than five-foot-six, maybe a hundred pounds with all his clothes on.

"I don't want to talk about her," Mark said.

"Don't blame ya." Pete sat down next to him, legs crossed like a little boy in front of the television. "They're like animals, sometimes. That's why they're here, I reckon. Ain't nobody here for bein' a gentleman."

Mark looked toward the huddle again.

"They're plannin' to attack the sheriff, you know," Pete said in a low voice. "They say we'll all be able to walk free. You think they can pull it off?"

Mark shivered at the thought of these prisoners let loose in Crockett all at once. "I don't know," he said.

"I gotta get outta here," Pete said. "My wife and two kids can't survive without me. She come up here yesterday and tol' me she got throwed outta the room we rented, on account of what I done. I don't know where she'll go, and it's mighty cold out there."

Mark's heart softened. He looked at Pete then, saw the sincere worry in his eyes. "What did you do to get put in here, exactly?"

"Defended her," he said. "Landlord's boy was comin' at her, forcin' hisself on her, and I fought him off."

"Did you kill him?"

"No, but almost. He claimed it was attempted murder, that I was tryin' to rob *him*. They believed him, of course. Why wouldn't they? He had money, and I'm a nobody."

"Did you tell the judge what happened?"

He laughed bitterly. "I ain't seen a judge since I been here."

"Well, you have a lawyer, don't you?"

Pete thought that was even funnier. "You think we have PDs poppin' up in here seein' if there's anybody they can help? No, I won't see a lawyer till I go to court, and the way things are movin' 'round here, that could be weeks. I ain't even been able to enter a plea yet." He glanced toward Tree House and his group of violent followers. "I just hope I survive long enough. I been in jail before, but that was easy time compared to this. Back when there were lights, and running water, and real toilets. We got showers every day and clean clothes to wear. Heat and air conditioning. Three meals a day. This here is my idea of what hell is like."

Mark had to agree.

"And if all that wasn't bad enough, we got Tree House and his boys, who love stickin' my head in the toilet and grindin' my face in the concrete."

Mark's cool gaze drifted back to the man. That explained a lot about Pete's misshapen nose and the bruises on his cheekbones, and his smell ...

If they attacked Pete again, Mark would have to fight. He couldn't let them do that to someone so defenseless.

Heaviness fell over him, and he knew this whole situation was going to get much worse before it got better. *God, please help me.*

Something was going to break loose soon. He only hoped he'd have the power to stop it.

TWENTY-NINE

WORD TRAVELED FAST. SOON ALL OF THE INMATES WERE IN on the plan. Though the room was cold, a thin sheen of perspiration made Mark's skin slick as he listened to the sinister scheme that would result in lost lives—and fifty criminals back on the snowy streets.

"Just so's you know," Tree House told Mark. "You do one t'ing to keep dis from happenin', and I'll snap dat Petie's neck right in two."

Mark's chest felt so tight he couldn't breathe. A threat against himself he could handle, but he couldn't stand the thought that Pete would take the brunt of it.

"Leave him out of this," Mark said. "Why don't we just let this be between you and me?"

"Oh, it is dat," Tree House said.

"You won't get away with it. Sheriff Scarbrough's too experienced to fall for something so stupid."

"Sheriff Scarbrough's sick as a poisoned mutt," he said. "He too weak to fight back."

"He has a family," Mark said, knowing his argument was weak. "So do the deputies. I don't know what you did to get put in here, but I don't think you want to add murder to your list of charges."

"*Add* murder?" Tree House laughed. "I already got t'ree life sentences breathin' down my neck. You tink I want to spend de rest of my life sittin' in dis cold, dark dump? I'm gettin' out, and I don't care who has to die. So don't get in my way."

Mark had never felt more helpless. He glanced at Pete, going into the Porta-John, and wondered if he knew he'd become a pawn in this game.

Lord, I need your help.

Over the next few hours, Tree House lay on the bed, pretending to be sick. When Scarbrough or one of the deputies would come in with cups of water for the inmates, Mark's cellmates all grew vocal about how sick he was and how they wanted him out.

"He got what Blatt had," they told the sheriff. "You got a epidemic startin' in here."

"You don't get him out," one of the men said, "we'll kill him ourselves."

Once, as Scarbrough considered the problem, he called Mark to the bars. "Just how sick is that man?" he asked.

Mark found it surprising that the sheriff trusted him to provide the truth while incarcerating him for attempted murder. He glanced back at Tree House, saw his slitted eyes on him, just daring him to give the plan away. Gus, one of Tree House's cohorts, inched up beside Pete, set his arm around his shoulders, and bent his forearm under his neck.

Yes, he could snap it with one movement.

Mark looked back at Scarbrough, wishing he could telepathically relate to him what was happening. But he'd have to think of another way.

"I don't know, Sheriff. I'm not a doctor."

He prayed that God would speak to the sheriff, tell him this was a setup. Surely Scarbrough had dealt with enough prisoners to know when he was being conned.

"Get him out!" one of the prisoners from another cell called, banging his tin cup on the bars. "You want more dead bodies in here? You want us all to drop dead of some plague?"

Tree House began to convulse slightly, like someone with a high fever.

Finally, Scarbrough succumbed. "I'll be back. We'll get him to the hospital."

Mark's heart stumbled. It was beginning. He couldn't let this happen. Rolling his hands into fists, he turned back to his cellmates. Pete was still under the arm of his tormenter, his blood-shot eyes pleading. Mark's throat grew tight, and every muscle went rigid.

Time ticked by, and the men in the cells grew quiet. Tension rippled on the air.

Finally, the big metal door creaked open again. Scarbrough and two deputies led in a couple of paramedics—George Mason and Will Truman—with a gurney. They drew their weapons as they came inside, just as they had when they removed Blatt.

"All right, everybody back against the wall."

Mark hesitated a moment, looking at Tree House, who lay curled in a fetal position on the bed, putting on an Oscar-worthy performance of shivering and convulsing.

"Go on, Mark. You too. Back against the wall."

Mark slowly backed across the floor. He stood beside Pete, who was again in Gus's loose headlock. Scarbrough pulled out his keys and started to unlock the door.

Suddenly, Mark thought of something. "I'll bring him to you, Sheriff!"

Everyone froze. Tree House's eyes opened and seared on him. Gus's arm tightened under Pete's neck.

Mark's throat felt suddenly parched. He couldn't swallow, and his breathing seemed restricted as his heart pounded in his head. Slowly, he went toward the bed.

"You might want to check Pete too," he said. "He's getting a fever, I think."

Scarbrough's gaze shot to the little man. Gus's arm loosened. At least that situation was now on his radar.

Tree House kept shivering, but he bit out a whispered warning. "Don't do it, white boy. Tell him I'm too heavy."

Mark ignored him. He bent down and pulled Tree House up, slipped his shoulder under the man's armpit, and tried to lift him. Tree House resisted, but Mark was strong, and he tried to force him to his feet.

The man went limp and fell to the floor.

"Just back up, Mark," Scarbrough said. "We'll come in with the gurney."

"No, I've got him." Determined, Mark bent, grabbed Tree House under his arms, and dragged him across the concrete. He knew this was a lethal decision. He'd probably wind up dead because of it.

"He's draggin' a sick man!" Gus shouted. "He's gonna kill him!"

The others joined in, a mob roar of protests. "Let go of him, Mark!" Scarbrough's gun came up. "Mark, I told you to back against the wall."

Mark let Tree House go and gave the sheriff a pleading look. Something changed in Scarbrough's eyes. He looked at the deputies. They got it, Mark thought. They knew he was trying to help them. He raised his hands and backed against the wall.

Scarbrough put the key into the lock.

Deputies Anderson and Jones kept their guns trained on the prisoners against the wall.

"Gus, let go of Pete and move to the corner over there," Scarbrough said. "Anybody moves, we'll shoot. Got that?"

Cold hard eyes registered the warning.

Mark held his breath as the door came open. Scarbrough told the paramedics to wait, then he came in slowly, rolling the gurney beside him. He went to the big man lying on the floor, felt his clammy skin. "Okay, men. Come give me a hand."

The deputies came in and bent to pick up Tree House.

Suddenly Tree House grabbed the gun in Scarbrough's holster. Mark lunged forward, but the gun went off. Scarbrough dropped with a thud.

"Freeze!" Jones shouted, but Tree House turned to the deputies and fired twice. Both men fell.

The plan had worked.

The cellmates rushed forward, trampling them, and crowded through the door. One of them grabbed the keys and guns from the bleeding men and unlocked the other cells. A stampede ensued as everyone rushed to escape.

Mark fell beside the sheriff and checked his pulse. He was still alive. "Sheriff, hang on!" he cried. "Somebody help!"

THIRTY

THE TWO PARAMEDICS WHO HAD HIT THE FLOOR RALLIED and made their way to the bleeding men. Mark held his breath as they worked on them, wishing he could help.

Suddenly, Milton Asher, the deputy who'd been out on patrol, rushed inside, his gun trembling in both hands.

"Three men down!" George Mason yelled. "The prisoners escaped."

As if Milt didn't know where to direct his terror, he turned the gun on Mark. "Get back, Green! Hands in the air!"

Mark got to his feet and raised his hands.

"He's not the one," George said, checking the pulses of the two fallen deputies. "Anderson's dead," he said, moving to Jones. "Dear God, Jones is dead too."

Milt looked as if he'd been kicked in the stomach.

"Scarbrough's still with us!" Will said. Mark's thoughts of the gun still held on him fled as he watched them intubate the sheriff, trying to open an airway. Scarbrough's lower jaw was bloody and broken, and panic seized Mark. The bullet had ripped through his face.

He held his own breath as they cut into the sheriff's trachea.

"Pulse is weak!" George cried, pumping on his chest.

Milt lowered the gun and took a heavy step toward his dead and wounded friends. "Oh ... my God."

Mark let his hands fall, and began to pray.

"Hold yourself together, Milt!" George cried. "Go get those prisoners before they kill more people!"

Milt gave him an astonished look. "I … can't."

George checked Scarbrough's pulse again. "It's stronger. Let's move him."

Mark noticed Milt's faltering. "Deputy, you have to go. They haven't gotten far. You could overtake some of them!"

Milt backed toward the door. "No … I have a family."

"*Do* it for your family!" George cried. "You have an obligation to this community!"

"Not anymore. I'm all alone here. Grady and Black walked off the job a couple hours ago after they got their pay. Nothing is worth this!" He sounded like a little boy.

Mark didn't know what to do. "Milt, please."

But the deputy removed his badge and dropped it on the blood-covered floor.

The paramedics moved Scarbrough onto the gurney. Milt waited for them to roll it past him. Then he made his own exit.

"Mark, we'll send somebody," George called as they rushed Scarbrough out. "You'd better stay here."

Mark stood helpless, looking at the bodies they'd left behind. This was madness.

He heard the front doors slam shut, and for a moment he thought of fleeing. But he couldn't do that. He couldn't be numbered among the escapees—the killers who had gunned these men down.

He looked down at the young fathers and husbands now lying dead and wondered who would tell their families. He thought of covering their bodies with sheets from the abandoned bunks. Then he realized he couldn't disturb the evidence.

His stomach churned, and he thought he might be sick. Struggling to hold it back, he knelt on the floor next to the bodies. He could guard them, he thought, until someone came to move them.

He heard the door again and looked up to see Brett Stampley, who owned the blacksmith shop across the street. Another gun pointed at him. He almost didn't care if Brett pulled the trigger.

But there was no fear in Brett's eyes. "George told me you're not to blame. He said you tried to stop it."

The small acknowledgement melted what was left of his strength. The tragedy of it all rushed into his chest, and he pressed the heels of his hands against his eyes.

"I can't let you go," Brett said. "But I can take you to clean up."

Clean up what? Mark looked down at himself, saw the blood on his knees, his hands, and the edges of his sleeves. Slowly, he rose. He was so tired his legs felt as though they'd buckle under him.

Brett's rifle at his back, Mark went out of the jail, through the desks, and into the defunct bathroom. There was some water there in a two-gallon jug. A towel lay on the counter; he wet it and tried to wipe off the blood.

It was impossible to remove it all, but he got it off of his hands. Taking off his jacket, he scrubbed the army-green cloth. It helped, though the edges of the sleeves were still stained. He scrubbed his knees and the tips of his Nikes.

Glancing up at the gun still trained on him, Mark said, "I appreciate it, Brett."

"No problem. I have to put you back in a cell now until they get more deputies over here."

"If I were going to leave, Brett, you know I'd have left by now."

Brett didn't answer him. Mark studied his face—he looked apologetic, but unwavering. Mark supposed he couldn't blame him.

Raising his hands, he headed back into the dark, smelly room. He stepped back into the cell he'd been in, but didn't close the door, and looked around at the place that had been packed so full before.

He sat down on one of the bottom bunks and dropped his face into his hands. Two good men dead. Sheriff Scarbrough might not make it.

The cell door clanged as Brett closed and locked it.

Loneliness fell over Mark like the darkness, and he fixed his eyes on the windows at the top of the room. There was still daylight, even though the room was dark. He had to concentrate on that.

There was still daylight.

THIRTY-ONE

"So where exactly was Mark standing when you saw him?"

Deni knew her voice had a gestapo edge, and Blake Mahaffey and Randy Kraft—the boys who'd placed Mark in the vicinity of Zach's shooting—were getting antsy.

"I don't know," Blake said. "It was in the woods."

"Third tree from the left," Randy said. "Is that what you want?"

So Randy was a comedian. The sarcasm rankled her. "I think people will expect you to have a little more than that when you accuse someone of murder."

"We never accused him of murder," Blake said. "We just said we saw him."

"In a place where he wasn't!" she pointed out.

The two boys looked at each other, rolling their eyes. "Get real," Randy said. "You're not here as a reporter. You're here as Mark Green's girlfriend."

Deni's chin came up. "The *Crockett Times* assigned me this story. I'm just trying to verify what you told the sheriff."

"Face it, Deni. Your boyfriend is a liar."

Fire rose to her face, and her eyes flashed. She wanted to take a swing at the smart aleck—but she knew a physical response wouldn't get the result she wanted.

Instead, she'd skewer them with words. Already today she'd collected a number of quotes from teens who had nothing good to say about these two boys.

Randy's ex-girlfriend said she'd broken up with him for hitting her. Blake's eighth-grade science teacher claimed he had little familiarity with the truth. A group of Jeff's friends told her both boys had had a drug problem before the outage.

The article she planned to write about them would amount to clear-cut character assassination—not her usual modus operandi. But the community had a right to know that they couldn't trust the boys' story.

She heard a horse's hooves galloping up the street, and she looked up and saw Blake's father riding up the dirt driveway.

"Dad, what's wrong?" Blake called out.

"I just heard there was a shooting at the jail. Two dead."

Deni gasped.

"Prisoners escaped. I have to warn your mother. You boys need to get inside."

He jumped off the horse and handed the reins to his son.

"Two dead?" Deni cried. "Who?"

"I don't know, but we have to stay armed. No one's safe."

She pictured Mark shot and bleeding. Without another word, she bolted for her bike. Pedaling with all her might, she flew through the streets of Crockett.

Please God, don't let Mark be dead.

Near the sheriff's station, she saw county vehicles parked haphazardly in the street. Deputies she didn't recognize were roping off the area, keeping her from getting closer.

"What happened?" she cried, ignoring the barricade.

"Stay back, lady," one of them ordered.

"Is Mark Green all right? Was he shot?"

They ignored her, so she shouted, "I'm a reporter for the *Crockett Times*! I demand to know what's happening!"

But her insistence fell on deaf ears as the deputies wrestled her back.

THIRTY-TWO

Sirens heralded the arrival of Chief Deputy Wheaton from Birmingham. Mark sat up and waited, his eyes on the metal door that closed him in. Finally, the door opened, and three uniformed men came in. Mark got up and went to the bars.

Hands on their sidearms, the men froze at the sight of their dead comrades. The deputy who seemed to be in charge cursed.

Mark stood quietly watching as they examined the bodies of Jones and Anderson. It had been about half an hour since the shootings. He wondered if the escapees had been caught—or the town warned. Had his mother and Deni been told?

After a few minutes, the chief deputy straightened and came toward his cell.

"I'm Chief Deputy Archie Wheaton," he said in a shaken voice. "Second in command to the sheriff. Why don't you tell me what happened?"

"Yes, sir. But first—is Sheriff Scarbrough gonna make it?"

"He made it to the hospital alive."

Mark let out a long breath of relief, then began to tell him the story, biting out the words with weariness that ached like toxins through his body. "I tried to stop it, Deputy. I really did. You have no reason to believe me. But George and Will, the paramedics, saw the whole thing. They'll tell you."

"They already did." The deputy studied him for a moment, then spoke. "Well, as you can see, we're in a mess here. The deputies here have walked off the job. I've pulled men from the substations to search for the escaped prisoners ... but I don't have the resources to keep you here. Mark, I'm gonna let you go for now."

Mark thought he'd heard wrong. "What?"

"I'm letting you go. I don't have a staff here to guard you, and my gut tells me you're not like the ones who left. Judge Myers is outside, and he agreed to release you under your own recognizance, waiving bond. I hope we're not making a mistake."

Mark's heart almost soared out of his chest. "You're not. You'll see. When Zach Emory is coherent again, he'll tell you I'm not the one who shot him."

Wheaton didn't comment on that. "Just don't leave the county." He unlocked the cell door, and Mark walked through it.

This time he appreciated the loud, echoing clang as it closed behind him. "I won't let you down, sir." His gaze strayed back to the bodies. "Is there anything I can do? Notify their families— "

"No, we'll take care of it." He led Mark past the bodies and into the office area. He picked up a letter off of his desk and handed it to him. Mark took it and read the handwritten scrawl.

To whom it may concern—

I, Judge Alfred Myers, have this day waived bond for Mark Green and released him under his own recognizance.

The judge had signed and dated it.

"This may not be any protection for you," Wheaton said. "But it's the best I can do right now."

The doors opened, and the medical examiner came in. Turning to the ME, Wheaton pointed to the jail door. "Bodies are back here," he said in a raspy voice.

Mark folded up the paper and shoved it into his pocket.

"Green?"

He looked back.

"I'm gonna have to call together a volunteer force. Otherwise, I'd have no way to replace these guys. Our staff is down all over the county, and even the state police are on a skeleton staff. If you know anybody who could help—"

"I'll tell Doug Branning and Brad Caldwell."

"Who are they?"

"They're good men who live in my neighborhood. They'll step up to the plate."

"Send them to see me." Deputy Wheaton shook his hand. "You be careful, Mark."

"You too, sir. I'll pray for you."

Wheaton went to the locker where they kept the prisoners' personal effects, found Jeff's bag that Mark had brought here with him, and handed it to him. Zipping up his coat, Mark stepped out into the cold.

THIRTY-THREE

MARK HADN'T EXPECTED THE CROWD THAT HAD GATHERED outside the sheriff's department, roped off and held back by a couple of deputies from other substations. Word had gotten around about the shootings, and people had gathered to demand answers.

"Mark!" He saw Deni ducking under the crime scene tape and running toward him. He opened his arms, and she threw herself into him. Warmth and relief rushed into his chest, washing like a balm over his body.

"Oh, Mark, you're all right. I thought you were dead!"

A roar arose from the crowd, angry, condemning voices demanding that he go back inside. Deputy Wheaton heard the din and came out behind him. "Wait a minute, Mark. This could get ugly."

"You ain't letting him go, are you?" someone shouted.

"He was there when the sheriff was shot!"

"You letting another prisoner run helter-skelter around this town?"

"How many dead bodies do you want?"

Wheaton raised his hands to the crowd. "Don't tell me about dead bodies! My friends are lying in there!"

The group quieted as the deputy chief walked down the steps and came to the edge of the barricade. "You're right. There's an army of escaped prisoners running around out there. But Green tried to stop the prisoners' attack, and he stayed behind when he could have escaped. He's been a help today—not a threat to anyone."

"But he tried to kill Zach Emory!"

Mark looked and saw the principal from his high school—the man who had once been his biggest fan when Mark led his track team to victory. "He talks a good game, Deputy, but he's a danger to society."

Deni turned on the man. "Mr. King, how can you say that? This is *Mark*! You know him."

Wheaton waved a hand for attention. "The judge has agreed with me that Mark can go home for now, since we don't have the resources to keep one lone prisoner. Nobody better lay a hand on him. If you want to protect the community, then sign up for the volunteer force and get deputized, and you can go out hunting criminals. We can use all the help we can get."

No one stepped forward, and Mark couldn't say he blamed them. It would take especially courageous people to go hunting crazed killers who had little left to lose.

Wheaton motioned for one of his deputies. "Stratton, give Green a ride home."

Relieved, Mark thanked the chief deputy and followed Deputy Stratton to his van. "Can she come too?" he asked as they reached the car.

"Sure, get in."

The deputy was quiet as he drove them home, and after her initial questions, Deni was quiet too. Stratton's face was pale as he drove. Mark wondered if he was considering quitting too. Unless he felt a calling to serve his community in a dangerous job with little pay—knowing he would have to go out looking for the murderers who killed his friends—Mark thought that there was a good chance he'd quit like the others.

On the other hand, maybe Stratton did feel that obligation to do the job he'd signed up to do. Maybe the ones who were left were men of particular courage.

He prayed that was true.

He held Deni's ice-cold hand, wondering if it was wise to let her be anywhere near him. "Any word on Zach?" he asked her.

She shook her head. "I haven't been able to get an update."

The car turned into Oak Hollow. Her hand tightened as she leaned forward. "Deputy Stratton, would you please take him to my house? Fifth house on the right."

"No," Mark said. "I need to go home. I need to change out of these clothes— "

"Mark, your mother's at my house. You can wear something of my dad's or my brother's. But going home is not smart right now, and you know it."

Stratton pulled up to the Branning house and idled at the street. "What's it gonna be?"

Mark sighed. "I guess I'll get out here." He stepped out of the van, helped Deni out, then got her bike out of the back and set it on the sidewalk.

He glanced toward the corner. Paul Burlin and his wife were walking their dog, and they'd stopped to stare. Paul was best friends with Lou Grantham and had probably been among those men who'd come after him. He saw the disbelief on the Burlins' faces as he and Deni thanked the deputy and started up the yard to the door.

Mark hoped word would soon reach the neighborhood that he'd had nothing to do with the shooting of the sheriff and his men. But as he stepped into the Branning house, he knew it wasn't over.

THIRTY-FOUR

An urgent knocking shook the Brannings' front door a few minutes after Mark came in. Deni knew trouble was on their doorstep.

"Here it comes," Mark said. "I'll get it."

"No, Mark!" His mother moved between him and the door. "Please, honey. You can hide. You can go out the back way again."

Mark went around her. "I'm not running again, Mom, and I won't let them terrorize us."

Deni turned to her mother. "Where's Dad?"

"Next door, talking to Brad," she said. "Beth and Logan, go upstairs."

"But Mom!" Logan whined.

"Upstairs, *now*!"

The two kids headed for the stairs. The banging came again. Mark reached the doorknob.

Deni stopped him. "Mark, wait for Dad to come back."

"I can't. They won't wait." He pulled Deni behind him and opened the front door, and Deni saw a group of men with baseball bats and guns, their faces seething in hatred. Lou Grantham stood at the front of the mob.

Mark stepped out on the porch. "Looking for me?"

Paul swung his bat. Mark caught it in his hand before it made contact. But someone else swung, hitting Mark in the stomach, doubling him over.

Martha screamed as more bats and sticks came down on him, knocking him to his knees.

Deni raced across the yard, screaming for her father. "Dad! Dad, help! They're beating Mark!" She threw herself at the Caldwells' door, banging with her fists.

The door flew open, and Brad and her father burst out.

"Please come!" she screamed. "They're killing him!"

Brad ran back in for his rifle, then chambered a round as he came out into the yard. He fired up into the sky, startling the men. It took one more wasted bullet before they backed off, leaving Mark in a heap on the ground. His forehead was bleeding and his cheekbone was swelling. He crawled on the ground for a moment, trying to get up.

Deni fell to his side. "Mark, are you all right? Mark ..."

He seemed dazed, unable to get up.

Brad and Doug stepped in front of Mark. Brad's teeth gritted as he chambered another round. "Now, if I were you, I'd be backing toward the street nice and easy."

Paul spat into the grass. "Put the gun down, Brad. You're not in this."

"Oh, yeah, I'm in it," Brad said. "See, I'm the attorney representing Mark in his conspiracy-to-commit-murder case against you people. It's about time somebody filed charges."

Deni kept her arms around Mark's shoulders as she looked up at the men. They all knew what Brad meant—just a few months ago Brad had been in Mark's place, when the same group of vigilantes had tried to make an example of *him*.

Lou Grantham wasn't fazed. "Doug, why are you fooled by the son of the maniac who kidnapped your daughter? You should be here with us, making sure he never hurts anybody again."

"He didn't shoot Zach!" Deni cried. "He's innocent! You're all crazy!"

The men eyed Mark again, then Brad's gun, and finally someone started to walk away. One by one, the group broke up.

Grantham was the last to leave. He pointed down at Mark's bleeding face. "I'm warning you, boy. Pack your bags and get out of town if you don't want your mama planning your funeral."

They watched him swagger away like the only law in the land.

And Deni knew he would be back.

THIRTY-FIVE

UPSTAIRS, BETH CRIED AS SHE WATCHED WITH LOGAN OUT the window as the drama in their front yard unfolded. When Brad's gun went off, she screamed and sat on the floor, holding her ears.

Squeezing her eyes shut, she imagined the scene outside—her family in danger, Mark bleeding, more people dead. Her head began to hurt as if a knife stuck through her brain, and she wanted it all to be over.

Logan shook her out of her thoughts, and she opened her eyes and looked up at him through her tears. His face was pale. "Chill out, Beth. It's over. Dad ran the men off."

She sucked in a sob. "What about Mark? Did they kill him?"

He went back to the window and peered out. "No, he's getting up. He doesn't look good, though."

She got up, wiping her face, and went to stand next to her little brother. She saw Mark struggling to get to his feet. Blood dripped into his eyes. He leaned on her dad as they came into the house.

"I'm going down," she said.

Logan followed her. They went downstairs slowly as her father walked Mark to the couch. His mother sat next to him, crying and dabbing at the gash. Deni stood over him, shaking like a trapped kitten.

"Mom? Is Mark okay?" Beth asked.

"Kids, go back upstairs. I don't want you to see this."

"I just want to know if— "

The front door came open, and Brad came in with Dr. Derek Morton, who lived and worked on the street behind them. His nurse Chris Horton, Deni's best friend, came in behind him.

"I knew this was gonna happen," Chris said. "Those old men think they're in the Wild West, playing shoot 'em up. Grantham's wife came in the other day with a bruised jaw and said she'd run into a door, if you can believe that."

Derek shot an angry look up at her. "Chris, that's enough."

She shoved her blonde curls back. "Oh, yeah. Confidentiality. They won't tell."

Realizing that she and Logan had dropped off her mother's radar, Beth stepped closer to the couch and watched as Dr. Morton examined the gash on Mark's forehead. "This is going to need stitches," he said. "And Mark, your collarbone's broken." He felt down Mark's bloody arms. "Humerus bone is broken."

Mark sucked in a breath and groaned as Chris came around the couch to help set it.

Beth felt sick. Her head throbbed, and she suddenly felt hot.

Thinking she had to get some air, she went into the kitchen, grabbed her coat, and stepped out into the garage. Tears rushed her again, and she pulled her coat on and zipped it up.

The Next Terrible Thing had come, and now there would be a next one, and a next one. It was like dominos, each one leading to something worse.

She decided to escape across the street to Eloise's house. Her neighbor, who'd died last year, had left her house to her son. Since he couldn't sell it during the outage, he'd given the neighbors permission to use the one-acre yard for whatever they needed to help them survive. The neighbors had pooled their resources and bought a bunch of rabbits, which they kept in cages in Eloise's yard and took turns feeding. It wasn't the Brannings' day to feed them, but sometimes Beth went over there just to hold the bunnies, pet them, and be by herself. They made her feel better.

The snow was beginning to melt, and slush ran in the gutters. She slid on some ice as she walked across the street. The tears on her face turned cold in the wind.

She made her way to Eloise's fence and opened the back gate. As she went in, her eyes scanned the yard for the cage with the youngest litter.

But something was wrong.

A few of the cages were gone, and several more were empty. She caught her breath and walked closer to the cages, making sure the little animals hadn't burrowed under something to get warmer.

But they were gone. Only a dozen or so remained.

Beth screamed, and ran back across the street.

THIRTY-SIX

DESPITE THE TRAUMA OF THE SHOOTINGS EARLIER THAT day, Deni found George Mason and Will Truman back in their ambulance, sitting in their usual spot on Keisler Street, waiting for the next emergency. They both stared into space as if shell-shocked. She knocked on George's window.

He rolled it down. "Yeah?"

"George … Will …" Out of breath, she tried to find her voice. "You've got to come. Mark Green's been beaten. He needs to get to the hospital."

The two paramedics wasted no time, and she followed on her bike as they drove back to her house. Derek had stabilized Mark and returned home to his living room full of patients, but Chris had stayed behind. She met them all at the door.

"It's an open head wound, and he's showing no evidence of concussion," she said as she led them in. "And it's a wonder, because frankly, I think they meant to kill him. If you ask me, we need to get our own vigilante gang, and make sure those men don't attack anyone ever again."

Martha moved away to give the paramedics room. George stooped down next to him, and Mark winced as he lifted the bandage that Derek had taped to his forehead. "Looks bad," he said. "Why didn't the doc suture it for you?"

"He said it needed a plastic surgeon," Mark muttered.

Chris leaned over the back of the couch. "It's deep enough to need several layers of sutures. He wanted it done right."

"He blocked the blows with his arms," Deni said. "That's why his arm is fractured."

"And if he hadn't, he'd be *so* dead," Chris muttered. "Those baseball bats would have shattered his skull. It's a classic case of a mob mentality, and these men have been allowed to get away with it too long."

George shot Chris a weary look. "We get it, okay?"

Chris's face fell. "I'm sorry … I just …" Suddenly, she caught her breath. "Oh no. I forgot that you two were at the jail when the shooting happened this morning. You're probably sick to death of … well, death."

George ignored her, but Will gave her a long, disbelieving look. Her hands came up to her chest, and remorse colored her face. Deni set her arm around her friend's shoulders to silence her. The more Chris talked, the more likely she was to dig herself deeper.

Mark seemed anxious to break the tension. "I think what Chris is trying to say … is you guys probably need some time off."

George studied Mark's broken collarbone. "We thought about it, but with convicts and crazies running around, we figure this isn't the time for a vacation."

Chris's hand came up to her mouth, and tears burst into her eyes. "You guys are such heroes."

George's agitation seemed to fade, and he swallowed hard. "Just doing our job."

Mark refused a gurney and limped out to the ambulance. Deni and Martha climbed in with him.

As George got behind the wheel, Chris came to his window. "Let me know if there's anything I can ever help you with," she said. "Really. I have a big mouth, but I'm a very good nurse."

George managed a smile. "I'll do that," he said as he pulled away.

THIRTY-SEVEN

Pain shot like fireworks through Mark's broken bones, but his condition wasn't urgent enough to warrant immediate attention. He sat in the waiting room for two hours, his mother and Deni taking turns pleading with the staff to move him up the list.

He gritted his teeth and tried to bear it—but it wasn't the physical pain that threatened to do him in. It was the humiliation of being beaten in front of Deni and his mother. He was supposed to be the protector, the guardian who kept his loved ones safe. He'd always prided himself in his strength.

But they had shown him to be weak.

Deni hovered over him, rivaling his mother in her attempts to make him comfortable. He didn't want her to see him this way. He would rather have her waiting at home until the doctors patched him up ... until he could gather his strength and pick up the pieces of his shattered pride.

The trauma of the last three days ached in him, and images of the dead deputies and Scarbrough's bloody, shattered face did a mocking dance through his mind. Along with those pictures, he saw the hatred in Tree House's eyes—so much like that in Lou Grantham's. Funny how the civilized and uncivilized had hatred in common.

When they finally called his name, he almost didn't hear them. Deni nudged him, and his mother grabbed his good arm and tried to help him up. "Come on, honey."

Deni got up to come with them, but Mark glanced back. “Why don’t you wait here?”

She looked hurt, but she didn’t argue. “All right.”

He tried not to limp as he left her in the waiting room.

THIRTY-EIGHT

DENI TRIED TO SWALLOW THE HURT WHEN MARK ASKED her not to go with him into the examining room. It wasn't a slight, she told herself. It was just a guy thing.

But as she paced in the waiting room, stepping around the sick and injured, she wondered if there had been another reason he didn't want her with him. Had she smothered him with too much attention? He'd hardly said a word since they'd been here, and he'd seemed impatient with her pampering.

She'd seen this before—when her dad was injured. Being weak made him so angry that he'd practically bitten their heads off as they'd tried to care for him.

But Mark wasn't weak. In spite of the last few days, he was still one of the two most courageous people she knew. It was that courage that kept getting him into trouble.

Out of the corner of her eye, she saw Deputy Wheaton coming in. She'd never met him before, but she recognized him from the sheriff's station earlier today. He seemed to be in a hurry as he cut through the crowd.

She made a beeline toward him. "Deputy, I'm so glad to see you. I'm with Mark Green. He was beaten this afternoon—"

"I know all about it," he said, not slowing his step.

She assumed George and Will had filled him in. "Have you arrested the men who did it?"

"Working on it. Right now I'm going to see Zach Emory. His brother just came and told me he's conscious and ready to talk."

Deni caught her breath. “That’s great. He can clear Mark!”

Wheaton nodded. “Ask him to hang around after he’s released. I may need to talk to him.”

“Okay, I will.”

“Also, let him know that Ralph Scarbrough is out of surgery.”

“Is he going to make it?”

“Looks like it,” he said, “but he’s not out of the woods.”

THIRTY-NINE

"IT WASN'T MARK." ZACH'S THROAT BURNED FROM THE ventilator tube that had been in his throat, but he croaked out the words.

He wasn't sure when the memory had made itself clear in his mind. It had come in images, fading in and out. The buck on the ground. His pride and excitement ... waiting for his brother ...

When he'd come fully awake, his parents had asked him to confirm that Mark was the one. His memories had been blurry, but he was able to get that much into focus. It wasn't Mark.

They stared at him now, as if they just couldn't believe it. "Are you sure?"

He tried to say yes, but nodded instead. What was the matter with them? Why would they think a guy like Mark would do a thing like that?

Deputy Wheaton didn't seem all that surprised. "Then can you identify who did?"

He pictured the shooter again, approaching him, raising his gun. He'd seen him somewhere before, but he couldn't think where. "No," he grunted.

"Can you describe him?"

Zach tried to focus. "Brown hair ... average height."

"What do you mean, average?"

"My height."

Ned looked at the deputy. "He's five-ten."

Wheaton nodded. "That's the same description Charles Hoyt gave us. What was he wearing, Zach?"

"Camo." His head began to ache with the effort of remembering, and fatigue tugged at him, threatening to pull him under.

"Zach, yesterday when your ventilator was shut off, did you see anyone in your room?"

He shifted his thoughts. He remembered images ... the guy over his bed ... the voices ... panic ...

"Yeah."

"Did you know him?"

He tried to picture the man again. He looked familiar too. "Maybe."

"Was it Mark Green?"

"No."

Wheaton looked at Zach's parents.

"Zach," his mother said. "The guy told your roommate that he was Mark Green."

"Then he lied."

Deputy Wheaton tried again. "Was he the same guy who shot you?"

Zach frowned. "Maybe."

"But you're not sure?"

Zach shook his head no.

"See there?" Ellen said. "He doesn't even know for sure."

Anger flared through Zach. Why wouldn't they listen? "Wasn't Mark," he tried to say louder.

Wheaton cleared his throat and stood up. "Looks like we locked up an innocent man."

"Well, it doesn't matter now, since you let him go," Ellen cried.

"The man's innocent," Wheaton said. "Didn't you hear your son?"

Zach closed his eyes, hoping his mother wasn't about to launch into one of her fits. Hoping to distract her, he rasped out, "Shoulda seen it. Ten-pointer. Beautiful."

"The buck?" Wheaton asked. "The one Mark Green brought home was eight points. Did you see the shooter take the deer?"

He didn't remember anything past the man raising his gun. His next memory was in the ambulance, gasping for breath. He shook his head again.

He faded out as the deputy talked softly to his parents.

FORTY

DESPITE THE EVENTS OF THE PAST FEW DAYS, KAY KNEW life had to go on. There were clothes to wash and more bread to bake, but there was no one around to help her. Doug had gone with Brad to volunteer at the sheriff's department, which meant that he'd be here less and less often. Deni had gone to the hospital with Mark, and Beth ... well, Kay hadn't seen her in hours.

She went out into the garage and raised the door to give her some light as she washed a load of clothes in the hand-cranked Maytag Doug had bought two months ago. Because of his careful planning with their FEMA disbursements and his investments in things that made them more money, he'd managed to raise enough to buy them a few luxuries. Though this machine wasn't as time-saving as the Kenmore she'd used before the outage, it was a far cry from washing the clothes by hand out in the cold. They had rigged it to run on kerosene, which was becoming cheaper and more readily available.

There was no reason Beth and Logan couldn't help her with this. Kay went back into the house, looked out the window, and saw Logan in the backyard feeding the chickens. She opened the door. "Honey, where's Beth?"

"I don't know. I haven't seen her."

She watched him for a moment. The snow was melting, and the temperature had warmed a little. It felt like it was in the upper fifties—a welcome change from the last couple of days.

"When you get finished there, come in and help me wash laundry."

He gave her that hangdog look he had. "Mom, no! I hate doing that. It's for girls."

"It's for anyone who doesn't want to wear dirty clothes. Now hurry up."

Resentment rushed through her as she closed the door. Why was it that she was the only one confined to the house twenty-four hours a day, baking and cooking and cleaning and washing, while everyone else was out in the fresh air, with a variety of things to do?

She did it for her family, and given the events of the last few months, she was glad to have all of them healthy and active. But sometimes she wanted to curl up on her bed and cry. The bad news that came so frequently—news of shootings and illness and the death of friends—took its toll and made her want to give up.

But she couldn't, not as long as there was work to get done.

She went to the bottom of the stairs and called up. "Beth?"

There was no answer, but she heard Beth's feet running across her floor. Maybe she couldn't hear her. Sighing, she went up the stairs. Beth's door was closed.

"Beth?" She knocked, and then opened the door.

Beth sat sobbing on the floor in the corner of her room, holding a rabbit in her arms and another in her lap. At least a dozen other rabbits sniffed and moved around her. "Don't be mad, Mom."

Kay wanted to scream. "Beth, what are you doing?"

Beth's chin trembled and she wiped her red nose. "I had to protect them. I couldn't just leave them over there, with killers and thieves in our own neighborhood, doing whatever they want."

Kay's anger faded. Had her daughter been up here suffering since Mark's beating this afternoon? She hadn't wanted the kids to see what was happening, but of course they had. She had ignored Beth after they'd gotten Mark inside, unaware that she was traumatized.

And then when the rabbits were stolen, Kay had decided to deal with it later. With two deputies dead, the sheriff fighting for his life, and Mark beaten with baseball bats, the rabbits had seemed unimportant.

But they were the one thing Beth could control.

Kay went into the room and knelt beside her. "How did you get them up here? I didn't see you bringing them in."

Beth sniffed. "I brought them two at a time. I tried to put four of them in a box, but they fought."

"That's why we keep them in separate cages."

"I know, but I couldn't sneak the cages in without being seen."

Kay tried not to focus on the droppings ruining her carpet. This was about her daughter exercising some control over the chaos of their lives. It was about protecting *something*, when she had no ability to protect the ones she loved.

She took the rabbit out of Beth's arms and set him on the floor, then pulled her child into her arms. Beth came willingly, clinging to her, weeping into her sweatshirt, wailing out her heartache.

"They beat him, Mom. They almost killed him."

Kay closed her eyes and stroked Beth's hair. "Oh, sweetie, I didn't want you to see that."

"Where's God? Why would he let that happen to Mark?"

"I don't know," she whispered.

"But things are getting worse and worse. They never end. Do you think God has a bet with the devil? That he's just daring him to do something to Mark, like Job?"

Kay pulled Beth back and looked into her wet face. "Honey, you're misunderstanding what happened with Job. It wasn't a bet. It happened for a reason. Job just wasn't told what it was."

"What reason?"

"So that we would be encouraged that God is in control. Thousands of years after that book was written, we read it and know that we're not alone in our suffering. That no one can do anything to us without God's permission. And that God uses things in ways we can't imagine. Job was an example to us. Do you think he would have ever dreamed that we'd be talking about him in the twenty-first century?"

Beth's hiccupping sobs eased up, and she shook her head. "I wish God would tell us more."

"I wish he would too. But you know that suffering has a way of making us stronger. Aren't we better people than we were eight months ago?"

"Maybe." She thought for a minute. "Nothing really bad ever happened to us before. We were kind of wimpy."

Kay laughed softly. "We're not wimpy now, are we? And don't we trust God more?"

"Sometimes."

Kay wished she could make Beth trust him more, but she knew she had a long way to go with that, herself. Kissing her daughter, she said, "We have to get these rabbits back where they belong."

"But Mom, what if they get stolen? Can't I keep them in the garage until Dad gets home?"

Kay didn't want them in her garage, but if it would make Beth feel better, so be it. "All right, just until he's home. Then he can figure out some way to lock the cages down so no one can take them. Maybe he can padlock the doors." She kissed her forehead again. "Are you all right now?"

Beth drew in a long, shaky breath. "Yeah, but my head really hurts."

"It's no wonder." She sighed and picked up two of the rabbits. "Come on, I'll help you get them out to the garage."

FORTY-ONE

"Well, son, you're off the hook."

Mark had waited in the lobby with Deni and his mother for the last half hour, anxious to hear if Zach had, indeed, been coherent enough to clear things up. Now he wasn't sure he'd heard Wheaton right. "So he told you what happened?"

"That's right. Guy who shot him was around five-ten, brown hair. The one who unplugged his ventilator might have been the same person. He was only sure about one thing—that neither of them was you."

For the first time in days, light broke through the clouds that seemed to hover over Mark. Deni shouted and threw her arms around him, but the pressure brought a sharp jolt of pain, and he gasped. She pulled back apologetically and hugged his mother instead. The two of them jumped up and down as though they'd just won a lottery. Mark laughed in spite of his pain.

Turning, his mother hugged Wheaton. "Thank you, Deputy. We're so grateful."

"Don't thank me, thank Zach. Now I have to find the real guy."

Deni's joy faded. "Not telling you how to do your job, Deputy, but you ought to question Blake Mahaffey and Randy Kraft. They lied about Mark for a reason."

"You bet I'm going to question them." He started to walk away, but Martha stopped him. "Deputy, will you please go tell our neighborhood so Mark can go home without being attacked again?"

"They'll find out when we start arresting Lou Grantham and the others. That's at the top of my priority list, almost as high as finding the escapees. But first I need to get some volunteers signed up."

"I want to be sworn in," Mark said.

Deni swung toward him, and Martha looked like she'd been slapped. "Mark, you're injured!" his mother cried.

Wheaton rested his hands on his hips. "Son, you're not in any shape to serve in the sheriff's department."

Mark wouldn't take no for an answer. "There must be something I can do. I could man the offices. I could go through the prisoners' files, getting their addresses and trying to figure out where to look for them. You need someone to do that, Deputy."

"But I don't need someone bent on revenge helping enforce the law."

"It's not revenge I want, Deputy. It's justice. Two men on your force were killed, and another is fighting for his life."

Wheaton stared at him for a long moment.

"I'm not saying that I'm not angry. But my anger won't keep me from enforcing the law. It'll just make me more determined to see justice done. Do you really have the luxury of turning capable men away? I can help you find those prisoners."

Wheaton looked at the floor. Mark knew he was considering it.

But Deni intervened. "Mark, *you* don't have to be the one who saves the world. Please—keep a low profile for a while so you can heal."

"Deni, somebody has to step up."

"Not you!" she shouted.

Mark grew silent. He looked at his mother, waiting for her to chime in. She was standing there, tears in her eyes, and her look told him she knew he was going to do what he had to do. She didn't like it any more than Deni, but she wasn't going to stand in his way.

Deni, on the other hand, wouldn't take it well. "Deputy, your instincts are right," she said. "He shouldn't be there. It would be irresponsible to swear him in."

"Deni, stop it!" Mark bit out.

She looked at him as if he'd betrayed her, her eyes pleading. He didn't like to see her cry, but this was important. Someone had to help them catch the escapees so she could ride the streets safely. Someone had to stop those men before they turned Crockett into a war zone.

If she couldn't understand that—

"Deputy," he said, "do you need volunteers, or don't you?"

Wheaton stared at Mark, then finally said, "All right. We'll give it a try. I'll give you a ride back to Crockett and we'll stop by the station and swear you in."

"I don't believe this." Deni took off toward the door.

Mark looked back at his mother and saw that her eyes were on the edge of grief. He hated making her worry.

"Mom, I need to do this."

She blinked back the tears misting in her eyes. "I know. That's the kind of man you are."

"You can stay with the Brannings when I'm at work."

She nodded. "I will. But for now, you need to go after her."

Holding his broken arm in its sling close to his body, and running his fingers under the brace on his collarbone, he went outside. He found her sitting on the curb near Wheaton's van. Her face was wet, and she wiped it with both hands.

He sat down next to her. Putting his good arm around her, he pulled her head against his chest. "It'll be okay."

"He's going to swear you in, isn't he?"

"Yeah, he is."

She crumpled against him. "I've been lucky until now. Of all the people I've loved who have been in danger, I haven't lost anyone yet. But I have a really bad feeling about this. You and my dad—in the middle of this mess."

"Deni, think of it this way. Who do you want protecting you?"

She closed her eyes. "You or my dad."

"So that's how I see it. I want to protect your family and my family, and the neighborhood and the town. I'm not the kind to sit back and wait for others to work things out."

"I wish you were."

"No, you don't." Wiping her cheek, he whispered, "Hey."

She met his eyes, dread coloring hers.

"You're one of the reasons I'm doing it, you know. I want you to be safe from people like Grantham and those murderers I was in jail with. I want you to rest easy at night."

He saw in her eyes that she probably wouldn't rest at all. But she didn't say it. Instead, she kissed him. Then stroking the stubble on his bruised jaw, she whispered, "Why did I have to fall in love with a hero?"

The sun banished the clouds, and he saw his life making a turn. Lowering his face, he kissed her, stroking her chin with his fingertips, tangling them in her hair. Had she really said she loved him?

After a moment, Wheaton and his mother came out, so he got Deni to her feet and, taking her hand, led her to the van.

When they reached the sheriff's department in Crockett, they found Doug and Brad waiting to be sworn in. Wheaton read the three of them the oath of the sheriff's department. They raised their right hands and repeated after him, swearing to uphold their duties to the best of their abilities.

Deni stood by, refusing to shed more tears. She would brace herself for whatever was to come.

When he was finished, Deputy Wheaton gave them instructions and keys to the department. "Brad," he said, "you know the law. I want you to be in charge of the volunteer force."

Brad nodded. "It would be my honor."

"You're all good men," Wheaton said. "It's a dangerous world out there. Let's get started making it safer."

FORTY-TWO

WHEATON INSISTED THAT MARK TAKE THE TIME TO clean up and change clothes before he started working. He dropped Deni off at her house, then took Mark and his mother home. As he drove down the street toward Mark's house, he stopped each time he saw people out, and let them know that Mark had been cleared.

The neighbors' reaction was cool and suspicious, but Mark was grateful that the deputy had done it. He hoped it would keep him safe until they came back to arrest Grantham and his men. If it didn't, the department-issued Glock he wore on his would.

But as his mother led him into their home, Mark's stomach plummeted again. He surveyed the mess the intruders had made of his family's things. A tornado seemed to have blown through the room, stirring it up in a vortex of anger, then dropping it all. They had knocked books off shelves, pulled open drawers, left the contents on the floor.

"They were looking for something," Mark said. "What could they want?"

His mother began folding the linens that had been pulled out of a hutch in the dining room. "They took all our food, and some cash I left on the counter. I can't imagine what else they'd want."

"How many do you think there were?"

"At least two, I think. I heard men's voices, but they were muffled."

He began picking up the pictures that had been pulled off the walls and tossed aside. If they'd been average thieves, they would have been satisfied with a vanload of food. And the cash—as little as it was—would have been pay dirt for them. They wouldn't have taken the chance of coming further into the house, with the possibility that someone was home. He stepped into the dining room; a cracked mirror lay on the floor.

Why pictures and mirrors? Were they looking for a safe?

"What would they have done if they'd seen me?" his mother asked, her voice wavering. "I heard them in the house, and I got my gun and hid. Maybe I should have gone out and shot them, I don't know. I just wasn't sure *what* to do."

Mark looked at his mother. She looked so vulnerable and tired. She'd lost a lot of weight in the last few months, and she'd aged five years in the last few days. Rage hammered through his heart as he pictured her hunkered in the closet, her gun shaking in her hand.

She should never have been left alone.

He couldn't blame it on his stepfather. John hadn't had much choice about where the government sent him to work. Besides, he'd left knowing that Mark could take care of her.

They just hadn't anticipated what would happen.

"I heard them come in the bedroom," she said, "and I got behind the shoe shelves in my closet and hid. They came in and looked around, took things off the shelves. I thought they were going to see me and I'd have to shoot them, but they didn't."

Mark's heart stumbled at the danger she'd been in. If they knew he was in jail and had come in expecting to find her, would they have killed her? Was that their plan?

"I've never been so scared in my life. I should have shot them. I should have had more courage."

"No, Mom, you did the right thing." He had never wanted to do violence to anyone before, but he could see himself killing the men who had terrorized his mother this way. "Mom, you can't be here alone when I'm working at the station. I want you to keep staying at the Brannings' for the time being. I don't want you alone in this house even for a minute. Someone was looking for something, and if they didn't find it, they might be back."

"But what? What in the world could we have that anyone would want—other than food and cash? I can't think of anything they'd be looking for."

Mark leaned back against the wall. Could it be the gold? No—he hadn't told anyone about it. Not even his mother. It had been carefully hidden in the tree stump since he'd found it. No one knew that it even existed.

At least, no one had known until he'd given some coins away.

He thought of that tent family and the little girl he'd given the coins to. Could she have told the others in their homeless community? Maybe her father or someone else from the area had figured out who he was and found out where he lived. Maybe they thought there was more where that had come from.

Yes, that had to be it.

His generosity could have cost his mother her life.

He thought of telling her about the gold, but he didn't see the point. It would only frighten her more. No, the best thing to do was to make sure she was safe and keep her out of this house. Maybe now that he was deputized, he could figure out who had done it and arrest them.

Until then, he would have to stay alert—and make sure his mother stayed safe.

FORTY-THREE

Deni would have given anything for a camera that worked as Deputy Wheaton took her father and Brad to arrest Lou Grantham. She knew that there were people who had working cameras, but they were few and far between, and neither she nor her paper had the money to buy one.

She stood on the sidewalk across the street from Grantham's house and watched with satisfaction as Lou tried to talk his way out of arrest. "I was taking care of this community, and y'all know it! If it wasn't for people like me and the men who were with me, this neighborhood wouldn't be a fit place to live!"

Wheaton wanted none of it. "You're under arrest for conspiracy to commit murder, and assault and battery." He cuffed Grantham's wrist, but the man recoiled.

"I didn't murder nobody! I was just sending a message."

"Mark Green is innocent," Wheaton said, wrestling Grantham's other wrist into the handcuff. "Zach Emory has cleared Mark's name. But even if he hadn't, you'd still be under arrest. Nobody in this county is gonna go around beating anybody they choose."

With his hands bound behind his back, Lou thrust his chest out and threw up his chin in arrogant pride. His western shirt was wet with sweat rings, and his mustang belt buckle glistened in the van's headlights. "I'm trying to help keep the law around here, since the sheriff's department has failed so miserably."

Neighbors came out of their homes and yards and stood in the street, watching. Squinting in the headlights, Lou tried getting their help. "Tell them how I've kept this neighborhood safe!" he shouted.

When no one came to his aid, he looked at Brad and Doug. "You men know me! Tell him I'm an asset to this neighborhood!"

That he would try to enlist Brad Caldwell's help was almost laughable. Deni moved closer to the Granthams' yard so she could hear Brad's response. But it was her father who answered. "Lou, you and your buddies should have been arrested eight months ago, when I had to fight you to keep you from killing Brad."

"Come on, Doug, the evidence pointed to him. You understand that, don't you, Caldwell? All's forgiven, ain't it?"

"You have the right to remain silent," Brad said in a calm monotone. "Anything you say can be used against you in a court of law by an angry attorney whom you once tried to kill."

Deni wanted to cheer.

"I want an attorney!" Grantham shouted.

"After we round up the rest of your gang," Deputy Wheaton said. "Then you can get all the attorneys you want."

Desperately, Grantham looked around at the neighbors standing in the street. "This is what you get for helping your community!" he shouted. "This is what happens when somebody tries to keep you people alive."

Stella Huckabee, wife of the neighborhood's president, came up beside Deni. "Your daddy's not going to let them take him to jail, is he? Lou was only trying to help."

Deni shot her a look. "By beating a neighbor half to death?"

"Oh, you always defend Mark Green. You think he's never done anything."

"He never *has*!"

"Get real, Deni!" Harry Goff yelled. "His father was a sociopath! It's in his genes."

Setting her chin, Deni went out into the street and came eye to eye with the man. "So I guess that would make you a lying adulterer, since your father, the pastor, ran off with the church secretary."

She knew it was a low blow. It had been a scandal of major proportions years ago, before she'd even been born, but she'd read it in an article the *Crockett Times* had framed on their wall. It was a story they were proud of, since they had broken it.

He looked as though he might slap her. Her eyes dared him to. Finally, his wife Merilee, said, "Deni, I'm beginning to think you're not the sweet young lady I thought you were."

"I don't care what you think," she flung back.

Grantham struggled as they dragged him to the van, his cowboy boots clicking on the concrete as he tried to dig his heels in. "Somebody find my wife," he shouted. "Tell her to get a lawyer. Tell her to hurry!"

Deni quenched her urge to applaud as they closed him into the van, then headed to Sam Ellington's house to make another arrest.

Word of the unfolding drama would spread like fire through the neighborhood. But would news of Mark's dropped charges make any difference in how they felt about him?

FORTY-FOUR

Mark waited at the sheriff's department while the others made the arrests. Deputy Wheaton had left him with the files of all the prisoners who had escaped, and he pored over them now, searching for addresses or any information that might lead Wheaton to them.

He opened a file with the name Miller on it and saw the Polaroid mug shot. The man staring back at him was Tree House. So that was his real name — Dante Miller. Mark flipped through the file and saw a long list of arrests on the rap sheet. Tree House was only thirty years old, but he had served prison terms three different times. Before he was eighteen, he'd spent five years in the juvenile detention center. His first arrest had been at the age of ten, when he and his own father had been caught robbing a liquor store.

Mark leaned back and tried to imagine a man enlisting his child's help in a criminal act. Miller's father had been arrested for armed robbery in that heist. He couldn't imagine being ten years old and following along while his dad put a gun to someone's head. No wonder Tree House had turned out this way.

But then he thought about his own father. Mark hadn't dreamed that his dad was capable of murder — until there was proof that he had been. But he had always known that most of his dad's business was probably not aboveboard. He remembered his parents' divorce when he was eight years old, and his mother's hysterical accusations: "You and those boys are going to wind up in prison! I don't want any part of it!"

He remembered wondering why his dad or his half-brothers would ever wind up in prison. That thought had haunted him for the next three years, until he found reason to be concerned himself. He'd been looking for his catcher's mitt one day in his father's SUV, and had discovered a dozen boxes of pirated videos of movies that were still being shown in theatres. Mark had been amazed at first and asked his father how he'd gotten hold of such treasures.

Vic had sworn him to secrecy. "Don't ever open your mouth about this, son. You'll get me and your brothers arrested."

Mark had kept the secret, though he couldn't imagine why a few boxes of videos could bring that much trouble.

When Mark turned twelve, Vic tried to enlist his help in some of his pornography trade. Mark hadn't understood it then, but now, looking back, he realized that his father's introduction to the images on his website had been a subtle and sinister way of drawing him into the family business. It was by God's grace that Mark had become a Christian a year earlier, and his youth minister had just given a talk about the covenant David had made with his own eyes, not to look upon anything sinful. Mark turned away from the images his father tried to show him, and told him that he wasn't interested.

"What do you mean you're not interested? You're a guy, aren't you?"

Mark found it difficult to explain his values to his dad or his brothers. When the accusation had flown back from his brothers—"Are you gay?"—he had decided that there was no point in trying to explain it further.

His father finally gave up. "But you let me know whenever you overcome your little religious experience. Puberty ought to take care of that."

His dad had tried again a couple more times over the years—Mark had been able to resist each time. But it would have been so easy to be taken in. He thought of his half brothers, who had probably fallen headlong into their father's pastime. Sometimes he felt sorry for them, and though he knew that they'd fled Crockett as fugitives from their murder charges, he often prayed for them at night—that the Lord would do his work in their hearts, and that they'd become true brothers. After all, he didn't have much family anymore.

He looked again at Tree House's file. That dangerous man who had killed two deputies right before Mark's eyes had once been an innocent child, lured into crime by a bitter, angry father with a skewed system of values. Now the community had to be protected from him.

Mark wrote down Tree House's address, though he supposed Wheaton had already gone there. Of course, he wouldn't be home anyway. Where would the man go? Mark searched the file for any references to family members or girlfriends …

Hadn't Tree House said something about having a girlfriend? Children? He tried to focus, to remember.

"I'll leave town. I got a woman and two kids live on a farm. They won't find me there."

There was no girlfriend or wife named in the file, but on one of the reports of a previous arrest, Mark found the names of Tree House's children. Rio and Cassandra had apparently been given their mother's last name—Ford. If Mark could find some record of the children's birth, maybe that would lead them to the mother's address … and to Tree House. Mark made copious notes, hoping someone would follow up.

He heard the front door opening, and his muscles went rigid as he reached for his gun.

A teenaged boy came in, clutching a shotgun. Mark had seen the kid before, but he couldn't place him.

"Hey," Mark said.

"Hey." The boy looked nervous, but he came in and lifted his chin high. "I came to sign up."

"For what?"

"For the volunteer force."

Mark got up and came around the desk. "How old are you?"

"Almost fourteen."

That would be thirteen, Mark thought. Not much older than Beth.

The boy thrust his chin up. "I know what you're thinking—that I'm too young. But I'm mature for my age, and I have law enforcement in my blood."

"How do you figure that?"

"My dad's the sheriff," he bit out. "I'm Jimmy Scarbrough."

Oh yes, now he remembered. Softening his voice, he said, "Hey, Jimmy. I'm Mark Green."

The kid shook his hand. "You were here when it happened, weren't you?"

Swallowing, Mark nodded. "Yeah, I'm afraid so."

"You tried to stop it."

Mark frowned. "How did you know?"

"George Mason, the paramedic, told me."

Mark's gaze drifted to the jail door. He couldn't let the boy go in there. There was still blood on the floor. "So how's your dad?"

Jimmy chewed on his lip for a moment. "They tried to put his face back together. It's all swollen and sewn up. Plus he has pneumonia, and he's having trouble breathing."

"I'm glad he's alive," Mark whispered. "Has he been able to talk to you?"

Jimmy cleared his throat and looked down at his feet. "He said I am the man of the house."

Mark wished he could help the boy with his pain. "Then you should be looking after your mom."

"She's going to be at the hospital most of the time. I'm staying with my grandparents."

"That doesn't change anything. Your dad wants you to look after the house."

Jimmy's gaze came back up and locked on his. "I want to catch them."

Mark sighed and sat back on the edge of the desk. "No way your folks are gonna let you do this. Look, Jimmy, I understand what you're trying to do. But I don't want to cause more stress for your mom. Deputy Wheaton would never sign up our wounded sheriff's kid. Besides, you're too young."

Jimmy tried to stand taller. "I've been taking care of my mom all these months, while Pop was out chasing bad guys. Ask her, if you don't believe me. I *know* there's something I can do here."

Mark stared at the kid for a moment, knowing that his grief over his suffering dad had brought him here. Maybe he could put him to work doing something, just to distract him.

"Look, if your parents say it's okay, I'll talk to Wheaton, and see if we can put you to work around here. You won't be out chasing killers, but if you're willing to do gopher work, run errands, clean up ..."

"I'll do whatever needs doing."

Mark could see that Jimmy was determined. "Okay, then. If your parents give the go-ahead, then come back and see me. As long as Wheaton says it's okay."

The grief on Jimmy's face seemed to fade as he raced out of the station.

FORTY-FIVE

When Doug, Brad, and Deputy Wheaton came back to the department, their van was filled with the men who had beaten up Mark. The prisoners were spitting mad, all of them, and fighting the cuffs that bound their wrists. Mark came to his feet as Wheaton led them in, grinding his teeth as he remembered the helplessness he'd felt as he'd struggled to fight back.

"You've got *him* working here?" Sam Ellington cried as he spotted Mark.

"Are you asking for trouble?" Paul Burlin said.

"Shut up and sit down," Wheaton said.

Mark sat back down, his jaw popping as he fixed his eyes on the file he was reading. He tried to ignore them as they were processed, but his pulse pounded in his broken arm, reminding him of what they'd done to him.

Finally, when Wheaton led them through the jail door, his tormenters began to cough and gag.

"You can't put us in there! That smell is horrible!"

"There's something dead in that place!"

Mark looked up. "It isn't anything dead," he said in a low, deliberate voice. "It's human waste."

"Come on, boys," Wheaton said as he ushered the men into the dark room.

Satisfaction rushed through Mark as he heard the cell doors clanging. Their cursing shouts echoed over the room.

Justice had been done, if only for a little while.

After a moment, Wheaton came back out. "Green, we're going to talk to Mahaffey and Kraft and check out the addresses you've come up with. Hopefully some of the escapees are stupid enough to go home. I want you to just babysit the prisoners and take care of whatever comes up. If their lawyers or family members come, let them in to talk. Hopefully, they'll bring food. But don't open the cell doors for anything."

Mark dreaded the duty but didn't argue. How could he, when he'd sworn to do whatever Wheaton needed?

"You got it. By the way, I meant to tell you that Sheriff Scarbrough's son came by." He told him what Jimmy wanted.

"If he comes back, give him something to do," Wheaton said. "Something safe. Keep him away from the prisoners, and don't leave him alone."

As Brad and Doug left with the deputy again, Mark prayed that people would start volunteering to help soon. The idea of him guarding the ones who'd beaten him was absurd. Through the steel door, he could hear their shouts: demanding attorneys, yelling threats. He thought of opening the door and screaming for them to shut up, but part of him enjoyed hearing them suffer.

His arm and collarbone ached, his brace was chafing his skin, and the stitches in his forehead were beginning to pull tight. He'd kill for a shower—it had been eight months since he'd had one. Washing with a bowl didn't cut it when you had dried blood crusted all over you.

He went into the department kitchen, wondering what he was going to feed these prisoners tonight if their families didn't come through. He knew what it was like sitting in a jail cell with disease festering in the Porta-John, his stomach growling. He wondered if any of Lou Grantham's men had been part of the break-in at his house. Had they stolen his food? If so, should he be expected to come up with something out of his own resources to feed them? Maybe he should just let them starve.

He went to the defunct refrigerator—empty. As many people as he'd told about turning refrigerators into solar ovens, he wondered why Sheriff Scarbrough hadn't done that with the departments' refrigerators. It would help keep the prisoners fed.

Maybe he could do it for them. All he would have to do was remove the door, take the coils and mechanics off the fridge and paint the metal liner black. The glass cover could be made out of old storm doors, or the big screen of a ruined television, or the windshield of a car. The whole contraption could be set on the refrigerator door to help insulate it, then wrapped with layers of cardboard, Styrofoam, or old newspapers to insulate it further.

All of those things were pretty easy to come by—it was the reflective panel that was tricky. For the ones he'd already made, he'd used three sides of a big cardboard box and covered it with reflective material—aluminum foil or old mirrors glued together. Set on top of the box, the three-paneled reflector could heat the box to 275 degrees Fahrenheit. An oven that size could bake twenty loaves of bread—or anything else a person would want to cook.

Maybe tomorrow he could get someone to help him drag the refrigerator out where he could work on it. If Jimmy came back, he could enlist his help. But even with the boy, he doubted he could handle it with a broken arm.

He heard the front door open and rabid voices as people came in. He picked up his gun and stepped out of the kitchen.

Sally Grantham, Lou's wife, led an entourage, and they looked ready for a fight. She froze as she saw Mark, and cried out, "What are *you* doing here?"

"I've been deputized." His tone dared her to protest.

"What kind of idiot would deputize someone like you?" She turned to the man with the bad toupee behind her. "This is ludicrous."

The man looked as if he'd suffered a personal affront. "Yes, it is. But maybe it's the basis for a motion to have them released. I'm Don Patton, attorney for Sam Ellington, Lou Grantham, Alan Newman, Mike Hinton, and Paul Burlin."

Mark recognized him from his personal injury commercials. He had a reputation for showing up at funerals and dropping his business card into the widows' hands. "I know who you are."

"Where is Deputy Wheaton?"

"He's out making more arrests."

"So you've been left in charge, with men you hold a grudge against?"

Mark breathed a sardonic laugh. "For the record, I'm not the one who's dangerous."

Sally bristled. "We demand to see our husbands."

Mark took slow, measured steps to the steel door and opened it. "Be my guest."

Sally stepped into the doorway. "Isn't there some light in here?"

"You may not have noticed," Mark said, "but we're in the middle of a power outage."

Sally looked like she could spit at him. Setting her teeth, she grabbed a lantern burning on one of the desks and carried it to the door. He heard her gag as she stepped into the cell room. The attorney pulled out a handkerchief and held it over his nose as he trailed her. Becky Ellington and Trish Burlin followed.

Mark sat back down at his desk as he heard one of them vomiting on the floor inside. He supposed he would have to clean it up.

Or maybe he'd just leave it there to add to the ambience.

He sat down at one of the desks, covered his face with his good hand, and tried to block out the sound of their angry voices.

God, help me to hate less.

The Biblical admonition flashed through his brain. *Love your enemies and pray for those who persecute you.*

Mark felt a stirring of resentment that the Lord would remind him of that passage right now. He didn't want to think about praying for those who had beaten him. He wanted to rub their noses in their plight, and make them as miserable as he had been. Unlike him, they were guilty of what they'd been charged with.

He stepped outside to get a little air. The temperature had risen—it felt like it was in the fifties. The snow was melting and the sky was clear, without a cloud. And this same sky was clear and pure for the prisoners who laughed at their exploits as they hid from the law.

Rubbing his eyes, he thought back over the last twelve months. It had been a nightmare for much of the civilized world. But for him it had gone much deeper. It had been a time of waking up to his father's true nature, then losing the dad that he couldn't help loving despite all his sins. It had been a time of overcompensating for his own unearned reputation, and of guarding his heart against Deni's on-again, off-again relationship with Craig. Now his house had been broken into, his mother threatened. And he was nursing broken bones when he hadn't done a thing wrong.

Why was God allowing all this? What had Mark done to deserve it?

And then a thought entered his mind. *To whom much has been given, much is required.*

"What does that mean?" he asked God aloud. "That in exchange for your grace, I have to be abused and insulted and humiliated?" He wondered if the cost was too high.

Almost as quickly as the thought came to him, he realized that it wasn't. No cost was too high for that grace. Jesus, too, had been abused and insulted, humiliated and beaten. Accused of something he hadn't done.

To this day, the name of Jesus was a curse word to some, a source of distrust, a reason for persecution.

How dare Mark think he was above that suffering? He'd given his life to Christ years ago, and gladly taken up his cross to follow him. He couldn't put it down now, declaring himself too righteous to carry it.

And where did he get the right to hate?

He thought of Jesus' model prayer—*Forgive us of our transgressions as we forgive those who've transgressed against us*. If Mark was indeed forgiven only as he forgave, then he was in a terrible mess.

Tears rushed to his eyes, but he blinked them back. "Dry up," his father would have told him. So he did.

Slowly, he stepped back into the building. The women and attorney were still in the cellblock with their men. He could hear the voices, angry and desperate. He was sure they were raking him over the coals.

He found a Gideon Bible on Gordon Jones's desk. Had the slain deputy been a Christian? He picked it up, and opened to the prayer that was tormenting him. He found it in Luke 11 and read the Lord's Prayer again. *Okay, Lord, I need to forgive. Show me how.*

He heard heels clicking on the concrete, and the group burst out. "You've got to do something about those toilets," Sally cried. "If my husband gets a disease, I'm going to sue the county, the town … I'll even sue you!"

"Good luck," Mark said. "I'm not worth much. And neither is the sheriff's department."

Trish stepped toward him, her eyes pleading. "Mark, don't you have any compassion?"

There he stood with his arm in a sling, his bruised and stitched face, his broken collarbone. Was she serious? Anger boiled in his chest again … and he thought of telling her what she could do with her compassion.

Don Patton wiped his oily face with his handkerchief. "I'm going to see the judge immediately. They'll be out of here within the hour."

That was it. Bitterness sliced through him. It was a clean cut, eliminating any hope of compassion. "Knock yourself out."

Furious, the women left with the attorney on their heels, slamming the door behind them. He walked to the jail door and slammed it.

But the Golden Rule flashed like a neon sign through his brain: *Do unto others …*

He turned his angry face up to the ceiling. "What is this, Lord? A day of Christian platitudes that don't work?"

Word of his innocence probably hadn't gotten around the neighborhood yet. If people knew that he was in charge of the jail, they would assume the lunatic was running the asylum. Someone else might come after him. He had bones that weren't yet broken.

It was all because of those men in there.

And because of Randy Kraft and Blake Mahaffey, who had deliberately lied about his whereabouts the morning of the shooting. And they were still free. He couldn't wait to hear that loud, iron door shut behind them.

Had they been the ones to shoot Zach? He pictured them in the woods the morning of Zach's shooting, one of them hearing the gun go off, finding the deer lying dead on the ground, coveting it enough to raise his gun and pull the trigger. Mark imagined the pact they'd made to pin the whole thing on him—a man people already distrusted. They deserved to be sitting in a dark jail cell that reeked of human waste and urine—with others like them. He hoped they'd be arrested quickly as all the escapees were rounded up. He would house the two boys with Tree House.

The men in the cells hollered and cursed, blaming, accusing, insulting him. How could he forgive men like that? How—and why—should he force himself to make it more pleasant for them?

I don't expect you to feel it. Just do it.

The thought, clearly from God, made him furious. "Do it *how*?"

The toilets. Clean the toilets.

He struggled against that thought, amazed that it would be asked of him. Hadn't he earned his anger? Wasn't it warranted?

He sat back down, leaning on his desk, rubbing his stubbled jaw as he wrestled with the prompting. The apostle Paul had been beaten, shipwrecked, run out of town. He called them his "light and momentary" afflictions, and said they were nothing compared to the glory that awaited him.

Mark wondered if he could ever learn to think like Paul. Wasn't that why he had the Holy Spirit? So he could do the hard things?

Clean the toilets.

It was ridiculous.

And yet . . .

He couldn't escape the thought that forgiveness wasn't a feeling. It was cleaning toilets for men who had beaten you.

Since he had all of them in one cell at the moment, he had the perfect opportunity to clean the other four. Just emptying the Porta-Johns would help the conditions immeasurably.

Just the thought made him ill. How could he go in there with a broken arm and clean out bacteria-ridden waste?

I'll help you, came that still, small voice again.

Mark wanted to raise his bruised fist at the ceiling and lash back, refusing to submit. But how would he dare? He had no right to argue with the one who had died for him.

Instead, he went into the kitchen and found a bucket and some dirty towels.

FORTY-SIX

Deputy Wheaton, Brad, and Doug found the judge at the courthouse and got a search warrant for the homes of Randy Kraft and Blake Mahaffey. The search would be twofold—to frighten the boys into confessing to lying about Mark, and to see if any of their guns matched up with the gun that shot Zach.

Luke Kraft, Randy's father, was in the backyard building a power-generating windmill. Doug looked at it with interest. His own attempt at harnessing the wind had ended in failure, since the winds in this area were too inconsistent. Maybe Kraft knew something Doug didn't know.

Deputy Wheaton got right to the point, wrenching Doug's thoughts back to why they were here. "Mr. Kraft, we need to ask your son a few more questions. Is he here?"

Luke didn't seem disturbed. "Yeah, he's in his room. Blake's over here too. I'll get them. You guys come on in."

It was clear the man wasn't threatened by law enforcement showing up at his door. The three of them stepped inside. The room was dim with only the window light, but a fire crackled in the fireplace.

The boys came into the room, looking even younger than Doug expected. They were both eighteen, but they were skinny and didn't look strong enough to carry off a ten-point buck. Randy was only five-six or so, much shorter than the men Zach had described, though Blake was probably closer to the shooter's five-ten. Neither of them seemed particularly well built.

Deputy Wheaton introduced himself. "How are you guys doing today?" he asked.

"Doing fine, sir." Randy looked troubled as he faced the deputy. "We already told the sheriff everything we know."

"The sheriff was shot, as you probably heard."

Randy nodded, and Blake's hands went into his pockets. "Yeah, that's bad. Is he gonna make it?"

"We hope so," Wheaton said. "We just wanted to come by and clarify a few things we're confused about."

Randy swallowed hard and looked up at his friend. Blake crossed his arms and took a step backward.

Wheaton scratched his head. "Grapevine's pretty active in this town, so you may have also heard that Zach Emory cleared Mark Green's name. Says it wasn't him that shot him."

Silence, then Blake cleared his throat. "Well, we don't know who shot him, Officer. All we know is that we saw Mark that day."

"Did Zach say who did shoot him?" Randy cut in.

Wheaton reminded Doug of Columbo as he rubbed his jaw in puzzlement. "He didn't know the name, but he described the guy. And see, the thing is, now I'm a little confused about your story."

Randy turned to his father, looking for help. Luke just stood there, waiting for him to clear things up.

"It's just ... we thought we saw him," Blake said. "Maybe it wasn't him, after all. Maybe it just looked like him."

Wheaton just stared at him. "See, there's the rub, boys. I read your statement, and it was emphatic. You said you were 100 percent positive that you saw Mark at the crime scene."

Doug held his breath. If they could just get the boys to confess to lying ...

The boys looked at each other again, then Blake nodded. Finally, Blake turned to Wheaton and cleared his throat. This was it, Doug thought. They were going to talk.

"Okay, we lied, but we didn't shoot Zach."

Luke looked incredulous. "*What?* You lied?"

Randy couldn't meet his father's eyes. "Some guys paid us to say what we said."

Bingo! Doug's heart leaped in his chest.

"What guys?" Wheaton asked Blake. "You got a name?"

"No, we don't know them. I wouldn't even know where to find them again."

Very convenient, Doug thought. Some "guys" they didn't know and couldn't identify had emerged out of nowhere.

Seeing the dubious looks on their faces, Randy tried again. "They came to *us*. We wouldn't have lied, but they promised us some gold coins if we would just go to the sheriff. After we told the sheriff about seeing Mark, they met us and paid us."

"Where did they meet you?"

"In the park," Randy said. "They had red ski caps pulled over their faces."

Wheaton asked them if he could search their house, and Randy and his father consented, clearly hoping to clear their names. They gave him the one remaining gold coin of the four they'd been paid, and he took it into evidence. He gathered their guns, checking to see if they were the same caliber as the one used to shoot Zach. One of them matched. Ballistics would show if the shells matched.

When Wheaton came back to the boys and Randy's father, he blew out a long breath. "I'm afraid you boys are under arrest for obstruction of justice and conspiracy."

The boys gasped, and Luke stepped in front of them. "Hold on, now. They're just kids!"

"They're legal adults, and they've just confessed to committing a crime," Brad said.

"But they voluntarily told you the truth! They didn't have to! They were trying to help."

"Yeah," Brad said. "Trying to help a killer cover his crime. And they did it for money. That, my friend, is a felony."

"I'm getting an attorney!" Luke said. "You can't take them until we've talked to an attorney."

"Think again," Wheaton said. "Come on, boys, let's go." He cuffed Blake and Randy, grabbed their arms, read them their rights, and pulled them out to the van.

Luke followed. "Don't say another word, Randy! Stay quiet until I get there with a lawyer."

FORTY-SEVEN

THE SOUND OF THE FRONT DOOR DREW MARK OUT OF the cells, where he'd been cleaning up the contents of Trish Burlin's stomach. The sight of Randy Kraft and Blake Mahaffey in handcuffs should have lifted the heaviness in his heart, but instead it made his burden heavier. The two looked so young and frightened, and when they saw him, they couldn't look him in the eye.

"They admitted to lying about you," Doug said as he sat them down. "They claim they were paid by some guys in red ski masks."

Mark walked closer to them. The boys seemed startled at his injuries—the stitches across his forehead, his arm in a cast ...

He wanted to smash his good fist into their teeth, and ask them if they had any idea what their lie had cost him. He wanted to accuse them of shooting Zach.

But he forced himself to stay quiet. When Wheaton had finished processing them, he handed them over to Mark to lock them in, then headed back out with Doug and Brad. Mark led them silently into the dark cellblock. Behind him, he heard Randy crying.

Lou Grantham looked up as Mark led them past his cell. "Now you lockin' up teenagers? What's the matter with you? Don't you have a conscience?"

Mark bit his lip, almost drawing blood. He went to the cell door and pulled out the pistol he'd been issued when he was sworn in. "Back against the wall, everybody."

The men got up and milled to the back wall. "You putting them in here?" Ellington asked. "We're already full."

Mark didn't intend to engage in a dialogue about how he planned to leave the other cells empty so he could clean them. Carefully holding his gun with his casted hand, he unlocked the cell door and motioned the two boys in.

"Are you deaf?" Grantham shouted.

Mark closed the cell door. The whispered voice of God came to him again, warning him to take his thoughts captive. *Don't answer.* Forgiveness was not an emotion. You didn't have to feel it. You just had to do it.

Holstering his gun, he opened the door to the cell next to theirs.

"You gonna torment us?" Lou Grantham's voice echoed in the room. "You gonna make us sorry we ever knew you?"

You were sorry for that months ago, Mark thought, but he said nothing. He opened the door of the Porta-John, and the smell made a fresh assault.

He wondered when it had last been changed. With all those men crammed into the cells, the receptacles would have filled up quickly. Left to fester for days, even in the cold, it was a breeding ground for bacteria and rot.

He pulled up the seat and looked inside. Nearly full. If these things were portable, then there was probably an easy way to empty them. He clicked on his flashlight and shone it around on the plastic walls, hoping there were some instructions.

Sure enough, there they were, slightly faded, but still legible.

The instructions warned that it needed to be emptied often. Clearly, the portable sanitation company was supposed to come with their trucks and hoses and clean the tanks out at least a few times a month. But that was before the Pulses. Now their vacuum trucks couldn't run, and if the company was even still in business, all their work had to be done with horse and wagon. Besides, it was doubtful the county could pay for such services. And not many service workers would go to the trouble for free.

If it was going to get done, he was going to have to do it.

Aware that he couldn't do it with a broken arm, he examined the unit to see how the tank could be taken out, since the instructions didn't explain. It looked like the whole back wall would have to come off.

"My mother said it was okay."

Mark turned and saw Sheriff Scarbrough's son standing in the doorway. He hadn't expected the boy to come back. He left the empty cell and walked toward him. "You're not lying, are you?"

"No. You can go ask her." Jimmy's voice amplified over the concrete room. "She said as long as I stayed in the office and hung with you, it would be okay."

Mark was skeptical, but he saw the pain in the boy's eyes and didn't want to disappoint him.

Jimmy looked past him to the men in the cell. "Is the guy who shot Pop in here?"

Mark shook his head. "No, they're still looking for him."

Disappointment clouded Jimmy's eyes.

"You gonna lock that kid up too?" Grantham called from across the room.

"Hey, I know a day care center you could raid," Paul Burlin added.

Jimmy's face flushed with fury. "I'm not a criminal like you," he shouted back. "I'm the sheriff's son." Pride rippled on his angry voice.

Grantham and Burlin had the grace to shut up then. Jimmy looked like he might cry, so Mark set his hand on the boy's back and ushered him into the office area. "Ignore them," he said. "They just have big mouths."

"Why are they here?" Jimmy asked.

"Some of them are in there for doing this to me."

Jimmy regarded his cast, then glanced at his stitches. "So you got revenge, huh?"

"I call it justice."

The boy walked to his father's office and stood in the doorway, looking at the empty chair. Mark stood behind him.

"So why don't they have everybody out looking for the killer?" Jimmy asked.

"They do. Except for me. Somebody has to hold down the fort." He nodded to the files on his desk. "I've been going through the files, trying to find addresses where we might find the escapees. I gave what I've already found to Deputy Wheaton and he's out looking for the prisoners."

Jimmy went to the desk, and Mark scanned it to see what Jimmy might find. On a piece of paper clipped to the front of Miller's file, Mark had written, "Ringleader and murderer."

Jimmy picked the file up. "Is this him? The one who shot my pop?"

Mark took the file back. "Look, Jimmy, you can hang around here and help with chores, but you're not going through the files."

"Why not?" He gestured toward the stack on Mark's desk. "I could help. You have a lot to go through."

"Because that's *my* job. You have a different one." He headed into the kitchen, looking for some cleaning supplies.

Jimmy followed him. "What's his name?"

"What's whose name?"

"The one who shot Pop and killed the others."

Mark didn't know if he should go on with this. But he'd been in Jimmy's shoes. When news came that his father was dead, he'd wanted to know the details so he could process it all. He supposed it wouldn't hurt to tell Jimmy what he knew. "His name is Dante Miller. The other prisoners called him Tree House."

"Tree House," Jimmy repeated, the words bitter in his mouth.

Mark found a mop and turned to hand it to the boy. But Jimmy was already back at the desk, looking at Miller's picture.

"Here, take the mop. I need help cleaning those cells."

The boy bristled. "If I go back in there I'll throw up."

Mark didn't doubt it. "So how are you with digging?"

"Good," Jimmy said.

"Then you can dig some holes for us to dump the waste in after I clean the toilets. Deep holes. Can you do that?"

Jimmy crossed his arms. "I guess so. Why are you cleaning them, anyway?"

"Because those cells are not fit for humans. I know firsthand what it's like to sleep in there with that filth."

"Who cares?" Jimmy asked. "Let them wallow in it like pigs."

Mark started to tell him that he'd felt the same way, but that God had given him orders. The kid wouldn't understand. He almost didn't himself. "Do you want to help or not? I told you what I need to have done."

The kid blew out a sigh, puffing his cheeks. "Where's the shovel?"

"It's leaning against the wall next to the back door."

Jimmy didn't look happy as he headed out the door. Mark went back into the jail cell and stepped into the Porta-John again.

Once again, he heard the front door. Had Wheaton, Brad, and Doug come back with more prisoners? Or were Blake's and Randy's parents bringing attorneys?

He abandoned the toilet again and walked toward the door.

Then he heard Deni's voice. "Mark? Where are you?"

He hoped she hadn't come to give him a hard time. He came out of the jail.

Deni looked relieved to see him. "Oh, thank goodness. I thought something might have happened to you, and I wasn't about to go into that place."

"I'm fine," he said. "I was just cleaning the cells. The illustrious Oak Hollow gang is here, and they're used to better accommodations."

She wasn't amused. "Are you kidding me? Let them sit there in it like you did."

He went to a bowl of water in the kitchen and washed his good hand. "Believe me, I thought about it. But I'm a Christian, so I can't."

She stood in front of him and looked him in the eye. "What does being a Christian have to do with cleaning out toilets?"

"It has everything to do with it." He looked around on the shelves in the kitchen—there were supplies there, so maybe there was a handbook for the portable restrooms. He saw some boxes stacked on a lower shelf and some large, five-gallon jugs of fluid with the Porta-John label on them. "There it is," he said. "Just what I need. Now I can figure out how to get those tanks out." He picked up the booklet he'd spotted and turned to the table of contents. "Here it is. 'Evacuating the effluent.'"

"Gross! You are not going to do that!"

He breathed a laugh. "Oh yeah, I am. I may not be in any condition to help enforce the law, but if I'm in charge of the jail, I'm going to treat the prisoners humanely."

Deni followed him out of the kitchen and into the office area. "So how do you plan to do this?"

"I'll manage. I'm resourceful."

"You have a broken arm!"

"Deni, you have to understand. It doesn't matter what else I do to clean up those cells—if I don't start with this, it's futile."

The sound of banging came from the cells, and someone's voice echoed through the place. Angry profanity reverberated out of one of the cells.

"You're going to go in there and do this for *them*? The same ones who beat you? Lied about you?"

Mark sat on the corner of a desk. "Deni, I've been praying about how to do what the Bible says and forgive them for what they did to me. It's not easy to turn the other cheek when I'm full of hatred." His voice broke, and he swallowed.

Deni tipped her head and took his hand. "Don't fake it, Mark. Jesus didn't mean for you to put on some big performance."

He knew she didn't understand. "I think maybe you do fake it. Maybe you get into the rhythm of forgiving, just by doing the things you would do if you cared about them."

She wasn't buying it. "Mark, why can't you just keep the jail door closed?"

He thought about coming up with more arguments, but he really didn't have any. It all boiled down to one thing, and he decided to give it to her straight. "Deni, I'm doing this because God told me to clean the toilets."

She breathed an astonished laugh. "He did not!"

"He did, Deni. I was praying, and it popped into my mind from out of nowhere. His still, small voice."

"Well, if it was still and small, maybe you heard wrong. Or maybe it wasn't even him."

"Who else would tell me to go in there and do for my enemies what I'd want done for me?"

Her amusement faded, and she stared at him, dumbfounded. "You're not going to be talked out of this, are you?"

"Nope." Moving away from her, Mark started back to the jail. "If you're going to stay, let me know if anyone comes in."

She stood frozen a moment, then blew out a disgusted breath. "All right!" she shouted. "If you're dead set on doing this, I'll help you!"

He turned around and almost laughed. "What?"

"I *said*, I'm helping you." Her voice was brittle and angry, as if he'd been begging her to for hours.

"No, you're not."

"Watch me." She took off her coat and tossed it on a chair, then rolled up her sleeves. "If you're doing it, so am I."

"Deni, you're not serious. This is smelly, dirty work."

"I know it is. It's absolutely gross, and it'll probably turn my stomach." She went into the kitchen and got a towel, then tied it around her face, mask-style, with a knot at the back of her head. She pulled on some rubber gloves and put one on Mark's good hand as well. "Now, let's get this stupid thing over with!"

"Deni, I can't let you—"

"Shut up, Mark! If I can't stop you, you can't stop me. If God told you to clean the toilets, then we're going to clean the toilets."

Mark couldn't help grinning at her furious determination as he led her back to the open cell. Strangely, none of the prisoners said a word as they passed. Mark supposed they'd heard the exchange, and didn't want to divert them from the filthy work.

Deni just gritted her teeth and got to work.

FORTY-EIGHT

There were some things so totally disgusting that you had to just hold your breath and dive in. Deni tried to make her mind numb out as she gasped for breath behind the towel covering her nose and mouth. They cleaned out the Porta-Johns in the four empty cells, dumped the waste into the holes Jimmy Scarbrough was digging, cleaned out the tanks, then filled them with fresh, sanitary liquid. With a bucket of water cut with bleach, they wiped down the mattresses and mopped the concrete floors. There were no clean sheets to put on the beds, but at least these cells were better than they'd been.

She was thankful when her father and Brad got back, bringing three of the escaped prisoners. They also had five new men with them, recent volunteers who'd come to be sworn in by Deputy Wheaton. Wheaton moved all the prisoners into the clean cells, leaving the other cell open for Deni and Mark to finish cleaning.

How thoughtful.

The cells already smelled much better, and even the new prisoners weren't complaining that much. All who had smelled the cells before Mark and Deni's work knew they were in much better shape than they'd been before.

Mark and Deni took the last receptacle out. Jimmy had finished digging his holes and the shovel was leaning against the building. Jimmy was nowhere to be seen. They dumped the "effluent" into the last hole, then covered the holes.

By the time they'd finished, their shoes and the bottoms of their pant legs were covered with dirt.

"Did you see Jimmy inside?" Mark asked.

"No, I saw him inside when they came in with the prisoners. But I thought he came back outside."

Mark frowned. Deni followed him back in and saw a group of men at the desks, filling out paperwork to volunteer for the force. "Have any of you seen Jimmy Scarbrough?" Mark asked. "The thirteen-year-old who was out back?"

One of the men looked up. "I saw him leave."

"Leave? Did he say where he was going?"

"No. But he seemed like he was in a big hurry."

Mark frowned and looked around the room, as if wondering what had prompted that.

"Maybe he just got tired of doing grunt work," Deni said. "He probably went home."

Mark's gaze drifted to his desk. Tree House's file was gone. The legal pad on which he'd written addresses was also gone.

"Oh, don't tell me." He went to his desk and started flipping through the files.

"What's wrong?" Deni asked.

"He took the file of the guy who shot his father!"

"What would he want with that?"

"An address," Mark said. "The kid is going to try to find him himself."

FORTY-NINE

"If anything happens to that boy, it'll kill Ralph and Mary." Wheaton grabbed his coat and pulled it on. "Doug, let's go look for him. You too, Brad."

"I'm coming too," Mark said.

Heading for the door, Wheaton glanced back at him. "What good will you do?"

"I can talk to Jimmy if we find him. I know how it feels to have that kind of bitterness churning inside you. I've been there."

Wheaton slowed his step, studying him. "And what if we're walking into trouble? You're in no condition to help."

"You'll still have Doug and Brad. Leave one of the new guys to hold down the fort."

Wheaton didn't have time to protest. "All right." He pointed to Glenn Reed, who had just been sworn in. "Reed, you stay here. Finish going through those files looking for addresses or clues to where the prisoners are. And if Jimmy comes back, don't let him leave."

It was five o'clock—not much daylight left. Mark hoped they'd find Jimmy on the way. If he made it to Tree House's apartment, would he go to the door? Break in? Kill the man who'd maimed his father?

They didn't see him on the way. It only took moments to reach Tree House's address—an old, abandoned warehouse that must have an apartment above it. A stairwell on the side of the building led to the upstairs rooms.

Dread tightened Mark's chest as he saw the boy's bike, dropped on its side at the bottom of the stairs. Had Jimmy gone in?

"God help him," Doug whispered.

They got out, closed the doors quietly, and drew their weapons. "Doug, Brad, you two split up and go around the building. Make sure any back windows or doors are covered."

Mark followed the deputy up the stairs. The door was open. Leading with his gun, Wheaton stepped into the doorway.

"Don't move!" The warning came from the boy, who stood across the barren apartment, his shotgun pointed at the door.

Wheaton caught his breath and raised his hands, gun pointed skyward. "Jimmy, it's me. Archie Wheaton."

Surprised, the boy lowered his gun.

Wheaton lowered his, as well, and entered the apartment. "What in the blazes are you doing?"

Jimmy dropped his gun and wilted to the floor. "I thought he'd be here. I thought I'd find him, but he's gone."

"And then what?" Wheaton asked. "What did you intend to do?"

"Shoot him. Right in the face, where he shot my pop."

Mark moved past Wheaton through the doorway and went to sit beside Jimmy on the floor. With a hand on the boy's shoulder, he said, "Jimmy, you could have been killed. What if he'd been here?"

Jimmy wiped his nose on his coat sleeve. "He's been here, though. I saw his shoes in there. And some potato peels on the counter. They weren't that old."

"Son, we've already been here, looking for him," Wheaton said. "If he comes home and sees that somebody's broken in, he's not going to stay. You're jeopardizing the investigation. Besides, you can't go around shooting people, not for any reason. Your daddy taught you better than that. Now get up and let's get out of here."

"Somebody has to wait here for him."

Mark looked up at Wheaton. The deputy was clearly moved by the boy's grief. "Someone will, Jimmy, now that I have some men. But right now, we have to get out of here and get you home."

Jimmy didn't want to go. Mark got up and pulled the kid to his feet. "Come on, buddy. Let's go." He led the boy out of the apartment and down the stairs, his arm around Jimmy's shoulders.

Doug looked up when he heard them coming. "Oh, thank God you're okay, Jimmy. You had us scared to death."

"I can take care of myself," Jimmy said.

"I can see that. But this wasn't smart."

Jimmy just wiped his wet face. "Can't you search the place? See if there's any clue where he could be?"

"Son, we already did. We were here earlier with a search warrant."

"And you didn't find anything?"

"We're still looking," Wheaton said. "We'll catch him, Jimmy. You can bet on that."

Mark opened the van door, and Jimmy climbed into the back bench seat. Mark sat next to him. Jimmy stared out the windows, crying softly.

"I know a little about how you feel," he said in a low voice.

"No, you don't. Nobody knows how I feel."

"Trust me, I do. I know what it's like to be so eaten up with anger that you feel like you have to do something about it or go crazy."

Jimmy set his jaw and kept his eyes fixed on a spot on the glass. "I just want to know why he did it."

"If you ask him, he'll probably do something real attractive like spitting in your face or growling like a dog."

Jimmy sniffed. "He growls?"

Mark smiled. "No. I'm just saying, he's probably not going to have some nice, organized explanation of why he did it. He just wanted out, and he figured out a way to do it."

Jimmy's face twisted as he turned back to Mark. "Didn't he know those men had families? That people were counting on them?"

"He didn't care. The guy doesn't have a conscience. That's why he has to be taken off the streets."

Jimmy's gaze moved to Wheaton, Brad, and Doug, who were still outside, talking at the bottom of the stairs. "If he'd only come home ..."

"Jimmy, we're gonna find him."

"He'll probably get off on a technicality. It happens all the time. Pop was always talking about how stupid the court system could be, letting killers go because they didn't cuff them right or something."

"Don't worry about that. I was an eyewitness to the shooting. I'll make sure there's no question that he's guilty."

The three men got back into the van. As Wheaton started it, he looked in his rearview mirror. "Jimmy, I'm taking you home now. If your mama's not there, I'm telling your grandparents to watch you like a hawk from now on. We can't have this kind of thing happen again."

As Wheaton pulled back onto the street, Mark saw himself in the hurting boy—the rage with no outlet, the grief that couldn't be assuaged, the confusion over things he could not control. And now Jimmy was embarrassed by his failed attempt to get justice. "Jimmy, it was the wrong thing this time," he said. "But I can see that you have what it takes to make a great cop someday."

Jimmy didn't answer.

"You do your dad real proud."

Jimmy's face tightened. "All I used to do was complain that he was never home. But what he was doing was important. The county needed him more than I did." He wiped his face. "My pop is a great man."

"Why don't you tell him that when you see him?"

"I will if I'm not grounded for life."

"Mothers have a way of offering parole, way sooner than you think."

FIFTY

After Mark left to find Jimmy, Deni went home and began praying in her room for the boy whose life was in danger. Her mother came upstairs and found her. "I just got back from the post office," she said. "You have mail from Craig."

Deni took the letter. She could see the disapproval on her mother's face. Her parents had never liked Craig and would have been glad if she never heard from him again. But the weary expression on her mom's face went deeper than that.

"Something wrong, Mom?"

Kay shook her head. "I don't know. I'm just worried about Beth ... and your father ... and Mark."

"What's wrong with Beth?"

Kay walked to Deni's window and looked down on the front yard. "She saw Mark getting beaten, and she kind of lost it."

"Didn't we all?"

"Yeah, but ... we can handle it. I'm not sure she can."

"She'll be all right, Mom. She's tougher than you think." She tore open the envelope and pulled the letter out.

Kay sighed. "So is he trying to get you back?"

Deni saw something else in the envelope. A ticket. She pulled it out and took it to the lantern on her desk. "What is this? A train ticket?"

Kay snatched it out of her hand. "What? Is he out of his mind?"

"Must be." Deni unfolded the letter.

Downstairs, Beth called out, "Mom!"

Kay looked at Deni. "Don't let him sway you, Deni. You have a good thing with Mark."

"Mom, I know." Deni watched her mother hurry back down the stairs.

Then she sat down at her desk and began to read.

Dear Deni,

I hope things are well with you. I've been very busy lately, too busy to get back to Crockett. The government is deep in the rebuilding process as you know, hoping to find workarounds to get things back to normal, or as close as they can be. Scientists who are studying SN–1999 tell us the Pulses are getting weaker. Soon, we hope, they'll stop altogether. At that point, we'll undergo a massive program to rebuild our infrastructure. The president is already hiring the staff who will supervise that rebuilding. I've just been hired to work on one of the top tiers of that program.

But that brings me to us. Deni, when the Pulses stop, people will depend on the government as never before. There will be good jobs for well-educated, intelligent people. If you were here, you would be on the inside track. I have the authority to hire anyone I want, and I want you. We need good communicators. The country needs you.

But more importantly, I need you. I miss you more each day. Please give our relationship another try. We've both changed. I've been thinking a lot about your religion, and believe it or not, I've been going to church and praying myself. I now see the comfort you find in it. As I've prayed, I believe God has shown me that you are the one he's chosen to serve our country in this way. But I also believe he's chosen you for me.

But I want you to come for selfish reasons too. My greatest prayer is that you'd give me another chance.

This ticket is one way to Washington on March 1. Please use it. If you decide you can't stay, I'll buy you a ticket home. But if you come, I can promise you a lifetime of happiness and success doing things you never dreamed of.

If you don't come, I'll come to you. I intend to win you back.

I love you, Deni. I hope I won't be disappointed.

Love, Craig

Deni stared at the letter, astonished. Craig was going to church? She couldn't even picture it.

She thought of the job he was offering her. It was a big deal, one she would have killed for eight months ago.

But so much had changed. She was in love with Mark now, and there was no way she could consider going back to Washington. How arrogant for him to think he could win her back.

Folding the letter up, she stuffed it back into its envelope and set it on her makeup table. She dropped the ticket on top of it and turned her thoughts back to Mark and Jimmy Scarbrough.

FIFTY-ONE

WHEATON INSISTED THAT DOUG, MARK, AND BRAD ALL go home, now that they had more volunteers to take the night shift. He dropped them all off at the Brannings' house, since Mark's mother was still there. But Mark didn't plan to stay. He'd been thinking about building a solar oven for the jail. He'd stored a lot of things he could use at his father's house. If he went over there, maybe he could find the things he needed to get started on that tonight.

But first he wanted to see Deni and his mother.

Mark found her sitting at the kitchen table with Kay, talking by the light of the solar lamps they'd left in the yard all day, then brought in at night. They'd stuck the pole lanterns into terra-cotta pots around the house, and it gave the rooms a sweet yellow glow. The fire in the living room added more light. It felt like a home.

Knowing it was Deni's home only made it warmer. He hadn't thanked her for cleaning the cells with him. When he'd discovered Jimmy missing, he'd hurried out without a word to her. But he was anxious to see her now.

He took off his holster with his Glock and laid it on the table. His mother fussed over him and fixed him something to eat while Kay took Doug to the garage to show him something. He was starving, but he didn't want to take the Brannings' food. "Mom, I'm fine. I don't need anything."

"Stop it, Mark. You're injured and tired, and I bet you can't even remember the last time you ate." She put a plate in front of him, and his stomach reminded him that his mother knew best.

"Where's Deni?"

"Upstairs. I'll go tell her you're here."

As his mother scuffed away, he ate the potato on his plate in five bites, then took a bite of the bread.

His arm and clavicle ached, and he longed to stretch out in bed for the first time in three days.

The door to the garage opened and Doug came back in, followed by Beth and Kay. Beth looked pale, and her eyes were swollen. She had clearly been crying. She sucked in a breath as she saw him. "Mark, are you okay?"

He smiled. "Sure, Sparky. I'm fine. How about you? You don't look so good."

She looked embarrassed and exchanged looks with her mother and father. "Did you catch the killers yet?"

"No, not the ones who killed the deputies. Although Jimmy Scarbrough gave it a heck of a try."

"Jimmy Scarbrough?" Beth took a step toward him. "I know him from school. He's in the grade above me. What did he do?"

Mark told her how the boy had taken matters into his own hands.

Her eyes rounded in wonder. "Wow, that was pretty brave."

"He could have been killed."

"But he's all right?"

"Oh yeah. He's back at home now. His mother may never let him leave the house again."

Beth just stared at the air, as if running Jimmy's heroics through her mind. Did Beth have a thing for the sheriff's son?

Mark took his plate to the sink and dunked it into the water bowl. Kay hurried over and took it out of his hand. "You go sit down in the family room, Mark. Let me do this."

He surrendered the plate and went into the family room. Doug sat in his favorite chair, and Mark took the couch. "Everything all right out there?" he asked Doug.

Doug put his feet up. "Yeah. Just a distraught daughter. And a garage full of rabbits."

Mark knew there must be a story.

He heard Deni coming down the stairs and he started to get up.

"Sit back down," she insisted. She came to him and hugged him. "How's Jimmy?"

He told her how they'd found him, and relief was clear on her face. "I came straight home and started praying for him," she said, sitting down next to him.

He put his arm around her and stroked her hair. "I haven't thanked you for helping me today."

She smiled. "You owe me big, Mark Green. Making me clean toilets, then running out on me like that."

"I really am sorry." It was amazing how much better her smile made him feel. He wanted to kiss her again like he had at the hospital. But not with her father sitting next to them.

"If I forgive you will I have to clean more sewage?"

"No, I promise."

Kay came and leaned in the doorway. "I've cleaned up Jeff's room for you, Mark. You look really tired. Why don't you wash up and get to bed? Your injuries will heal better if you're not exhausted."

"Thanks, Kay, but I'm not sleeping here tonight."

Deni grunted. "Why not?"

His mother came into the room. "Mark, you need rest! You've earned it."

"I know I do. But I want to sleep at Dad's house. I have some things I need to do over there."

Martha looked as if she might cry. "Mark, that place feels evil."

"It's not evil, Mom. It's just a house. It's no big deal. I have a lot of stuff over there I need to check on."

Clearly aggravated, Deni got to her feet. "Can I talk to you alone, Mark?"

He stood up. "Sure."

She led him into her father's study and dropped into a loveseat. "Mark, why do we have to keep going over this? You demanding to go into danger, and your mom and me begging you not to?"

"My father's house is not dangerous, Deni. I just want to work on a solar oven for the sheriff's department. If I'm there anyway, I might as well sleep there."

"But if the neighbors see you there they might attack you again."

"The neighbors have heard about the arrest of Grantham and his gang. No one's going to hurt me."

"What about whoever broke into your mom's house? What about Zach's shooter? Or the escaped prisoners? They could come after you."

"I'll be armed. Besides, they wouldn't even know to look for me there."

Sighing, she just looked at him. "Mark, you're so stubborn."

He smiled. "I know."

She touched the skin around his stitches. "This is swollen. Does it hurt?"

Her touch sent a current through him—grabbing his full attention. "No."

"Liar."

"Okay, maybe a little."

She leaned closer. "It's okay for you to acknowledge pain, Mark. It doesn't make you any less heroic."

Her breath was warm against his face. "Me? I'm no hero."

"Yes, you are, in every way. Everything you've done for the last two days was heroic."

He thought of the hate-filled thoughts he'd had about Grantham and his men today, before God had made him clean toilets. Those thoughts hadn't been very heroic. He was glad she didn't know about them.

"You're the one who was heroic. Never in a million years would I have imagined that Deni Branning would voluntarily clean out filthy Porta-Johns for people she couldn't stand."

"Hey, it wasn't my idea. I did it for you, not them."

"The fact that you did it at all was major. You've come a long way, you know that?"

She seemed to appreciate that. "I had a long way to come."

He took her hand. She brought his fingers to her lips. Fire shot through him, and he swallowed hard.

"I didn't much like cleaning the toilets," she whispered, "but I did like being with you so much today. And that's why I want you to hang around here tonight."

His mouth was suddenly dry again. He leaned toward her, and their lips touched. He kissed her then, a soft, slow, long kiss that melted the pain out of him, but the pain of his longing for her seared through his heart.

When the kiss broke, he pulled back and brushed her hair out of her eyes. She was beautiful. He remembered sitting in sociology class and watching her across the room. Whenever she'd catch his eye, he'd mouth some benign message to her and pretend he was planning a prank on one of their classmates. Then he'd have to come up with one. Their friendship was too important to be ruined with a crush.

She'd been way out of his league.

Now she sat here, holding his hand and stroking his skin with her thumb, her mouth brushing his. He wanted to linger at her lips.

"You were the brightest spot in the last two dark days," he whispered. "You made everything bearable. You were a gift."

Her smile was soft. "A gift? From whom?"

"From God, of course."

She looked back at him with expectation and mirrored longing.

Her words at the hospital played through his head. He hadn't had time to dwell on them, but they'd sunk deeply into his heart. *Why did I have to fall in love with a hero?* Was it true? Had she fallen in love? Or was it just a figure of speech?

He hadn't answered her. His feelings had trapped themselves in his throat. He thought of telling her now, but what if he made too much of it? What if she pitied him for misunderstanding?

But that kiss was no misunderstanding. Deni had made it clear that she wasn't just his friend. Hadn't she?

He had stood face-to-face with killers—but he'd never feared anything more than rejection from her.

As if coming to his rescue, Doug stepped into the room. "Sorry to interrupt, but I need my reading glasses."

Mark took the reprieve and got up. "No problem. I was just about to leave."

Deni looked disappointed. She stood up, her eyes round, vulnerable. "Can't talk you out of it, huh?"

He took her hand, squeezed it. "No, I need to go."

She followed him to tell his mother good-bye, then trailed him to the door, and stepped out on the porch with him.

His heart pounded as he looked down at her. "Well ... good night," he said.

"Good night." She raised up to kiss him one more time.

He was almost lost then. Declarations of love rose to his head, flushing out reason, banishing fear. He stroked her face with his knuckles as he gave himself to that kiss.

Suddenly, she pulled back. "Wait. You forgot your gun." She disappeared inside, got his holster he'd laid on the table, and one of the solar torches. He gratefully took his gun, and she helped him strap his holster on. Then he took the torch, realizing his feelings for her were killing his brain cells. He'd never forgotten his weapon before.

Pulling himself away from her, he stepped off the porch and walked out into the darkness.

FIFTY-TWO

MARK'S FATHER'S VICTORIAN WAS UP THE STREET FROM his mother's house. It had been purchased as an act of spite, to plague Mark's mother after her new marriage. Vic had purchased the biggest house in the neighborhood, and at first, Mark believed that his dad had moved to Oak Hollow subdivision just to be closer to him.

But Vic hadn't spent all that much time with him, which had been baffling. It had taken a few years to figure out that the move had nothing to do with him.

He'd inherited the house after his dad's death, and it had sat just as Vic left it, except for the pornography. After his father's crimes were exposed, Mark had taken the boxes full of smut and burned them in a pit in the backyard. He planned to sell the house after the Pulses, when banks reopened and the economy rebounded and real estate prices returned to normal. Now he wondered if he should make it available to a family like little Ruth's.

Instead of going in the front door, he went around back. In the light of the torch, he saw the pool thick with algae, and all the patio furniture his father had bought for the parties he loved to throw. Against the back fence, Mark had stacked up parts he'd gathered for the solar equipment he'd learned to build—old doors, windshields, broken and discarded mirrors, television boxes, broken microwaves. It was beginning to look like the yard in *Sanford and Son*.

He walked across the grass, still wet with melted snow, and looked through the items he had collected. It was all still there.

He'd learned about solar energy when he sought out the owner of a solar panels store in Birmingham a few months ago. He'd found the store closed, but questioned other merchants in the area and found out who owned it. Finding the man's name in the phone book, Mark went to his house. He found Norman Phillips doing what almost everyone else with land was—planting vegetables in his yard.

Mark introduced himself. "I want to talk to you about what it might take to build homemade solar panels for energy," he said.

Delighted at his interest, Norman walked him around his house, where he showed him all the ways he was using solar energy. Most of his equipment had been professionally manufactured and installed by his own crew long before the outage, but he allowed Mark to examine them to learn how they functioned. Mark realized that if he could find someplace to get glass panels, reflective items like chrome sheets or tin foil, and things that could pass for insulation, he could harness the sun to bring energy back to homes.

Norman took Mark back to his empty store. Digging through his file cabinets, he found a stapled booklet that he handed to Mark.

"Some guy had a website that I printed this from a couple of years ago. Tells how to assemble free stuff you can find around town—like glass storm doors or cracked mirrors—to make everything you need to use solar energy."

Mark skimmed the booklet. The information was pure gold. "Would you mind if I take this and give it to my friend who's a reporter for the *Crockett Times*? It'll help a lot of people."

Phillips considered that for a moment. "If I ever intend to open my business again, letting you publish that would be pretty stupid."

Mark wasn't surprised, but he didn't give up. "Mr. Phillips, do you have any idea how many people are going to die this winter? The families living in apartments already have it bad enough. This could save their lives and make the winter bearable."

Norman nodded. "Maybe I should go back into business. Start making these things for money."

"The people I want to help can't afford to pay for them. Come on, Mr. Phillips. Don't you want to help keep people alive during such tough times?"

Phillips had finally told him to take the booklet, as long as he brought it back.

Mark had promptly given it to Deni, and her editor had put out a special edition of the paper to publish it. After that, as Mark rode through the streets of Crockett, he'd seen dozens of people implementing the ideas in one way or another. He'd sent a copy of the paper to the mayors of large metropolitan areas in the north, hoping it would help the millions of apartment dwellers there. Whether they'd used it or not, he had no way of knowing. But he hoped they'd seized the information as he had.

Mark had spent the next several weeks showing those in the apartments in Crockett how to make solar panels for their windows using black garbage bags and other easy-to-find items. He hoped it had lowered the mortality rate when the temperatures dropped.

Crossing the yard to the patio, he went to the back door and unlocked it, leading his way in with the torch. As the light illuminated the living room, Mark froze.

His father's house had been ransacked, just like his own. Holding the lantern's post under his casted arm, he closed his hand around his pistol, and walked through the living room. His father had hired an interior design student to decorate the place, and ignoring the Victorian architecture of the house, she'd decorated it like a tropical beach resort. The wet bar with a Tiki roof covering it remained intact, but all the cabinets beneath the bar were open, the contents pulled out. The red Hawaiian print couch cushions were pulled off the sofa, and once again, pictures had been removed from the walls. The sand-colored shag rug had been rolled back—exposing the mahogany wood floors beneath. A few of the floorboards had been pried up.

What were they looking for?

A chill ran through him as he realized that the ones who'd robbed his mother's house had come here, as well.

He went upstairs, looking through each bedroom. Some of the more valuable items his father owned had been taken, but other valuables had been left behind. Things lay all over the floor in every room. There hadn't been one nook or cranny they hadn't emptied or explored in some way.

He went to his father's bedroom. The chest at the foot of the bed had been opened, the front of it kicked in. He looked inside—empty.

And then it occurred to him. That was where he'd found the gold.

The thought backed him up against the wall, and he stared at the chest for a moment. Why would anyone kick in the chest that used to hold the gold coins, unless they knew they had been there?

His heart raced as he leaned the solar light against the wall. Sitting on the bed, he tried to think. No one knew about that gold. He hadn't told a soul.

Could someone from under the bridge have found out about his dad's house? But why would they have kicked the chest in? That was the act of someone enraged that it was empty.

It couldn't be the escaped prisoners, since the first break-in happened while they'd all still been incarcerated. But he couldn't tell when this break-in had occurred. It could have been the same night, or as recently as today. Or it could have been long before. He hadn't even been in the house in over a month.

Yes, it had something to do with the gold. The knowledge throbbed through him, making his bones ache. What did that mean? Would neither of his homes be safe until the robbers found the gold?

He went around the house, checking the windows and doors, trying to see how they had gotten in. There didn't seem to be any sign of forced entry.

He thought of the gold, hidden in the tree stump. Was it still there?

Locking the house, he used the torch to find his way into the woods surrounding Oak Hollow. It was difficult to see at night, but he made his way down the path he'd trod so many times before. In moments, he reached the stump. He looked back through the trees, hoping no one could see him. Without leaves, the trees provided little cover.

When he was satisfied that he hadn't been followed, he pulled out the leaves stuffed into the stump, and saw the tool box. He opened it.

The gold coins were still there.

If he knew who wanted them so badly, he would take the stupid box and give it to them. The gold wasn't worth all this.

He closed the box and placed it back inside the stump. As he covered it back with dead leaves, paranoia crept over him.

When he'd found the gold in his father's bedroom, he hadn't expected it to bring him such trouble. He should have known that everything his father touched did that.

Making his way back through the woods to his mother's backyard, he stuck the torch into the ground and got his bike and a flashlight out of his garage. His ski cap sat on the table, so he grabbed it and pulled it on. Riding was hard with one arm, but he made it to the bridge on I–20, to see if Ruth and her family were still there. If they were, he could talk to her father and find out whom they'd told about the gold.

He left his bike hidden in the trees and made his way to the indigent community. A fire rippled in the same pit as the other night, and several sat huddled around it. He pulled the ski cap low over his forehead, careful not to irritate the stitches. Hiding his cast under his jacket so he wouldn't look vulnerable, he ambled through, looking for the family to whom he'd given the coins. Their brown tent was gone, and he didn't see little Ruth.

He did see one of the other men who'd been here that night. The toothless man with one false eye sat beside the fire, picking through a bag of garbage.

Mark stooped down next to him. "How ya doing?"

The man glanced up at him. "I ain't got nothing you want."

"I don't want anything."

The man regarded him in the firelight. "Hey, you're the dude brought us meat. You got anymore?"

Mark wished he did. "No, not tonight."

Crestfallen, the man went back to his garbage.

"Hey, listen," Mark said in a low voice. "When I was here the other night, there was a family here. Had two little girls. One of them named Ruth. Are they still here?"

Preoccupied, the man didn't look like he was going to answer. Finally, he said, "They moved on. Came into a windfall somehow, wound up gettin' a room."

Mark's eyebrows shot up. "Really? A windfall, huh? What'd they do, win the lottery?"

"Got me. I thought the lotteries went out with the electricity."

Maybe they'd used the coins as he'd intended. "Good for them," he said. "I'm glad to hear that." If the man didn't know about the gold, maybe they'd kept it to themselves. If that was true, then who had come looking for more?

The man found a brown apple core and scarfed it down.

A conversation was growing heated on the other side of the fire, and Mark looked over and saw a group of men huddled in the trees. He couldn't see their faces, but one accented voice rose above the others. It sounded like Tree House.

He backed away from the fire, stepping back into the shadows. Making his way around the fire, he got in close enough to the huddle to hear what they were saying.

"We can't be seen in town in de daylight. If we gon' do our stealin', it has to be in de night."

"But I can't go tonight." It was Gus, who'd held Pete during Tree House's charade. "I got two kids and a wife fit to be tied. Night's the only time I can go see them without being caught."

"Hey, we stand together or we fall. Now, are you in dis wit' me or not?"

Mark held his breath as he waited for Gus's response.

"I *said*, are you in dis wit' me or not?"

"I'm not, man."

Mark moved around a tree and saw the two men facing off.

"I'm sick of this," Gus said. "I want out. I'll go get my family and we'll leave town. But I don't got to put up with this. They catch you, you're going down for life. Killing two deputies? Almost killing the sheriff hisself? What you got to lose? I don't want to be with you when you start gunning down more people, bringing attention on all of us. You ain't got fear, man, but I ain't ashamed to say I do."

Tree House grabbed Gus's throat and slammed him against a tree. "Man, I broke you out. You owe me."

Gus wouldn't back down. "I don't owe you nothing!"

"Hey, man, calm down." It was the third guy, one of the men who'd been in a different cell. He came between them and made Tree House let go. Gus rubbed his neck.

"We have to stick together, man, like brothers. Tree House is right. There's just no other option."

So what did that mean? More people dead?

Mark's mind raced. He had to get word to the deputy before these men carried out Tree House's plans—whatever they were. Mark couldn't possibly arrest them himself, not with his injuries. No, he'd have to hurry to the sheriff's department and hope Wheaton was still there.

Quietly, he went back through the woods, got on his bike, and with one arm on the handlebars, headed for the sheriff's station.

FIFTY-THREE

Four of the escaped prisoners were sitting in the front room of the sheriff's department, hands cuffed and feet shackled, when Mark dashed in. Six volunteer deputies were processing them. They'd clearly been hard at work since he left the station.

He found Wheaton in the jail, where he'd just locked up another three. "Deputy, I found Dante Miller, Gus Cole, and one of the other prisoners. We've got to go get them now, because they won't be there long."

Wheaton looked exhausted, but his reaction was instant. Hurrying out of the jail room, he started barking out orders. "Roberts, Hernando, Jackson, and Ward—you guys come with me. We've got some more prisoners to round up." He glanced back at Mark. "Where are they?"

He told them of the tent community under the bridge. Surprisingly, Wheaton knew all about it. The men grabbed extra boxes of ammunition, and Mark followed them out to the van. He started to get in, but Wheaton stopped him. "Hold up, Green. You're not coming. With your injuries, you're a liability."

"But I have to show you where they are."

"I know that place better than you do. I can't tell you how many arrests I've made there."

"But the men—do you even know what they look like?"

"Those men have rap sheets as long as my arm. I've gotten to know Cole and Miller real well over the years." The others climbed in and slammed the door.

Mark stood there, frustrated, as they drove away. Under his breath, he prayed that they'd capture the three criminals without any bullets flying.

He went back inside and helped the two remaining volunteers march the shackled men into the jail cells. When they were locked up, and he wasn't needed anymore, he decided to go to the Brannings' house. Maybe Doug could help him figure out what was going on with the break-in at his father's house.

It was 12:30 a.m. by the time Mark knocked on the Brannings' door. He knew the family was probably sleeping. He hoped those in the upstairs rooms wouldn't hear him. But Doug and Kay's bedroom was downstairs. Maybe Doug wasn't a heavy sleeper.

He heard movement in the house, and he shone his flashlight on his own face, so Doug could see through the peephole that it was him. The deadbolt clicked and the door came open. Doug looked out at Mark. "What's wrong?" Doug stood barefoot, his rifle at his side, wearing a T-shirt and a pair of sweatpants, his hair mashed on one side and sticking up on the other.

"Doug, I'm really sorry to wake you up. But I need to talk to you."

"Sure," Doug said. "Come in."

He led Mark to his study, and quickly lit an oil lamp on his desk. "Has something happened?"

"Yeah, something has." Mark told him about finding Tree House and the others. "But there's more. I was at my dad's house tonight, and it's been broken into also. Something occurred to me that may explain some of what's going on."

Doug leaned on the desk, the shadows deepening the lines on his face. "I'm listening."

Mark leaned on the other side of the desk, locking into Doug's gaze. "When I was going through my father's things a few months ago, I found a chest with some gold coins. They were U.S. Eagle gold bullion. They weighed an ounce each and there were a hundred of them."

Doug whistled. "Wow, that's a lot of gold."

"Yes, it is."

"What did you do with it?"

Mark glanced down at his hands. "Well, I thought of sharing it with Mom and John, but I worried that spending it might be a little dangerous."

"Dangerous how?"

"If people knew I had it, they might come looking for more. So I hid it away."

"Okay," Doug said. "That makes sense."

"If we'd been starving or something, I probably would have used it. But let's face it. My family's done pretty well through the outage. I was tempted to use it to help the people in the apartments, but what they really needed was my labor and ideas. Again, I worried that some of the shadier guys there might turn on me if they knew I had gold. I've kept the family fed, John has been sending money home to my mom, and we haven't been desperate. But the other night I used some."

"Yeah?"

"The night before I was arrested, when I sneaked off to get away from Grantham's gang, I went to this place under the bridge on I–20. There were lots of people living under there, out in the elements. Families and children."

Doug hadn't heard this before. He sat up straighter. "Mark, it was snowing that night."

Mark nodded. "I had taken three of the coins with me, in case I had to pay for a place to stay. There was this little girl who kept trying to talk to me. I felt like she was in jeopardy, being there around homeless men, some who looked pretty dangerous. And I wanted to get her family out of there."

"So you gave her the coins?"

"Three of them. I told her to give them to her dad, and then I disappeared."

Doug stared at him as he processed that. "Wait a minute." He pushed back his rolling chair and came around the desk.

"What?"

"Mark, today when we were arresting Blake and Randy, when they told us about the two guys who hired them ..." He looked at the wall, as if running the conversation back through his mind. "They said the guys paid them with gold coins."

"They *said* that?"

"Yes, four coins, and they had one left. Wheaton took it into evidence."

Mark slowly stood up. "Doug, did you see the coin?"

"I did. Mark, it was a U.S. gold Eagle. I know these coins. It was an ounce."

"No way!" How could that be? Mark stared at Doug, his mind reeling with possibilities. "Where is the coin now?"

"I don't know. Wheaton has it somewhere."

Mark rubbed his jaw. His stubble was softening into a beard. He didn't even remember the last time he'd shaved. "If their story is true, and they were paid with four coins, then that had nothing to do with the family I gave mine to."

"Maybe they lied. Randy and Blake could only produce that one. Maybe the person that family rented the apartment from used the coin."

Mark couldn't make all that compute in his head. "Why would Randy and Blake lie about how many coins they were given? I mean, they admitted to accepting payment to lie about me. What difference would it make how much they were paid?" He shook his head. "No, I don't think they lied."

"Do you think Blake and Randy could have found the coins where you hid them?"

That made even less sense. "If they did, why wouldn't they take all of them?" He sat back down, trying to work through this new information.

Ruth's family had spent their three coins on a new place to live.

Randy and Blake had four of the same coins.

Who else would have a stash of U.S. Eagle gold bullion coins weighing one ounce each?

Suddenly, clarity dawned. He got back up, shaking his head. "No way. It can't be."

Doug's eyes were intense as he locked his gaze on him. "What, Mark?"

Mark didn't want it to be true, but he had to say it. "My brothers."

Doug's mouth fell open. "Do you think they're back?"

Mark paced across the carpet. "I don't know. But I found a receipt that my father had for the gold bullion. That's how I knew he'd bought them and not stolen them. My dad and my brothers were in business together. It would stand to reason that if Dad had found a good source for gold, he would have told them. Maybe they bought some at the same time."

"That's possible. It might even be likely. So do you think they're the ones who paid off Blake and Randy?"

"Two guys," Mark said. "In ski masks, so they couldn't be identified."

Doug swallowed. "Mark, do you realize what this means? If they were the ones who paid off Blake and Randy, then one of them is probably Zach's shooter. But why?"

Mark shook his head. "I don't know. Maybe they just wanted the meat. My brothers never were good hunters."

Doug sat on the edge of his desk. "I can believe they did it. I met them once, when Deni disappeared with your father. The things they said about her were vile. I wanted to kill them myself."

Mark thought of the boys he'd known his whole life. He'd never gotten along with them … but they were his brothers, nonetheless.

"The Abernathys dead in their dining room," Doug went on. "The Whitsons, robbed for their food. No one thought your father did that alone. That's why they suspected your brothers … and even you."

It was all becoming clear. "They set me up," Mark whispered. "My brothers set me up. They had a bike trailer with the same design as mine. And according to the Emorys, there was a drunk guy in the hall, creating a ruckus just before Zach's ventilator was unplugged. It drew the nurse out of the room. Then the other one went in and unplugged the ventilator. Two guys—one to divert attention, the other who claimed to be me as he was trying to shut Zach up."

"Did Zach know your brothers?"

"Probably. They were at Dad's house all the time before he died. Zach just lives a few houses down. They were probably afraid he'd recognized them."

"It's them," Doug said. "I know it is. Your brothers are killers, Mark, and they're looking for that gold that was supposed to be in your father's house. They know you have it."

Mark realized his brothers had hated him since the day he was born. The thought sank deep into his psyche and settled next to the realities about his father.

"You're not safe until they find it, son."

Mark's throat was tight as he forced the words out. "That's why we've got to find them first."

FIFTY-FOUR

EXHAUSTED AS HE WAS, MARK RODE BACK TO THE SHERIFF'S department with Doug. Wheaton's van arrived the same time they did. The deputy chief saw them as he got out of the van.

"We got 'em, boys!"

Mark and Doug helped get the three shackled, angry men out of the back seat. As they led them inside, Tree House kept up a vicious, profane monologue. Mark had never been so happy to see anyone behind bars. He hoped they'd never let him out.

When things settled down, he told Wheaton about his brothers and the gold. Wheaton took notes but decided to wait until morning to try to find them, so they could all get some rest.

As he and Doug started home, Doug insisted that he spend the night at the Brannings'. "You're not safe at either of your houses, Mark. I won't take no for an answer."

Mark couldn't argue with that. "All right, but I'm sleeping on the couch. No way I'm putting anybody out of their bed in the middle of the night."

"Fair enough," Doug said. "The couch it is."

At the house, Doug brought him some blankets and a pillow, and Mark sank into the cushions. Despite troubling thoughts about his murderous brothers, Mark fell into a deep, exhausted sleep.

NEXT MORNING, WHEN THEY HAD ALL FINISHED BREAKFAST, Mark took his mother and Deni upstairs to Deni's room and broke the news of his brothers' involvement.

"It never ends." Martha fought back tears as she paced across Deni's room. "I'm telling you, Larry and Jack have been jealous of you since you were born. When they would come for their weekends with us, I lived in fear of their hurting you. I had to watch you like a hawk. They hated me too, even though I didn't even *meet* your father until years after his divorce from their mother."

Deni sat on her bed, writing the facts on a notepad. "Mark, does Wheaton plan to interview their wives?"

"I'm sure he will today. I hope he'll let me go with him."

His mother slapped her hand over her mouth. "Mark, I'm worried for your life. They're evil, just like your dad. And all the sheriff's department has is a bunch of volunteers. How will they ever find them? They're *smart*!"

"I'm smarter."

A vein in her forehead bulged, and her mouth trembled. "They're desperate. Just give them the gold, honey."

"How?"

"I don't know."

"Even if I knew how to get it to them, it wouldn't solve the problem. We have to get them off the streets."

She burst into tears, and he pulled her into his arms and held her. Over his mother's head, he glanced at Deni. Her head was down, and she wrote furiously in her notebook.

What was she working on?

His mother finally pulled away and, wiping her face, went downstairs. Mark turned back to Deni. "What are you doing?"

"Making a list," she said. "Brainstorming ways to get word to them. We could use the gold to lure them out. I could post something on the message boards or put it in the paper. If they're in town, maybe they'd see it."

"They'd know it was a trick."

"Yeah, but if they want it badly enough ..." Her voice trailed off, and she brought her troubled eyes back up to him. "Your mother's right, Mark. You're in a lot of danger. Even more than we thought."

He lowered himself into the chair in front of Deni's makeup table and picked up a bottle of perfume. Bringing it to his nose, he recognized her scent. Feminine, fresh, clean ... She must not use much—just a dot behind her ears, like his mother. Just enough to implant that scent in his brain.

"I think besides talking to the wives, you need to talk to Larry's child. If he's been home, even for a little while, his wife might not say so. But children are more likely to spill the beans."

He set the perfume down and touched her hairbrush. "Yeah, I guess that's a good idea."

"Maybe you could tell the wives about the gold. Make up some story about how you feel bad taking it, and you want to share it with them or something. If they have contact with Larry and Jack, they'd get word to them. You know they would."

"Yeah, but what if they're not in contact?"

"It's worth a try."

Yes, she was right. He imagined how that would work. Laura, Larry's wife, would deny seeing the brothers. Maybe he could leave her a deposit of one coin, and give her a fake location for the rest of the gold. They could post men in the woods around the fake location and catch his brothers when they came to get the gold. But without leaves on the trees, there was too much visibility, and it would be too difficult to hide.

No, there had to be another way.

As he tried to think it out, his eyes skimmed the surface of Deni's makeup table, lingering on the lipstick she wore on special occasions, the mascara, the tint for her cheeks ...

The train ticket.

He picked it up, read the destination. Washington, D.C. His heart plummeted.

Deni sprang off the bed. "Oh, I meant to tell you about that."

He read the date. It was for March 1—three weeks away.

One way.

Deni grabbed the ticket, along with the envelope containing Craig's letter. "Mark, I got this yesterday. I came to the station to tell you, but I got sidetracked with the toilets. I'm not going, of course."

He tried not to look hurt. "Are you sure?"

"Of course I'm sure. Here, read the letter. I haven't even given it a thought since I got it."

He took it and read the handwriting of her former fiancé. His mouth went dry as he got to the part about the job offer. "Great offer," he managed to say.

She just looked at him. "Mark, please don't start thinking this means something. I'm going to send it back and tell him to get his money back."

"He said he'd come here."

"I'll tell him it's a waste of time."

He didn't know what to say. Slowly, he read back over the letter. The job was something Deni was made for. What a stepping stone it would be for her career. If she took it, she would be on the fast track to success. There would be no stopping her.

Swallowing hard, he said, "Maybe you should go."

She snatched the letter out of his hand. "Don't be ridiculous."

He met her eyes. "It's not ridiculous, Deni. It's what you've wanted since you went to college."

She grunted. "Mark, I don't want the same things now that I wanted then. You know that."

He hoped that was true. But looking at her now, so beautiful, so intelligent, so full of the greatest kind of potential … What if she went? Could he hold it against her?

And if she stayed for him … wouldn't she always regret it?

He got up, slid his hands into his jeans pockets, and walked to the window. "If the outage hadn't happened, you'd be there already. You'd be married and on television in the heart of the nation."

"Not on television," she said. "I was just going to be an intern. It's not like they were putting me on the Nightly News."

He felt her behind him. She touched his back.

"Mark, the outage did happen. I'm not the same person I was. The Pulses have brought out the worst in a lot of people, but I think it's brought out the best in us. It's changed my priorities. I'm not even sure I want to go into television journalism anymore. I may want to keep working for a paper."

He swallowed the lump in his throat and turned to look down at her. "That would be a crying shame. You have a face for television."

A smile flashed across her eyes. "But I love the power of the printed word. It used to be all about me wanting to make my mark. I wanted to be famous. But that's not important to me anymore."

His gaze drifted back to that ticket. "But the job isn't reporting. It's communications. It would be such a great position for you."

Her smile faded, and her eyes grew serious. "Are you trying to talk me into this?"

Was he? "No, I'm not. I just don't want you to have doubts … regrets."

"If I'm so gifted, I can get a job anywhere. But this isn't about the job, is it, Mark? It's about him. And about you."

He blew out a hard breath and looked at that ticket in her hand. "I come with a lot of baggage, Deni."

Her eyes softened. "Mark, when Craig was here, he felt inferior to you. You're stronger, more capable, more inventive, more giving. You're the one with integrity and faith and ingenuity. You're like my dad, and he's the greatest man I know."

High praise, Mark thought. If only it were true. People were always accusing him of being like *his* dad. To be like Doug …

Just the thought filled him with a fragile pride.

Deni took his hands and made him look at her. "Mark, tell me we have a future together."

His heart raced with longing, and he wanted to hold her and tell her that they did, that they would be together forever. "We can have a future even if you go. If we're meant to be together, we will be."

"Would you come with me?"

He chuckled softly. "Craig didn't send a ticket for me."

"Hey, you've got a pot of gold."

She was joking, he knew, but his smile faded. "I need to stay here until the Pulses are over. There's no place for me in Washington. I'd be so out of my element."

He didn't like seeing the pain in her eyes.

"So you're telling me to go without you and take a job 750 miles away, working with a man I was once going to marry?"

Mark knew the whole thing was stupid. What was he thinking?

"You still think I'm shallow, don't you, Mark? You think the glamour of a job like that, a man like Craig, will lure me. You don't believe I've changed."

"It's not bad to have ambition, Deni."

She tossed the ticket down and went into her closet. "I cleaned toilets with you yesterday," she said as she emerged with her tennis shoes.

"I know you did, Deni. You were a trouper. I just don't want life to go back to normal, and have you feel like you're settling for Crockett ... or for me."

Tears burst into her eyes. She sat down on the bed and pulled her shoes on. Tying them with furious motions, she said, "It's just the opposite, Mark. If I had married Craig, I would have been settling for him. And he would have known it. He would have spent his life comparing himself to *you*."

Getting back to her feet, she faced off with him. "I'm staying here, and that's that."

Relief flooded through him, but he couldn't believe she meant it.

She let out a hard sigh. "I have to go to the well. My family needs water."

He just nodded. "I think your dad and I are going with Wheaton to look for my brothers."

Crossing her arms, she started for the stairs. At the doorway, she looked back at him. "Be careful, Mark."

"I promise," he said.

FIFTY-FIVE

DENI DIDN'T GO STRAIGHT TO THE WELL. INSTEAD, SHE went to her parents' bedroom door. Knocking, she said, "Mom? Dad?"

Her mother called, "Come in, Deni."

Deni stepped inside. Her mother sat in the center of the bed. Her father was pulling on his boots. "What is it, honey?"

"I need advice."

"About what?"

She sighed. "That letter I got from Craig yesterday?"

Kay's eyebrows shot up. "Yes, I wanted to read it, but I got busy and forgot."

"Yeah, well. He sent me a train ticket for March 1, and a job offer working for the government in communications. Mark found the ticket, and got all weird about it, telling me that I should go."

Doug stopped tying his boot, and Kay slid to the edge of the bed. "And you want to know if you should?" she asked weakly.

"No! I know I don't want to go. The advice I need is about Mark. I don't get why he thinks I should take this job."

Kay looked at Doug, relief in her eyes.

"I mean, if he loves me, wouldn't he want me here with him?"

"Has he told you he loves you?" Kay asked.

Deni groaned and dropped into a chair. "No, but I've told him."

Doug smiled and pulled his other boot on. "I don't think you have anything to worry about, sweetheart. He may not say it with words, but every time he looks at you, it's apparent."

"I don't think he trusts me. When the power comes back on, I think he expects me to go back to the way I was. And frankly, that's a little insulting."

"Well, you can't blame him for wondering about that," Doug said. "I've thought it myself."

"Dad!" She sat up rigid in the chair. "Mom, tell him. I wasn't a real Christian before the outage. Christ has molded me and taught me that it's not about me. I know I'm not perfect, and I still have a long way to go. But I've *come* a long way."

"Of course you have, honey." Kay got up and came to sit on the arm of the chair. "It's just that when the power comes back on and things start going back to normal, you'll have the whole world in front of you."

"But I don't want the whole world. I want Mark."

Kay's face glowed. "That just thrills me, Deni. I'd like nothing better than to see you married to him. And I don't want you to leave here in three weeks."

"Neither do I," her dad said. "But don't blame him for worrying about the future."

She felt betrayed. "Never mind." Getting up, she started back to the door.

"Honey, wait," Kay said. "You know Mark loves you. He just wants what's best for you, even if it hurts him. We've all seen how he is with you. He'd give his life for you."

"But that's how Mark is. He'd give his life for *anybody*. I want to be special to him. I want to be the one he's chosen, not the one he flippantly sends away to test her wings."

"I think you are the one he's chosen," Kay said. "He just wants to make sure *he's* the one *you've* chosen."

FIFTY-SIX

Coming down the stairs, Mark saw Deni go into her parents' room and knew they were talking about the train ticket, Craig ... and him. He glanced out the back window and saw his mother helping Beth and Logan feed the chickens. He pulled his coat on over one arm and draped the other side over his cast and sling. Stepping out on the front porch, he drew in a long breath.

The wind was cool, sweeping across the wet ground, blowing his hair against his stitches. The sleep had done him good, but soreness had crept into his muscles and bones, leaving him feeling more bruised and battered than before. With his Frankenstein scar, his collarbone brace, and the sling and cast, he looked like something out of a horror movie.

Why would Deni be attracted to him?

He tried to push the ticket and job offer out of his mind and concentrate on what he had to do today. He needed to find a picture of his brothers to take to the sheriff's department and the hospital. If he could get Zach to ID one of them as the shooter, and ask Zach's hospital roommate if this was the guy who claimed to be Mark; if Blake and Randy could tell them if these were the guys who'd paid them off ...

Then maybe they could manage to find them, and this nightmare could come to an end. He got on his bike and rode to his father's house to look for a picture.

But the melancholy that had shadowed him for days still hung over him, pressing down on his spirit. Anger swirled afresh in his heart, mocking the forgiveness he'd shown yesterday. The temporary peace it had brought to his heart seemed as fragile as lace today.

And new anger layered itself on the old. This time, it was anger at himself. Telling Deni she should take the ticket and go back to Washington?

What was wrong with him?

He didn't want to believe he had done it to bait her, to see if she would take him up on it. Was it some kind of sick test he was giving her, to see if she really loved him?

Or was it a test for *him*? If so, who was testing him? God or Satan?

He thought of what Jesus had told the apostle Peter, before he betrayed Christ: *Simon, Simon, Satan has asked to sift you as wheat. But I have prayed for you, Simon, that your faith may not fail. And when you have turned back, strengthen your brothers.*

There was so much to learn from those statements. First, Satan had to ask permission before he could sift. Satan's power was limited. That knowledge comforted Mark. But an even greater comfort was the fact that Jesus had been on Peter's side—praying for him through his trial. Mark knew that Jesus was interceding for him as well.

Peter's faith had wobbled before the crucifixion, when he'd denied Christ three times. But it had rebounded, and the apostle had gone on to strengthen so many others. He'd even written those famous words that warned Christians of the warfare around them: *Your enemy the devil prowls around like a roaring lion looking for someone to devour.*

Peter knew of what he spoke. And so did Mark. Satan was after him, but as Joseph, one of the great Old Testament heroes, had said, *What Satan meant for evil, God intended for good.*

Even knowing these things, Mark felt more devoured than sifted, and he prayed that his faith was strong enough to withstand the enemy's flaming arrows. He could take his brothers' murderous greed and hatred. He could take the disdain of his neighbors and friends.

But losing Deni might just do him in.

Telling her that would be the height of selfishness. But he didn't know if he had the faith to put their relationship in God's hands. To believe that if it was meant to be, no job or geography—and no man—would stand between them.

He pulled his bike around behind his father's house. Unlocking the door, he stepped into the tropical living room and searched the debris on the floor for the framed family pictures that had been pulled off the walls.

Vic hadn't been big on memory preservation, but there had been a few pictures of himself and the boys. The ones that had made it into frames had been the ones that had brag value, like the shot of his brothers holding a twenty-pound bass between them. His dad had gotten the picture blown up and framed.

Where had he hung it?

Was that the one he'd put over his bed?

He hurried up the stairs, stepped over the clutter in the hallway, and went into his father's room.

There it was, the only picture the marauders had left hanging—an eleven-inch-by-sixteen-inch picture of Larry and Jack, matted and framed in bamboo. It had been taken a year ago, when his brothers and father had taken a trip to Alaska. Mark had opted out.

Though he hadn't seen his brothers in about seven months, they couldn't have changed much. They may have lost some weight, and their hair might be longer. They may have grown beards. But he was sure they would still bear a striking resemblance to his father.

He took the picture off the wall, peeled off the cardboard back, then rolled up the photo and slid it into his coat pocket. Quickly, he looked around for more pictures. He found two and stripped them out of their frames.

Then he headed back to the sheriff's department.

Deputy Wheaton was still there, along with the men who'd worked the night shift. Brad Caldwell and a few fresh recruits had already reported. Mark knew Doug would be along soon.

He unrolled the pictures and flattened them on a desktop. "Here's who we're looking for," he told Wheaton. "Larry and Jack Green."

"Great." Wheaton picked up the biggest picture, got a flashlight off his desk, and took it into the jail. Mark followed him.

The smell was considerably better than it had been yesterday before Mark and Deni cleaned the toilets. Instead of human waste, the smell of bleach filled the air. So far the jail wasn't too overcrowded, so each man had his own bunk. Most of them still slept.

Tree House was stretched out on a bottom bunk, all alone in his cell. Wheaton must have decided to keep him isolated so he couldn't kill anyone else. Mark was glad of that. But the man looked way too comfortable for a cold-blooded killer.

Mark followed Wheaton to the cell where Blake and Randy were housed, along with some of the men from the vigilante group. Blake and Randy looked like children sacked out on their beds. Blake was on the top bunk, his arm slung over the side, his sheet tangled around his legs. Randy lay on his side in a fetal position, his hand cradling his head.

"Mahaffey, Kraft, get over here." Wheaton turned on the flashlight, adding to the light coming in from the windows at the tops of the walls.

Blake sat up, bleary-eyed. Randy stirred and lifted his head. "Are we getting out now?"

"Dream on," Wheaton said. "I want you to take a look at this picture."

Randy looked crestfallen as he got off the bed. Blake dropped from the top mattress and walked barefoot across the cold concrete.

"You ever seen these two men before?"

Randy shrugged. "Faces aren't familiar."

"But I recognize the jacket," Blake said.

Mark held his breath.

"One of the guys who paid us to lie was wearing a brown leather bomber jacket just like that. But we couldn't see their faces because they had those ski masks on."

"Same jacket," Wheaton repeated. "Guys, take a good hard look. Do you remember anything else about them?"

Randy began to look hopeful. "Well, it's not in the picture, but they had these cool alligator boots. I remember wondering where they got them."

Mark knew those boots. He looked at Wheaton. "Those are their favorite boots. They strut around in them like Butch Cassidy and the Sundance Kid."

"Are you saying you believe our story now?" Blake asked Wheaton.

Wheaton rolled the picture back up. "I'm just reviewing your statement. Anything else you want to tell us?"

"No," Blake said. "We told you everything we know. Who are those guys, anyway?"

Wheaton didn't answer. He turned off his flashlight and headed back to the door.

"Mark," Randy called as Mark started away. "Do you know them?"

Mark didn't think they deserved an answer. He closed the jail door behind them. "It's them, Deputy. I'm telling you, my brothers are the ones who shot Zach and pinned it on me. They broke into my house looking for the gold, and they unplugged Zach's ventilator. Zach said the guy who shot him looked familiar. He's seen them at my dad's house. He lived just a few houses down."

Wheaton nodded. "I'll get over to the hospital and show the pictures to Zach and his roommate. If they confirm it, you can come with me to the DA's office and tell him about the gold. There's already a warrant for their arrest for the murders in your neighborhood months ago."

"Right—and that's why they're hiding. It's not going to be easy to find them."

"We'll start in the most obvious place," Wheaton said. "We'll get a warrant to search their wives' houses again."

FIFTY-SEVEN

As Mark expected, Zach confirmed that Jack had been the one who shot him. Charles Hoyt, Zach's roommate, was certain Jack was the man who'd unplugged the ventilator. And a nurse who'd been on the floor that day identified Larry as the drunk man who'd drawn attention from Zach's room.

Armed with search and arrest warrants, Kevlar vests, and enough ammo to take out a small army, Wheaton, Doug, Brad, and Mark headed to the homes of Mark's sisters-in-law.

Brad sat up front with Wheaton, and Doug sat in the back with Mark. Tension hung over them all. Mark thought of Deni's admonition to be careful and knew his mother had probably been on her knees all morning.

As they drove down the country road to where Jack's wife lived, he looked over at Doug. Over the rumble of the engine, he asked, "So did she tell you about the train ticket?"

Doug met his eyes. "Yeah, she told us she doesn't intend to go. That you're encouraging her to."

Mark looked out the window.

"Is that true? Do you want her to go?"

"Of course not." Mark sighed. "I just don't want to hold her back from the job of her dreams."

"Even if it's there with him?"

Mark swallowed. "I want what's best for her."

"Well, that's not what's best. Living 750 miles away with some guy who would bring her nothing but emptiness and misery? And this song and dance he gave her about going to church, praying—"

"Maybe it's true," Mark muttered. "Maybe God's working in his life."

"I don't trust him." Doug's eyes were angry as Mark turned back toward him. "Deni can do anything, get a job anywhere. She doesn't have to work with him."

"I don't want her to go, either, Doug. I just don't want her to wonder someday if she should have. I don't want her to settle for something and regret it later."

"What would she be settling for, Mark? You?"

Mark didn't want to answer that. He leaned his head back on the seat and closed his eyes.

"You don't give yourself enough credit, son."

Mark didn't want to talk about it anymore. It wasn't that he lacked confidence in himself. He knew he could make Deni happy. But part of that included giving her the freedom to be who she was. She was born to shine, gifted for greatness. If he loved her, how could he cause her to be less than she was born to be?

He saw Jack's house through the trees and tried to shift his thoughts to what he would say if he saw his brothers. Would they fight? Fire on them? Try to get away? Or would they come willingly? What if Larry's children were there? He didn't like the idea of their seeing their dad in handcuffs.

They pulled off the dirt road into the driveway of Jack's house. It was a much bigger house than Jack could afford, at least according to his income on paper. But his father had taught his two older sons not to report everything, and with their shady dealings, Jack probably made a lot of unreported cash. He'd built the house just before his marriage to Grace a little more than a year ago, and it was situated on three acres. Mark had been here only once before, with his father. His sister-in-law was an insecure woman full of jealousy and bitterness, and she'd never been a friend to Mark. He knew she wouldn't be happy to see him … especially with the sheriff's department in tow.

Doug and Brad went behind the house to cover the back doors in case the men attempted to escape, and Mark followed Wheaton up the sidewalk to the plantation-style front porch. Wheaton knocked on the door.

After a moment, Grace came to the door. Her blonde hair had grown out and four inches of brown roots crowned her head. Her gaze shot past Wheaton to Mark. "What do *you* want?"

"We're looking for Jack and Larry," Mark said.

She let out a sardonic laugh. "Join the crowd."

Mark looked into the house beyond her and saw a man he didn't recognize coming into the foyer. Despite the cold, the man had his shirt off with a pair of jeans, and he walked barefoot through the house. He clearly felt at home here. Had he replaced Jack?

Wheaton identified himself, then asked, "Are you Jack Green?"

"Jack?" The name seemed bitter in his mouth. "No way, dude."

"I haven't heard from Jack," Grace said, "and I don't care if I never do again. He ran off and left me to deal with all the fallout of what him and your maniac daddy did. I don't care if he rots."

"But he's back in town, all right." The boyfriend stepped into the doorway beside her. "We do know that much. Tell 'em, Grace."

Grace crossed her arms. "He broke into the house a week ago."

Wheaton shot Mark a look. "This house?"

"Yeah, and Laura says they broke into her house too. Went pillaging through all our stuff."

Before the shooting, Mark thought. "How do you know it was him?"

She smirked. "I recognized his handwriting."

"His handwriting?"

She chuckled and exchanged looks with her boyfriend. "Come in, and I'll show you."

Mark hesitated, wondering if this was a trick, an ambush. No—she wouldn't have her boyfriend here if Jack and Larry were here, would she?

He glanced at Wheaton and saw his hand moving to his weapon as he stepped into the house. Mark trailed behind them, watching the shadows for any surprises.

She led them through the house to the master bedroom. As they walked in, Mark understood. On the wall over the king-sized bed, someone had written:

Die, you cheating tramp.

"He got the spray paint out of the garage," Grace said. "Unfortunately, I didn't have any paint to cover it with. So I'm trying to sew a wall hanging to cover it up."

The boyfriend looked livid. "If I ever get my hands on that little— "

"Mrs. Green," Wheaton cut in. "Why didn't you file a complaint about this?"

"And tell them what? That my husband broke into his own home and wrote on the wall? That he stole his own gold?"

Mark's mouth fell open. "Gold?"

"Yeah. He apparently came back for the coins he left here. Cleaned me out. Didn't even leave me a single one. I guess when he saw that I wasn't living here alone, he got a little hot under the collar."

So he was right about them having their own stash of gold. Mark looked at Wheaton, saw him looking around the room. "Show me where the gold was."

She went into her closet and got out a shoebox, opened it up. "They were in here, what was left of them. I'm glad I spent so much of it. They only got a few. Laura said they got hers too. She'd spent almost all of hers, what with the kids and all. What did they expect us to do, taking off and leaving us at a time like that?"

That explained it, Mark thought. They had come back for their coins, but when there weren't very many, they'd come looking for his.

The evidence was falling into place, giving their case a solid foundation. Now all they had to do was find Larry and Jack.

When they finished searching the house, they got back into the van and headed over to Laura's house.

Mark liked her better than Grace. She had always been friendlier to him. More than once, he'd wondered why a nice woman like her had married a cad like Larry. Now, as they drove up to her ranch-style house, sprawling on ten acres, he wondered how she had gotten along all these months. There was no garden here, with all this land. How had she provided food for her family?

As they pulled into the circular driveway, Mark saw his eight-year-old nephew shooting hoops outside, his little dog Scrappy running and jumping beside him. Mark smiled and called: "Hey, Trent, how you doing, buddy?"

The boy caught the ball and peered at him.

"It's me, Uncle Mark."

Trent dropped the ball and ran into the house.

"Nice to see you too," Mark muttered under his breath. Scrappy ran to him, wagging his tail. Mark bent down to pet the Yorkie that had once belonged to his dad. He was glad they had taken care of him.

Doug and Brad went around back, as they'd done at Grace's house, and Mark followed Wheaton to the front door. It flew open before they reached it.

Laura stood there with her toddler on her hip, her face anxious as she looked from Wheaton to Mark. "What's going on?"

Mark was stunned at how bad she looked. Abandonment had clearly not agreed with her. She looked anorexic. Her hair, which had once been thick, silky, and straight, was now frizzy and thin. Her skin was pasty, and dark circles sank into her face under her eyes.

"This is about Larry, isn't it?" Dread deepened the pain in her eyes. "Is he dead?"

Wheaton frowned, and Mark stepped forward. "Laura, why would you ask that?"

Her face almost relaxed, and she brought her bony hand up to her chest. "Because ... you show up here with the sheriff ..."

"I'm Chief Deputy Wheaton." The deputy showed her his ID. "We're looking for Larry, but we have no reason to believe he's dead."

Tears filled her eyes and a trembling smile crept across her face. "Oh, thank you, God."

She still loved him. After all he'd done, she hadn't let him go. Mark suddenly felt guilty for not checking on her and the kids. He could have helped them out. He *should* have.

"Laura, when's the last time you saw Larry?" Mark asked.

She set the baby down, and he toddled back into the house. "Seven months ago, when he and Jack disappeared."

"Grace told us he broke into your houses and stole the coins," Mark said.

Quickly, she shook her head. "Oh no, I'm sure it wasn't them. If Larry were back, he would have told me. He would have wanted to see his children." She looked over her shoulder. Trent stood behind her. He had a toy gun in his hand, and it was pointed at the door.

"Tell us about the gold," Wheaton said.

Her face twisted. "Grace shouldn't have told you that. It's none of her business."

"How much gold did they take?"

"I only had ten coins left. It could have been anyone, though. Lots of people knew I had them. I've used them all over town."

Mark looked at Wheaton, realizing that any merchant who'd gotten those coins could have paid Blake and Randy. Maybe his brothers weren't the culprits, after all. But as that thought took hold, he remembered something else. "But why would a stranger write 'Die, you cheating tramp' on Grace's wall?" he asked.

That stumped her for a moment. "I don't know." She tossed a look back at him. "Maybe *you* wrote it. You've always been judgmental."

Mark's breath hitched. "*Me?* Laura, you know I didn't break into Grace's house!"

Laura thrust her chin out. "How do I know that? Maybe Jack told you where his gold was. Maybe Larry told you where mine was."

"They never told me anything! They hated me, and you know it!"

"Maybe for good reason," she said. "Larry and Jack had nothing to do with your father's crimes, but maybe you did."

He hadn't expected such a slap-down from her, but as it sank into his gut, he told himself he shouldn't be surprised. Larry and Jack's poison had infected the whole family.

Wheaton showed her the search warrant. Reluctantly, she let Wheaton in. Mark went back to the van and waited, knowing he wasn't welcome inside.

Now he realized why he hadn't come to help her before. He had sensed how he would be received. He wondered if she believed the things she'd said.

It seemed like an eternity before the three men returned to the van. Doug again took the seat next to Mark.

"Nothing?" Mark asked.

Doug shook his head. "He's not there. Looks like he came in and got what he wanted. Laura seems close to a nervous breakdown."

Wheaton and Brad got into the front seats, and as they closed the doors, a rock hit the windshield.

Trent stood across the yard, another rock in his hand. He flashed them a profane gesture.

"Sweet kid," Wheaton said. "In a few years, I'll probably be back for him."

Mark looked at the kid who seemed so angry. "It's not his fault. He's just mimicking his dad. Doing what he was taught."

"Hating cops?"

"No. Hating me."

The boy reared back and hurled another rock at the window. This one left a nick.

"Come to think of it," Wheaton said, "I might just put the fear of God into him now."

"I'll come with you," Brad said.

Mark watched as Wheaton and Brad got out and chased the boy around the house.

Doug chuckled, but Mark didn't find it amusing. Doug's smile quickly faded. "You okay?"

"Yeah, I'm fine. It's just sad, that's all."

Doug nodded. "Yeah, it is that. So how did your brothers treat you when you were a kid?"

Mark's throat was tight. "Jack was twelve, and Larry was fourteen when I was born. I can't really blame them. My dad had dumped their mother for a string of other women. My mom came a few years after the divorce. She wasn't like the others. That's probably why he married her. When I came along, Larry and Jack felt replaced, I think."

"That explains a lot."

Mark leaned his head back on the seat. "I remember one time when I was nine or ten years old, my dad took us all hunting. There was a deer camp over near Tuscaloosa, and I thought it was going to be a great time. And the first day, it was. I shot my first rabbit, and realized I was a good marksman. But that night, things took a turn."

"What happened?"

"They all started drinking and playing poker, and all three of them wound up drunk. Larry and Jack got into a fight, rolling around on the floor like idiots, and my dad just sat back and laughed his head off. Then they turned on me. Told me I had to be initiated into their hunting club. Took me out and tied me to a tree in the middle of the woods. Made me spend the night there."

Doug gaped at him. "At ten years old? Your dad didn't do anything?"

"No, I think he was passed out drunk by the time they went back in. Next morning, I guess he realized what had happened, because he came and found me and untied me. He told me I needed to be more of a man. I decided I wasn't going on any more hunting trips with them."

Doug was silent for a moment. "So how did you learn to hunt so well?"

Mark looked down at his cast and adjusted his sling. "There was this man who was my Sunday school teacher all through junior high. My best friend Jason's dad. He used to take me hunting with them. He led me to Christ and showed me there was a better way to live."

"Thank God for him," Doug said.

Mark couldn't believe he was telling Doug all these things. He'd never felt free enough to talk this way with anyone else.

But Doug reminded him of Jason's dad. He knew Doug would understand and not see him as some kind of victim who'd never gotten over his past.

He'd gotten over it long ago. He thought of all the times after that that his dad tried to talk him into going hunting with them. He wondered if that camp still existed.

Then a thought slammed him.

"Oh, I can't believe it," he whispered, sitting straighter. "I never even thought of it. They're probably hiding there."

Doug frowned. "Where? At the deer camp?"

"Yes. I mean, *think* about it. It's out in the woods on a lake. They could hunt for food and get water, and no one would think to look for them there. They're close enough to make it home in a couple of hours if they want to, and then they could disappear again."

Doug opened the van door to get Wheaton. "Do you remember the way to the deer camp?" he asked before he got out.

Mark thought about that for a moment. "No, but my dad owned it. There's got to be a record of it somewhere in the house."

FIFTY-EIGHT

Mark found the directions to the deer camp tucked away in a folder in one of his dad's massive file cabinets. In the garage was a pegboard with a dozen keys. Mark took them all, hoping one would open the door.

Then they armed themselves with AR–15s in addition to the .40-caliber Glocks the department had already issued, and drove as fast as the old van would carry them.

On the way, Mark tried to work through what was likely to happen. It might come to a shoot-out, and he knew his siblings wouldn't hesitate to shoot their little brother.

As they turned down the dirt road to the deer camp he hadn't seen in twelve years, he began to wonder if *he* could shoot *them*. He thought of all the times he'd looked up to them, even though they hated his guts. The times he'd sought their approval in spite of their treatment of him.

Would he really be able to pull the trigger? He honestly didn't know. *God, give me the strength to do what I have to do.*

He read out the directions—fourth dirt road after the radio tower; go five miles down, then the third dirt drive past the Feed Mill.

"I think we're close," he said as they turned onto a gravel path. "The camp is less than a mile from here. Leave the van here, and we can go the rest of the way on foot so they won't hear us."

Wheaton pulled the van over. The road from that point on seemed overgrown, but fresh bike tracks were imprinted in the dirt, along with wider tires.

When they came to the little house on the lake, it was just as Mark remembered, only smaller and dirtier. Wood was chopped and piled beside the house in a loose mound. An ax blade was stuck in a stump where someone had recently left it.

And off to the side of the yard was the bike trailer with big tires, just like his.

The four of them stayed in the shelter of the trees but made their way to the back of the house. Mark gripped his pistol in his sweaty hand as he moved.

A dozen or so homemade rabbit cages, built with chicken wire and fencing pickets, stood four feet off the ground behind the house.

"Your rabbits," Mark whispered.

Doug nodded. "Looks like it."

"No smoke coming out of the chimney," Wheaton said in a low voice. "If they were here, there'd probably be a fire. Spread out and go around the house. Look for bicycles, fresh footprints. Count the windows and doors and see if any are open. Meet me back here."

They spread out. Mark kept to the back side of the house, staying in the trees as he counted the windows. None of them was open. His eyes raked over the landscape, down to the lake with a small pier.

What if Larry and Jack were in the woods, waiting to ambush them? He looked through the barren trees. No, it wouldn't be that easy for them to hide in the winter forest.

The three men returned to their starting place.

"I saw some towels hanging on a line on the south end of the house," Doug whispered. "They were dry. No open windows that I saw."

"I got a look through the windows," Wheaton said. "I didn't see movement, but they could still be in there. Let me see those keys, Mark."

Mark pulled the keys out of his pocket. "I don't know which one."

"I got close enough to see the doorknob," Wheaton whispered. "It's a Yale." He sorted through the keys and found one that had the word printed on it. "This is probably it."

"So what are you gonna do?" Brad whispered, keeping his eyes on the house. "You can't just walk in there."

"I could kick the door down if I wanted. I have an arrest warrant."

"But that could get you killed," Doug said.

"That's why I'm going to use the key. If I can get the door unlocked as quietly as possible, we may be able to surprise them." Wheaton looked back at the house. "Now, I know you men don't have any police training, so listen carefully. You lead into rooms with your weapon. You don't go around corners until you've looked carefully to make sure no one's about to ambush you. Keep your firearm pointed at the ceiling or the floor to make sure you don't kill each other."

Mark began to think this was a bad idea. His brothers weren't stupid. Wheaton might be dead before he let go of the key. He and Doug and Brad weren't experienced enough to do this right.

There had to be another way.

"I have a better idea," Mark said. "If Larry and Jack see you at the door, they'll kill you without a thought. But if I go to the door and they see me, they might not shoot right away. Remember, they want my gold. They'd have to keep me alive long enough to find it."

Wheaton shook his head. "I don't want them taking you hostage, Mark. That's the last thing I need. You're injured, and they might overpower you."

"But I have a gun. If anything happens, I can defend myself. And you guys can cover me."

Wheaton thought it over for a moment.

"I don't like it," Doug said. "It's a real bad idea."

"But it could work," Brad said.

Finally, Wheaton made a decision. "All right, Mark. We'll do it your way."

FIFTY-NINE

MARK'S HEART WORKED IN OVERDRIVE AS HE STEPPED OUT of the trees and headed for the front door. As he approached the house, his eyes shifted from one window to another, looking for movement.

He stepped quietly onto the porch and felt the filthy boards giving beneath his weight. He listened, trying to hear footsteps—a shifting of weight, a creak of a board. But there was nothing.

Blowing out his tension, he brought the key up and slipped it into the lock. Wheaton had been right—the key fit. Slowly, Mark rotated the lock, and the doorknob clicked.

The others joined him within seconds, their weapons ready. Wheaton took a breath, then plunged the door open. Silently he led through the house, careful as he passed doorways, looking for some sign of life.

The beds were unmade but seemed recently slept in. Two pairs of muddy alligator boots cluttered the bedroom floor. The bathroom was empty, but toothbrushes lay on the sink. They moved about the house quickly, cautiously, looking in closets and behind furniture, under beds.

"No one here," Wheaton said finally as he came back into the living area.

Mark looked at the sparse furnishings in the room—the table where his brothers and his dad would play poker at night. The couch where Vic would pass out after too much to drink. They'd found a different use for the refrigerator than Mark had. They had turned it on its back, placed it under the window, and filled it with dirt. A small crop of beans grew there.

"Interesting use of the fridge," Doug said. "Looks like they've turned it into a mini-greenhouse. Wonder why they didn't just clear a place to plant a crop outside. All they'd have to do is cut down some trees and clear an area for a garden."

"Too lazy," Mark said. "Why work that hard when they can steal other people's game?"

Doug touched the soil. "The plants are a little dry, but not too bad. They probably watered yesterday or the day before."

Wheaton checked the fireplace. The ashes were cold. No one had had a fire in here today.

Disappointment rivaled the adrenalin pulsing through Mark. He had so hoped to find them here. "Maybe they're back in Crockett."

Wheaton shook his head. "If they are, they're up to no good."

The men didn't move anything in the house or leave any evidence that they had been there. It wouldn't pay to tip the brothers off that the law was on to them. What Mark wouldn't give for surveillance cameras, working radios, and enough men to stake out the place and wait for them to return.

But Wheaton's small force was stretched too thin as it was, and without technology, they were too limited. There were still almost two dozen escapees on the loose ... and way too few men to look for them.

•

FOR THE RIDE HOME, MARK SAT ON THE BACK BENCH SEAT ALONE, and Doug took the seat in front of him. Over the rumble of the old engine, Doug caught pieces of Wheaton and Brad's strategizing up front, but couldn't hear well enough to join in.

Besides, he was tired, and he had no brilliant schemes for luring the brothers out. Still—as tired as Doug was, he knew Mark was even worse off.

Doug leaned back against his window and set his arm on the back of the seat. He looked back at Mark, who was staring out the window as if looking for his brothers. Doug knew Mark wouldn't rest until they were found.

Mark was holding his sling close to his body, cradling the cast in his other hand. "Arm hurt?" Doug asked, even though he knew Mark wouldn't tell him if it did.

"Not bad." Mark shook his head. "I can't believe we're going back empty-handed."

"Me too. I thought we had them."

The swelling on Mark's forehead had gone down around his stitches, leaving a purple bruise the width of a baseball bat. Anger rippled through Doug as that scene came back to him. Not many men could have survived that kind of an attack, but Mark had defended himself valiantly.

Still, it wasn't Mark's physical strength that impressed Doug so much. It was his spiritual strength. His acts of forgiveness yesterday had put Doug to shame. It was the stuff sermons were made of. Yet he could still see the pain in Mark's weary eyes.

Doug's conversation this morning with Deni ran through his mind, and later, when he and Mark had discussed it before visiting Grace, he knew he'd come across as angry. Selfishly, he'd tried to put a guilt trip on Mark for encouraging Deni to take the job. But his concerns went deeper than the distance to D.C. He was concerned for his daughter's future.

And he was also concerned for Mark's.

Knowing the guys up front couldn't hear him, he said, "Mark, about Deni ..."

He saw the tension on Mark's face. "Yeah?"

"I just want you to understand. A year ago, when Deni told me she was going to be marrying a lawyer who worked in a senate office, I was excited and proud—at first. I thought, great, she'll have a wonderful, prosperous, exciting life. I loved the whole idea of it. And then I met Craig."

Mark couldn't help chuckling. "He was a nice enough guy."

"He was arrogant and proud, and he seemed a little bit narcissistic to me. And I started to worry about my daughter and her future." He shifted in the seat. "And then after the Pulses, when he came here, I realized that if she married him, he would bring her nothing but misery. That's why I did everything I could to talk her out of going through with it. So did Kay."

He had Mark's full attention now.

"The thing is, Deni was smart enough to see it too. And when she broke up with him at the train station that day, I realized that she had the guts and the maturity to do the right thing. She had changed, and a high life in Washington with Craig just wasn't what she really wanted."

"How do you know?" Mark asked. "She's stuck here, really. There aren't that many options. Why should she hold back when her life's dream is being dangled in front of her? She says she doesn't want that anymore, but I find that hard to believe." He leaned his head back and raked his hair. "I don't want her to go, Doug, but who am I to stand in the way if this is a God-given opportunity?"

Doug shook his head. "Opportunity for what? Mark, it's not just a question of being selfless and letting her fly. It's about letting her be lured into a life that will bring her heartache and emptiness."

The moment the words were out, Doug knew he'd laid it on too thick. He sounded like a desperate father, afraid to let his daughter grow up.

"I think you're selling Deni short," Mark said. "I think she's smarter than that." Mark's eyes grew shiny with unshed tears, and he rubbed his mouth. "She's going to follow God's guiding, and do what he leads her to do. Whether that's with me, or someone better, I want her to have God's best for her life."

"And so do I," Doug said. "But Mark, I don't think there is anyone better."

Mark looked jolted by the declaration. He blinked back the mist in his eyes and swallowed hard. "Wow. I appreciate that."

"No, *I* appreciate it." Doug turned around in the seat to fully face him. His eyes were intense as he locked into Mark's gaze. "I might as well just lay this out on the table, Mark. You're the kind of man I want for my daughter. A man I would consider it an honor to call my son."

Mark's pale eyes locked with his, and his forehead rippled as he let those words sink in. He opened his mouth to speak, but couldn't. Finally, he got the words out. "That means a lot to me."

Doug smiled, reached back and gripped Mark's good arm, then turned back around in his seat.

SIXTY

"GREAT," WHEATON MUTTERED AS THEY PULLED INTO THE parking lot at the sheriff's department. "Jimmy Scarbrough. Just what I need."

Mark saw Jimmy sitting on the steps, and his heart went out to the kid.

As they all got out of the van, Wheaton called out, "Jimmy, I told you not to come back here. Does your mother know where you are?"

Jimmy got to his feet, ignoring the question. "I heard you arrested Dante Miller. I want to see him."

Wheaton took in a deep breath, letting it out in a long sigh. "Jimmy, you know I'm not gonna let you in that jail."

"But why not? My dad is your boss! Those men in there are volunteers. They have no right to keep me out of my own father's station."

Mark was glad the men holding down the fort had done their job, but he worried what it was doing to the boy. "How's your dad?" he asked.

Jimmy turned his troubled, angry eyes to Mark. "I think he's gonna live, but he's in a coma right now. They made him that way, with medication."

"A medically induced coma?" Mark asked. "Did they say for how long?"

"No, they don't tell me much."

That was too bad. Details might be just what Jimmy needed.

"Well, I'm sure Ralph's in good hands." Wheaton trudged up the steps to the front door.

Jimmy's eyes followed him. "Deputy Wheaton, please let me come in. I don't want to do anything to him. I just want to see what he looks like."

Wheaton turned back. "Why, Jimmy? How will that help you?"

"I don't know." The corners of his mouth trembled. "But it will."

Mark set his hand on Jimmy's shoulder. Knowing he was going out on a limb, he said, "I'll walk in with him, Deputy."

Jimmy's hopeful eyes looked up at Mark.

"I'll go with them," Doug said.

Wheaton stared at the boy, considering it for several seconds. Mark braced himself for Wheaton's answer. Finally, he said, "All right, Jimmy. You let Doug and Mark walk you in there." He looked up at the two of them. "You boys need to frisk him, make sure he isn't trying to pull some heroic stunt."

"Frisk me?" Jimmy grunted. "What do you think I'm gonna do?"

"The same thing you intended to do when you showed up at his apartment," Wheaton reminded him.

Jimmy looked down. "Okay, fine."

Mark took him inside. In the kitchen, he and Doug searched him. He wasn't carrying anything. "All right, we'll walk you in there," Mark said. "He's in the back cell, alone."

Jimmy's brows came together. The kid was nervous, despite how tough he tried to appear.

"Jimmy," Mark said, "the reason I said I'd go with you is that I knew you'd handle this like a man. With dignity and integrity, like your dad would do. Do I have your word that you'll do that?"

Jimmy stood straighter, and his expression took on a new resolve. "I will."

Mark nodded at Doug, and they escorted Jimmy in. They walked past the men from Oak Hollow, past Blake and Randy, past the escapees who'd been brought back in.

Jimmy's eyes locked on the cell at the back of the room. Tree House was on the floor doing push-ups; his arms bulging as he came down and up, down and up. He looked up and chuckled as the trio walked toward him. "Dey puttin' you in here wit' me, white boy?"

Mark didn't answer.

"Dat's right. You workin' for de other side now. You watch your back now, you hear? Or you might wind up like de sheriff and his deputies."

Mark didn't take the bait. He felt Jimmy's shoulders going rigid, felt the tremor of the boy's rage. "Dante Miller, I want you to meet Jimmy Scarbrough," Mark said.

"Scarbrough?" Tree House seemed amused. Stepping toward the bars, he said, "De sheriff's boy, huh?" His face grew serious, and he took hold of the bars, and pressed his face between them. "What you doin' here?"

Jimmy took a step toward him and spoke through his teeth. "I wanted to see you in a cold jail cell, locked up tight, where you'd never get out."

Suddenly, Tree House spat. A wad of phlegm hit Jimmy in the face.

The boy snapped and lunged forward, looking like he could strangle Tree House with his bare hands, or die trying.

"Jimmy, don't!" Doug wrestled him back. The boy kept fighting to get away, but Doug pulled him back to the door.

Mark turned back to Tree House. "You're a real class act."

Another wad of spit came flying at Mark, but it only hit the floor.

Slowly, Mark turned and went back out.

Jimmy was still raging.

"See there?" Wheaton said. "I told you that was a bad idea."

Jimmy kicked a chair and sent it rolling across the room. It crashed into a metal desk. Turning to Mark, he shouted, "Why'd you have to clean out those cells?"

Mark knew Jimmy would never understand. "Because it was the right thing to do."

"He doesn't deserve the right thing!"

Mark sighed. "No, he doesn't."

Jimmy grabbed his coat and started for the door.

Wheaton tossed Doug the car keys. "Doug, Mark, drive him home. Make sure he's delivered to his grandparents."

Mark hurried out and caught the boy before he could get on his bike. "Jimmy, wait. We're taking you home. Get in."

Frustrated, Jimmy got off his bike. Doug picked it up and put it into the back of the van. Jimmy just stood there, refusing to move.

"Jimmy, I know how you feel," Mark said.

"You keep saying that, but you don't. If you did, you wouldn't have cleaned out those cells."

Mark bent to look into his face. "Jimmy, yesterday, when they brought those men in who did this to me, I had the same feelings you're having right now. I felt like killing somebody. But God showed me that cleaning those toilets was a way of separating myself from the men who beat innocent people with baseball bats ... or spit in the face of grieving sons."

Jimmy fought back his tears.

"You have to take the high road, Jimmy. It's the only way you'll find any peace over what's happened. It's what your dad would do."

The tears pushed forth, and Jimmy looked at his feet. Mark put his good arm around him, holding him for a moment. Finally, he felt strength seeping back into the boy. Jimmy wiped his face on his sleeve and got into the van.

SIXTY-ONE

Jimmy's grandparents weren't at the Scarbrough's when they took the boy home.

"They probably went out looking for me when they realized I wasn't in my room," Jimmy said.

"Well, we're not leaving you here alone," Doug said.

"Why not? I stay by myself all the time! I'm not some little kid."

"Your judgment is slightly off-kilter right now," Doug said. "We'll leave them a note. I'm taking you to my house where my family can keep an eye on you."

Jimmy didn't argue. They got back into the van. His silence made Doug uneasy. Did he intend to bolt and run the minute they turned their backs? If so, what would he do?

When they got to Oak Hollow, they found the Brannings' garage open. Jeff was crossing the street with a rabbit cage in his arms. Doug pulled the van into his driveway. Kay, Beth, and Logan were in the garage, taking care of the rabbits.

Beth straightened when she saw Jimmy getting out of the van. "Jimmy, what are you doing here?"

His face changed. "Hey, Beth. You live here?"

Doug looked from one to the other. "You two know each other?"

"We went to school together, before the Pulses," Beth said. Her face absorbed the pain on Jimmy's. "I'm sorry about your dad. I've been praying for him real hard."

He tightened his lips and looked at his feet.

"Jimmy's gonna stay with us until his mom or his grandparents come to get him."

A smile tugged at Beth's lips. "Can you help us lock down these rabbit cages?"

Jimmy shrugged. "Sure, I guess."

"Jeff found some heavy chain, and we're gonna put it through the cages. He traded two rabbits for some padlocks."

Jimmy picked up the chain and examined it. "This could work," he said.

Beth showed him Jeff's sketch of the plan. It was the most animated Doug had seen his younger daughter in days. He shot a surprised look at Mark, and Mark winked.

Maybe the project would provide the necessary distraction for both of these traumatized kids.

SIXTY-TWO

Mark found Deni at the typewriter in her father's study, working on an article about the arrests of Tree House and the other prisoners. When he came into the room, she sprang up and threw her arms around him. "Mark, I've been so worried! Did you find Larry and Jack?"

Her greeting brought a smile to his lips, and he savored the feel of her hug. "Not yet. We found where they've been staying, but they weren't there." He filled her in.

Letting him go, she leaned back on the desk. "Mark, I've been thinking about this all day, trying to figure out where they might be. Didn't they have a warehouse in town where they kept all that smut they sold?"

Mark hadn't really considered that. "They must have, I guess. They kept a lot of it in my dad's house, but they had so many stores."

"If they had a warehouse, you might find the address on an invoice or something."

Mark thought that through. Maybe Deni was onto something. He looked into her anxious eyes. "I told you you were gifted."

She grabbed the front of his shirt. "Let's go over there and look right now. There's no time to waste."

Deni's parents were across the street working on the rabbit cages when she and Mark came out. She didn't take the time to tell them where she was going—dusk was beginning to fall, and she didn't want to be at Vic Green's house after dark.

It only took a few moments for them to walk to his father's house, and Mark handed Deni his Glock as he fished the keys out of his pocket, found the right one, and unlocked the front door.

The sight of the living room took her breath away. "Wow, you were right. This place is a mess." She knew Mark must dread the thought of cleaning it up. Maybe when Larry and Jack were safely behind bars, she and her mom could come in here and put it back together, so he wouldn't have to.

He lit an oil lantern—one of the few items left intact. He handed it to her and took the gun back.

Memories rushed back to her as she stepped over the mess. She had made friends with Vic for his swimming pool when water was so scarce—putting her life in the hands of a killer so she could wash her hair. Such stupidity.

"Let's hurry," she said as she followed Mark upstairs. "This place creeps me out."

He led her to the room his father had used as an office. File cabinets lined the wall. This was the room where he and her parents had found the boxes of pornography when Deni was on the road with Vic.

Her skin chilled at the memory of the horrors she had walked into.

Mark went to a file cabinet and pulled out a drawer. "I was here earlier today when I got the address to the deer camp, so I know which drawers it's *not* in."

"Is there a file for receipts?"

He scanned the file labels in two more drawers. "Here it is." He took it to the desk, and she set the lamp down so they could read.

Suddenly, they heard a creak overhead.

Deni caught her breath and grabbed Mark's arm. "Did you hear that?" she whispered.

He raised his gun. "Maybe it was the wind," he whispered. But he chambered a round and pointed the gun toward the sound.

Another creak. Her heart stumbled into triple-time as terror shivered through her. "Mark, they're in the attic."

He motioned for her to be quiet and follow close behind him. She held her breath as he led her out into the hall and toward the stairs that would take her to safety. She kept her eyes on the ceiling, wondering where the attic door was.

Mark stayed close beside her as they descended the staircase. She stumbled as they reached the first floor, righted herself, and stepped over things to get to the door.

Suddenly, she heard a gun cocking.

Her heart stopped as Jack stepped out of the dining room, his revolver at her head.

Deni screamed.

She heard a whack and spun around. Mark hit the floor, and she saw Larry standing over him. Breathing hard from his descent down the stairs, he held a rifle in one hand, and Mark's Glock in the other.

"Well, this is gonna be real fun," Larry said.

She screamed again. Jack's hand slapped around her mouth, muffling her as he pulled her against him.

Mark scrambled to his feet. "Let her go, Jack. She hasn't done anything to you. It's me you want."

"Oh, it's you we got," Larry said. "Right where we want you. Don't we, Jack?"

"Where's the gold?" Jack bit out.

Deni struggled under Jack's arm, fighting to get away, but he clamped his arm across her throat, subduing her in a death grip. He pulled her back to the table and grabbed a roll of duct tape. Larry covered Mark with his rifle.

Jack ripped a piece of tape off with his teeth and slapped it over Deni's mouth. She squealed, but she knew no one would hear. He got more tape, wrapped it around one of her wrists. Roughly, he wrestled her other hand behind her and wrapped them together.

Duct tape. It had been Vic's favorite way of binding his victims. The thought made her nauseous.

"Let her go!" Mark said. "I'll take you to the gold!"

Jack shoved Deni to the floor. She kicked and fought as he wrapped her ankles together.

"I've only spent three coins," Mark said. "There are ninety-seven left. They're all yours."

Now he had their attention. "Where is it?" Larry asked.

"It's not here." Sweat dripped into his eyes. "Let her go and I'll take you to it."

Jack laughed. "You've got it backwards, little bro. I'll stay here with your hot little girlfriend. You take Larry to the gold, and when we have it in our hands, we let her go. You pull any tricks, and we kill her."

"We've got nothing to lose," Larry snapped. "We're already wanted for murder. We've lost our wives and our children, our homes and our inheritance."

Deni got her feet under her and started to rise, but Jack's gun came back to her head. Squeezing her eyes shut, she waited for him to pull the trigger.

"It's not far," Mark said. "It's hidden in a tree in the woods near my house."

"A *tree*?" Larry almost spat the word. "Who do you think you're dealing with?"

Deni opened her eyes again and saw the front door. If she could just get to that door, open it, squeal with all her might.

"I'm telling the truth." Mark's voice wobbled. "You know I don't have it at either one of these houses, because you tore them both apart looking for it. Where else could I have it? I'll take you to it, but you both come with me. Once you have it in your hands, you can take off from there."

Deni had gotten to her knees. Jack grabbed her by the neck, jerked her to her feet, and pressed the revolver up to her ear. Her mind raced for an escape.

God, please ...

Cursing, Jack said, "You're not calling the shots, Mark! We're in charge here. Larry'll go with you, and I'll stay here with her."

Deni met Mark's eyes. She had never seen such fear. The terror was for her, she knew—as if he knew in his heart that he had set her up for murder.

But she nodded her head, telling him to go.

She had no idea what Jack might do to her while Mark was gone, but this was at least a way of buying time. Maybe someone would see him on the way. Maybe her father would come looking for them. Maybe she could figure out a way to turn the tables.

She couldn't communicate all that to Mark—but he nodded, as if he understood. *I'll hurry*, his intense eyes seemed to say.

Jack laughed and buried his face in her hair, nuzzling against her neck. She shrank from his touch. She would kill him if she could, she realized. She had fought his murderous father, and she could fight him.

"Forget it," Mark said. "I'm not going unless she comes too."

Larry hit him across his stitches and Mark stumbled back, but he quickly righted himself. "Unbind her!" he yelled.

"She's staying here!" Jack said.

Mark's eyes flashed. "Then find the stinking gold yourself."

Larry thrust the pistol into Mark's throat. Jerking his chin up, Mark spoke through his teeth. "Kill me, if you want. You'll never find it then."

Deni saw the look pass between Larry and Jack. Suddenly, Larry tossed the rifle to Jack. Keeping the Glock against Mark's head, he took Mark's broken arm, tore off the sling, and wrenched his cast behind his back. Pain twisted through Mark's bones.

Deni tried to scream, but only a muffled squeal came out.

Grabbing Mark's collarbone brace, Larry jerked it until the bone snapped again. Mark arched in pain.

Larry dragged him to the door and looked over his shoulder. "If we're not back in ten minutes, Jack, you know what to do."

SIXTY-THREE

DENI WATCHED MARK LEAVE WITH HIS BROTHER. SHE turned back to Jack, raising her chin and trying to look stronger than she was.

It was a mistake, because he saw it as a challenge. Hanging the rifle from its sling, he shoved his revolver against her neck. "What's the matter, darlin'?"

She pressed her head back against the wall.

"I've known since the first day you came to this house to swim in my dad's pool that you were salivating for me."

She grunted out her protest and shook her head hard. She'd been stupid then, but not that stupid.

"Remember when my little wife Grace was so jealous of you and your friend?"

He came closer to her, touched the inside collar of her shirt.

Twisting away from him, she threw herself on the floor, breaking his hold on her. Pushing with her knees, she tried to crawl to the door.

Jack was on her in an instant, picking her up by her waist and carrying her up the stairs. "You're feisty, aren't you, baby? My dad had good taste."

She kicked and bucked her head, trying to make him drop her. He got to the top of the stairs and tripped over some books on the floor. She fell out of his grip again and rolled to her back.

"Want to play rough?" he said through his teeth as he grabbed her again.

She squealed and flailed and fought. But she didn't know how long she could hold him off.

SIXTY-FOUR

STRUGGLING WITH THE PAIN FIRING THROUGH HIM, MARK led Larry through the trees as fast as he could. The sooner he could get to the gold, the sooner he could get back to Deni.

Ever aware of the gun at his back, Mark prayed as he ran. *God, please protect her!*

He saw the stump up ahead. "There it is," he said, slowing down. He reached it and started pulling out the leaves with his good hand.

Larry was out of breath. "You've got to be kidding. Are you setting me up?"

Mark reached inside for the metal box. He tried to pull it out, but it was heavy, and agony shot spears through his broken bones.

"Hold it!" Larry cocked his pistol. "You got a gun in there? You trying to put one over on me?"

Mark raised his good arm and took a step back. "Open it yourself, if you want. It's full of gold."

Larry moved closer, keeping the gun on Mark, and opened the box. There they were, all ninety-seven coins. Larry's eyes rounded lustfully as he took in the sight. He grabbed some of them, let them fall through his fingers. Perspiration rolled down his temples as he started filling his coat and pants pockets with the coins.

Mark knew his brother had no reason to keep him alive now.

Taking advantage of Larry's distraction, he took off running, each footstep jolting his fractured bones.

He heard Larry drop the toolbox, footsteps pounding the earth behind him.

Mark didn't look back. He kept running, moving from left to right through the trees, knowing that Larry could kill him at any moment before he could get back to the house and save Deni from Jack.

SIXTY-FIVE

DENI PUSHED WITH HER FEET, BACKING INTO THE OFFICE, sliding across the carpet until she reached the wall with a window. She struggled to get to her feet, but Jack grabbed them out from under her, knocking her to her back.

She kicked him in the mouth.

He stumbled back, bumping into the desk. The oil lamp she'd left there tumbled onto the floor. Flames spilled across the carpet.

But in his rage, he didn't see them. He swung and slapped her, knocking her head back against the wall. She kicked him again, but he grabbed her feet and dragged her toward the door.

She twisted helplessly, looking up at the window through which she could call for help, if she could just get it open.

Smoke began to fill the room, and suddenly, Jack let her go.

She looked back and saw that he was stamping out the flames that had now crossed the doorway. The fire spread as if it had life, ravenously devouring the carpet, creeping toward her. She slid to the side, away from the window as the flames grew taller, licking up the walls.

SIXTY-SIX

LARRY WAS RIGHT ON HIS HEELS AS MARK MADE HIS WAY back to his father's house. As he ran, he expected Larry to fire. But his brother must have been leery of drawing attention. Bent on reaching Deni first, Mark crossed the yard and burst in through the back door. Smoke filled the house, and Mark saw flames devouring the staircase. "Deni!" he screamed.

He saw Jack stomping through the flames upstairs, scaling the banister, leaping to the first floor. As he hit the ground, his revolver went off.

Time seemed to slow into still pictures. Jack's gun recoiling, the bullet tearing through Mark's flesh, wrenching, agonizing, exploding pain doubling him in two, throwing him back into the glass door ... glass shattering ... flames reaching ... Jack getting to his feet ... Larry kicking Mark out of the doorway. Opening the door. Running.

Mark struggled to sit up. Blood seeped into his shirt, and he pressed his hand against the wound in his gut. Fire ... Deni ...

He heard her squealing at the top of the stairs. He got to his feet, stumbled through the flames. The fire was spreading across the carpet, ripping up the walls, spreading to the curtains.

He couldn't breathe.

His hand was wet with blood, his shirt soaked. His mind raced.

God, save us!

He jerked a curtain off a wall that hadn't yet been hit by the fire, and used it to try to smother the flames on the stairs as he made his way up. He felt the flames licking at his skin, singing the hair on his arms, licking up the denim of his jeans.

Dizziness hit him as he reached the top of the stairs. Pressing a hand against his wound, he tried to go on. Gasping for breath, he fought the flames. There was a fire extinguisher somewhere. He had seen it on the floor in one of the rooms, pulled out with everything else. Where had it been?

The bathroom!

He lurched into the room across from the office and saw the red tank lying on the floor. Letting go of his wound, he reached for it with his blood-covered hand.

He pulled the pin and squeezed the trigger.

The white foam cleared a way into his father's office, smothering the flames. Now he could see her—Deni was hunched in a ball with her face in a corner. He staggered to her and ripped the duct tape from her hands.

She fought her way upright, coughing...

The room began to spin. He felt himself hit the floor. Darkness closed in on him as he heard Deni screaming.

SIXTY-SEVEN

Deni ripped the tape from her mouth, got to her feet, and opened the window. "Help!" Her hoarse scream tore across the neighborhood. "Someone help!"

She fell to Mark's side, mashing her fist into his wound to stop the bleeding. Smoke still billowed into the room, telling her that, although the fire was mostly out in this room, it was still raging elsewhere.

She could take the fire extinguisher and go for help. But by the time she got back, Mark would have bled to death.

No, she had to stay here and stop the bleeding. As she kept her hands on Mark's stomach, she screamed until she had no voice left.

SIXTY-EIGHT

On his way back home from the well, Hank Huckabee heard screaming. He saw the smoke pouring from the window of Vic's house and ran toward it. As he approached, he saw flames engulfing the first floor, but the screaming came from upstairs.

He dragged his garbage can full of well water into the house and used it to extinguish some of the flames. By that time, Merilee Goff had appeared with a fire extinguisher. Rushing in, she covered the stairway, killing the flames. Hank ran up the slippery stairs and found a hysterical Deni Branning—and Mark Green bleeding to death.

Deni didn't know how much time had passed before the paramedics arrived. Someone had gone to get her father, and Doug jumped into the sheriff's van, still parked in his driveway, and flew out of Oak Hollow to find the paramedics.

Prayers, bargains, and desperate pleas tumbled through Deni's mind as she tried to keep Mark alive. It seemed like an eternity before she heard the sirens, and the paramedics ran in with a gurney. Pushing her out of the way, they rushed him into their ambulance. Doug and Kay intercepted her as she tried to follow, but she pushed past them. "I have to go with him!"

"Deni, you're bleeding!" her mother cried.

Deni looked down at her wet hands. "It's not me. It's him!" She started to sob and looked up at her dad. "Go after Larry and Jack, Dad. You can't let them get away."

SIXTY-NINE

DOUG DIDN'T WAIT FOR BACKUP BEFORE GOING AFTER Larry and Jack Green. Their tracks led him into the woods. These men who had tormented his daughter and almost killed their own brother would not get away this time.

He heard sirens on the other side of the trees, dogs barking, voices yelling.

And then he saw the brothers, running back toward him. Doug raised his gun. "Freeze!" he shouted. "Don't move!"

Larry fired. Doug dove and felt the bullet whistle past his face. He returned fire from the ground, and Larry dropped.

Jack raised his hands in the air, his gun pointed at the sky.

"Drop the gun!" Jack looked from side to side. Wheaton and his men were moving toward him from the other side of the woods. He lowered the revolver ...

And put it to his head.

The gun went off, and he hit the ground with a thud.

Doug couldn't believe what he'd seen. Slowly, he got up, keeping his pistol trained on the two bodies on the ground. He moved closer, watching to see if either of them moved.

Wheaton ran through the trees toward him. When he saw the two bodies on the ground, he knelt to check their pulses. He nodded up at Doug. "They're gone," he said.

Doug leaned against a tree, letting his weapon drop to his side.

It was over now.

SEVENTY

WHEATON LET DOUG TAKE THE SHERIFF'S VAN TO BIRMINGham so his family could ride along. As he drove, he heard Martha weeping in the backseat. Kay sat next to her, comforting her as they flew through town.

Beth sniffed behind him. He looked in the rearview mirror and saw her eyes, hollow and vacant. Jimmy Scarbrough sat next to her, his face white. Doug hoped Jimmy's mother was still at the hospital with his dad.

Logan sat on the other side of Beth, holding his sister's hand. "They can't kill Mark," Logan said. "He's tough. He's probably better already."

Doug stayed quiet. The opposite was probably more likely. As tough as Mark was, Doug had seen the blood on the carpet.

Jeff, in the passenger seat, seemed to sense Doug's thoughts. "He's gonna make it, Dad."

Doug stared through the windshield. "I hope you're right."

It would be so unfair if Mark died, after all he'd been through. It would destroy Deni, devastate Martha, demoralize Beth.

And Doug himself would never get over it. What would he tell his family? How would he explain such tragedy to his church?

He struggled to see through the tears in his eyes as he drove the dark, deserted streets. *Please, God. Don't let him die. He means so much to all of us.*

Finally, Logan broke the silence. "Daddy, when is this ever gonna be over?"

He glanced back at his youngest. "When will what be over?"

"The stinking Pulses. I'm sick of this. I want things back like they were before."

Doug looked through the glass to the stars sprinkling the night sky, and he wished the same thing. If they could only turn back time, to the days of peace and prosperity, before evil ran so rampant, when everyone he knew was thriving and healthy.

Had it really been that way? Or had he just viewed the world through the filter of his affluence, through the lenses of American technology, hurrying along so fast that he didn't have time to see the suffering around him? Was it bliss or merely ignorance?

The work God was doing in them all was important. Purging out the waste, intensifying their purpose. They were all stronger for it.

But like Logan, he longed for it to end.

He thought of his sermon last week, on the reason for God's testing. The Scripture he'd used was from Deuteronomy 8, verses 2 and 3.

> Remember how the Lord your God led you all the way in the desert these forty years, to humble you and to test you in order to know what was in your heart, whether or not you would keep his commands. He humbled you, causing you to hunger and then feeding you with manna, which neither you nor your fathers had known, to teach you that man does not live on bread alone but on every word that comes from the mouth of the Lord.

Though he had trouble embracing the theme of that sermon now—that this time of testing was to make them more righteous, more useful for the kingdom of God—he knew it was true. God was doing a work in them all. And there might be more yet to come.

SEVENTY-ONE

DOUG AND KAY FOUND DENI ON A TABLE IN AN EXAMINING room, breathing into an oxygen mask, her hands and clothes still covered with blood. She reached for Kay, trembling.

"We got them," Doug told her. "Larry and Jack are dead."

Her forehead wrinkled as she stared into her father's eyes. "Are you sure?"

"Absolutely. They won't cause any more trouble for Mark."

She squeezed her eyes shut and tears rolled down her face. "The doctors took him as soon as we got here. I don't know if he was dead or alive."

"Oh, honey, he's alive," Doug said. "They have him in surgery. They took his mother back when we came in."

Deni opened her eyes and pulled off the mask. Tears streaked through the soot on her face. "They can save him, can't they? They saved Zach and Sheriff Scarbrough."

"I hope so, sweetheart."

"He was bleeding so much ... but he came up the stairs and saved me."

Kay got a paper towel and some alcohol and began to wipe the blood off Deni's hands. "If we had some water, we could get you cleaned up. But this'll have to do for now."

She scrubbed hard, rubbing off every spot. "Rubbing alcohol is good for so many things," Kay said. "Did you know you can wash mirrors with it? Or is that hydrogen peroxide?

I always get the two mixed up. I never have tried it because there's never much of either one around, but I think I heard Martha Stewart say once—"

Deni took her mother's hand, stopping her chatter. Kay turned her distraught face up to her.

"Mom, I can clean myself up," Deni whispered.

Kay's face twisted and her lips stretched tight. "I just ... let me ..."

Deni gave in and let her mother clean her, weeping quietly over her daughter's hands. As Kay scrubbed, Deni closed her eyes and sent her silent, anguished pleas up to her sovereign God. She remembered all Mark had done to honor Christ, the truths he had taught her about forgiveness and integrity, the selflessness he wore like a clean, white cloak. There was so much pain in his life—so much abandonment, betrayal, abuse ... But he had overcome it.

The world needed him. *She* needed him.

I'll do anything you want if you save him, she told the Lord. *I'll be a missionary. Go to Africa. Or Washington, if you say. Whatever you want, Lord, I'll do it.*

"Deni Branning?"

Deni opened her eyes. A doctor in scrubs, with his surgical mask pulled under his chin, stepped inside.

"Yes?"

"Mark Green's mother asked me to let you know that he made it through surgery. He's very lucky. The bullet missed all of his major organs."

Deni came off the table and into her mother's arms. Her dad caught her and swung her around. Letting him go, she threw herself at the doctor. He laughed and stepped back to keep her from knocking him over.

"He's lost a lot of blood," he said. "We're giving him a transfusion as we speak. If any of you are O positive, you could help us out with that. Our blood supplies are dangerously low."

Relieved that hers would help, she followed him out of the room, weeping with gratitude as she went.

SEVENTY-TWO

THE FLAMES WERE LICKING HIGHER, WIDER ... DESTROYING ... devastating.

Deni's face loomed in terror within the flames. White foam rained down on her, but it didn't extinguish anything. Instead it ignited, consuming her.

Mark heard her screams echoing in his ears ... Larry and Jack laughing ... his father's cold, sharp voice.

It's time you were a man.

Tree House emerged through the flames, spitting.

Satan roams around like a roaring lion ...

You are precious in my sight ... you are honored and I love you ...

And then he heard Deni's voice, soft and steady. "And my mouth offers praises with joyful lips ..."

She was reading Psalm 63. The flames died away and he felt cool air on his face, comfort in his spirit. "For you have been my help," she read, "and in the shadow of your wings I sing for joy ... Your right hand upholds me."

He forced his eyes to open.

"Mark? Can you hear me?"

He saw the blur of Deni over him ... her eyes round and anxious ... alive ... beautiful.

Life came into soft focus.

"Hey," he whispered.

Her voice was hoarse, raspy. "They're dead, Mark. Larry and Jack are gone."

His brothers dead. Loss clouded his thoughts, but relief was fast in its wake.

"You saved me," she whispered.

He reached up to her. His arm felt heavy, clumsy, but he touched her face, felt the satin skin, her lips against his fingers. She took his hand, pressed a kiss on his palm. "I love you, Mark," she said.

"I love you too." The words drifted deep into his spirit, settling things in his heart.

She laid her head against his chest. "I feel so safe with you."

Her words banished the lingering feelings of loss. Illuminated what was gained. Framed the miracle.

As he held her and stroked her hair, he knew the strength that came from weakness ... the courage that came from fear ... the faith that came from doubt ...

God had come through.

And in the shadow of his wings, Mark could sing for joy.

A NOTE FROM THE AUTHOR

Sometimes I don't feel fearfully and wonderfully made. There are days when I feel like a disappointment to God, a frustration, a prodigal that he'd rather not see come home. Those are bad days, and I admit I fall prey to them way too often.

Tonight at church I watched a sculptor take a lump of clay and sculpt it lovingly and skillfully into an image of Jesus. I knew going in what she was going to do, yet when his features emerged, I found myself moved to tears. Delight filled my heart as I thought, *I know him! I recognize those features!*

As I watched her work, I felt God whispering into my spirit, "This is how I made you. You were a lump of unformed substance. I sculpted your face out of clay, my fingers forming your cheekbones, your nose, the shape of your eyes. And when your face emerged, I smiled, because I already knew you. I delighted in you, because I created you so carefully."

In Psalm 139, David said:

> My frame was not hidden from you
>   when I was made in the secret place.
> When I was woven together in the depths of the earth,
>   your eyes saw my unformed body.
> All the days ordained for me
>   were written in your book
>   before one of them came to be.

When I think of my life as a book that has already been written, I'm even more moved. It makes me wonder how I can ever despair or question God, how I can ever lose my trust that he will answer my prayers, how I can ever fear or worry. If God knows me by name, if he knows me by touch, if he knows the number of days ordained for me on this earth, if he wrote the book of my life and knows what will happen on all future pages, if he can see around corners and over hills and knows what's coming ... what is there *ever* to fear?

Yet, I do sometimes, and he knows it. I fear and worry and cry out and question ... and he understands because he knit my personality in just this way. He gave me a questioning mind, an emotional heart, a cautious spirit. And he's not finished with me yet.

He's still sculpting, still editing, still knitting ... and when I let him mold me in that special way, when I succumb to his loving, skillful, strong, and sometimes harsh fingers, I become more like *his* image. I begin to take on the features of my Creator, the one who knows me by name, the one who took on human flesh because something had to be done about my sins. Someone's blood had to be shed. Someone had to die. I was that precious to him.

And so are you. God knows when you sit and when you rise. He perceives your thoughts from afar. He discerns your going out and your lying down. He is familiar with all your ways. Before a word is on your tongue he knows it completely. He hems you in—behind and before; he has laid his hand upon you. He created your inmost being, and knit you together in your mother's womb.

We—you and I—are fearfully and wonderfully made. His works are wonderful (Psalm 139:1–5, 13–14).

No mistakes. No regrets. No surprises.

I think he wanted me to tell you that today.

TERRI BLACKSTOCK

READING GROUP GUIDE

1. In the opening scene, Zach Emory is shot after killing a deer. When you read the book, what were your initial thoughts about who shot Zach and why? Beth Branning reacts strongly to the shooting. Do you have similar fears about death? What stokes or soothes those fears?
2. Many people assume that Mark is the killer. What drives their accusation? Did you believe there was a chance that Mark could be the killer?
3. When neighbors in Oak Hollow hear that Mark was seen near the site of Zach's shooting, what is their reaction? How does Mark react to this display?
4. Mark willingly turns himself in, then finds himself in the middle of a dangerous plot. How would you react if you were in Mark's shoes? Would your trust in God waiver at any point?
5. It never occurred to Deni to think of the needs of inmates after the Pulses. Discuss your own town. What ministry is needed that you've not considered? How do those in your city aid the less fortunate?
6. Again, Beth witnesses violence as neighborhood men assault Mark at her home. How would you help Beth cope? Is there any explanation to the violence occurring?
7. After the prisoners shoot Sheriff Scarbrough, his son Jimmy wants revenge. Where else in *True Light* do you see this desire for revenge? How does revenge influence our actions and behaviors?

8. Discuss Mark's choices regarding the treatment of his enemies. How has God spoken to you in your life when you've dealt with enemies? Does God really give instructions like "Clean the toilets?"
9. If you'd been abused the way Mark was, would you be able to clean the cells where your attackers are imprisoned? Discuss Mark's choices and motivations. Where do you think Deni's motivation comes from?
10. Mark finds out that Deni's ex-fiancé has written, asking her to come back to him. How does Mark react? Discuss how different characters' dreams have changed since the Pulses.
11. Discuss the value of family in *True Light.* How has Mark's family affected his life? How has the Branning family affected his life? What impact does your family have on your loved ones?

ACKNOWLEDGMENTS

SPECIAL THANKS TO ALL THOSE WHO ENTERED MY *LAST Light* contest at www.terriblackstock.com. The five winners were Valerie Chess, Michelle Rowe, Angelina Linthicum, Bette Hammang, and Esther Huibers, who gave me great ideas to use in the books. I also want to acknowledge Steven E. Harris of www.knowledgepublications.com for his books *Sunshine to Dollars* and *Surviving the Blackout of 2003*, along with his disaster preparedness resources. His website is full of great ideas and was a great help to me in writing this book.

An Excerpt from *DAWN'S LIGHT*

PROLOGUE

ON MAY 24, CIVILIZATION AS WE KNOW IT COMES TO AN end. Plumbing doesn't work because the water treatment plants run on electricity. Trucks and trains don't run, so stores run out of food. Generators are rendered useless. In this major meltdown of life, people are stranded where they are, with no transportation, no power, and no communication. Crime runs rampant as evil fills the void, and desperation becomes the only moral guide many people recognize.

Eventually, word makes its way to Crockett, Alabama, that the event was caused by a star—a supernova named SN-1999—which is emitting electromagnetic pulses every few seconds. With no assurance of when the star might burn itself out and allow them to rebuild, people are left with a choice: will they hoard what they have until it all runs out, or will they share with those around them who are in need?

The Brannings, an upper-middle-class Christian family, who pride themselves on their righteousness, respond like everyone else at first: they hole up at home, hoarding their food, paranoid that interacting with others will force them to share the few provisions they have. The children are angry that their lives have been disrupted. They're bored without visual and audio entertainment. Deni, the twenty-two-year-old, is frustrated that she won't be able to get to Washington to start her new job and be with her fiancé, who lives there.

When Doug Branning finally comes to grips with the fact that this is not going to end soon, he breaks down before God, realizing that he's not equipped to function without technology. How will he support his family? How will he provide food? How will they survive? As he struggles to find answers, he begins to realize that God has a purpose for him and his family through this trial. People around him have great needs—physical and spiritual. The Brannings begin to understand that they have much to learn, and much to give.

When Deni's eyes open to the true character of Craig Martin, her fiancé, she breaks her engagement. She's begun to fall in love with Mark Green, a high school friend who lives in her neighborhood. But Mark is the son of a convicted killer, and when a neighbor is shot by an unknown assailant, people assume that Mark committed the crime. He's thrown into a dark and broken prison system. Deni and her family help to find the true killer and clear his name. As they do, Deni sees Mark's noble acts of forgiveness toward those who persecuted him, and falls more deeply in love with him.

The blackout continues for a year, and the Brannings learn to work together to survive, until God gives them their ultimate test ...

ONE

THE PROMISE OF VIOLENCE RIPPLED LIKE STEAM OVER THE hungry, sweating mob, waiting in the rain at the door of Alabama Bank and Trust. The May thunderstorm was ruthless, pounding and cracking like a symphonic movie score foreshadowing catastrophe. Beth Branning wasn't supposed to be here. It was no place for a thirteen-year-old, her parents had said. She was better off staying home with her brothers.

But she couldn't resist one peek at the anxious crowd. Even from a block away, she could feel the tension and thrill of those who would go from poverty to plenty in a matter of minutes. Armed deputies surrounded the place, along with the few running vehicles in the town—sheriff's department patrol cars, ambulances, fire trucks. Clearly, they expected the worst. Though accountholders were only able to withdraw two percent of their holdings, it was the first time in a year that people around Crockett had any cash to carry. Criminals were bound to strike.

Her parents had charged her brother Jeff with two jobs today. Watch Beth and Logan, her ten-year-old brother, and take ten loaves of bread they'd baked to the Sheriff's Department, to help feed the prisoners. Jeff had been in the middle of a jam session in his room with two of his friends, and hadn't wanted to go, so Beth convinced him to let her do it instead.

"All right," he said, "but don't go near the banks. Straight there and straight back. No detours to see all the hoopla. Got it?"

"Got it," she said, though she made no promises.

The rain had almost dissuaded her, but she knew the prisoners had to eat. On days like this, the ladies of the Crockett Apostolic Church, who usually cooked for the prisoners, weren't able to bring meals. Beth's dad had been working as a volunteer deputy last night and knew the men hadn't been fed. They were probably starving to death.

Leaving the crowd, she rode her bike through the pouring rain, her tennis visor keeping the water from her eyes. The raindrops pricked her skin, soaked her T-shirt, and made her shiver. The sheriff's department was only another two miles.

A bolt of lightening flashed in front of her, thunder cracking simultaneously. Her heart kicked through her chest.

Okay, this was crazy. She had to get to shelter. She was too far from home to turn back now, but she'd never make it to the Sheriff's station with lightning hitting so close. She pulled her bike onto the parking lot of a Cracker Barrel restaurant that hadn't been open in a year and rolled it up to the porch. Lightning flashed and thunder cracked again, too close for comfort. She backed up against the wall and checked the garbage bag she'd wrapped the bread in, hoping it had stayed dry.

"Don't shoot!"

She heard a man's muffled voice, a choked cry. She looked around and saw no one.

"No, please! I'll give you the money!"

It was coming from behind the restaurant. Quietly, she stole to the end of the porch and peered around the side of the building.

She saw two men standing among the trees—a young man who looked like he was in his early twenties, holding his hands out with his wallet. A man with a black do-rag and a gray goatee stood facing him with a gun. He took the wallet, then raised the gun.

Beth froze, unable to move or breathe.

The gun went off, and the younger man dropped to the ground.

Beth screamed.

The gunman turned and saw her.

She turned and stumbled toward her bike, dragged it off the porch. Suddenly the killer was on her, knocking over the bike. It clamored to the ground and she fell over it.

She screamed again, and he rammed the barrel of his pistol against her forehead.

"I won't tell!" she squealed out. "I didn't see anything!" She squeezed her eyes shut. "Please!"

He was going to kill her. One shot, and she would be dead, just like the man.

Suddenly, she heard the sound of a car engine, turning onto the street. *Help, please help.*

The man looked toward the vehicle, cursed, then shoved his gun into his pocket. Grabbing her silver necklace with her name on it, he jerked and broke the chain. "You so much as utter a word about what you saw, and I'll kill you and your family, *Beth.*"

The van rattled closer, and he took off then, disappearing through the trees. She scrambled to her feet, righted her bike. The van tooled by, its driver not noticing her on the ground with her bike. She thought of flagging it down, but what would she say? If the man could hear ... he would come after her and her family.

Rain soaked through her clothes, making her shiver. She got back on the bike. The bread had been smashed and lay flattened in a puddle. Leaving it, she flew home, praying the man wasn't following her.

About the Author

Terri Blackstock is an award-winning novelist who has written for several major publishers including HarperCollins, Dell, Harlequin, and Silhouette. Her books have sold over 6 million copies worldwide.

With her success in secular publishing at its peak, Blackstock had what she calls "a spiritual awakening." A Christian since the age of fourteen, she realized she had not been using her gift as God intended. It was at that point that she recommitted her life to Christ, gave up her secular career, and made the decision to write only books that would point her readers to him.

"I wanted to be able to tell the truth in my stories," she said, "and not just be politically correct. It doesn't matter how many readers I have if I can't tell them what I know about the roots of their problems and the solutions that have literally saved my own life."

Her books are about flawed Christians in crisis and God's provisions for their mistakes and wrong choices. She claims to be extremely qualified to write such books, since she's had years of personal experience.

A native of nowhere, since she was raised in the Air Force, Blackstock makes Mississippi her home. She and her husband are the parents of three adult children—a blended family which she considers one more of God's provisions.

Terri Blackstock, a *New York Times* bestselling author, has sold over six million books worldwide. She is the author of numerous suspense novels, including *Intervention*, *Vicious Cycle*, and *Downfall* (the Intervention Series), as well as the Moonlighters Series, the Cape Refuge Series, the SunCoast Chronicles, the Newpointe 911 Series, the Restoration Series, and many others. (www.terriblackstock.com)